GUIDE TO THE DRAFT

Selective Service rules and practices change frequently. To the best of our knowledge, this book has correct information to the date given below. The general procedures and practices are unlikely to change greatly, but specific rules may be changed at any time by administrative decision or court ruling.

You can keep up to date by subscribing to *News Notes* or the *Reporter for Conscience' Sake* (see page 255), by reading current newspaper and magazine reports, and by staying in touch with a good draft counselor (see list on page 256).

This edition of *Guide to the Draft* was finally revised on August 21, 1970.

Dedicated to those who struggle,
against all odds, to be human beings.

Guide to the Draft

THIRD EDITION

by
ARLO TATUM
and
JOSEPH S. TUCHINSKY

Beacon Press   Boston

Copyright © 1969, 1970 by Arlo Tatum and Joseph S. Tuchinsky
Library of Congress catalog card number 69-17998
Simultaneous casebound and paperback editions
International Standard Book Number: 0-8070-2790-1 (casebound)
0-8070-2791-X (paperback)

All rights reserved

Beacon Press books are published under the auspices of the Unitarian Universalist Association

Printed in the United States of America

First edition, February 1969
Second edition, December 1969
Third edition, October 1970

ACKNOWLEDGMENTS

The authors are grateful to all who have laid the groundwork for this book over the past twenty years. There are too many to list by name, but we especially thank those who have researched and written the memorandums, articles, and books used by draft counselors and attorneys, without whose efforts this book could not exist.

We are particularly grateful to the draft counselors, lawyers, and other friends who have read our manuscripts looking for errors and suggesting possible improvements, and to many readers of the previous editions whose ideas have been helpful.

For endless hours of devoted manuscript typing, we thank Yuriko Hohri.

And to our wives, for understanding and forbearance, our indebtedness can never be repaid.

Although the efforts of many people were indispensable to the compilation of this book, only the authors are responsible for any errors or shortcomings in it. We encourage readers to send to the authors or the publisher suggestions for improving future editions.

PREFACE

We have written *Guide to the Draft* because we believe that, as a draft-age man, you need to know your rights and obligations under the Selective Service System if you hope to have some control over your own destiny.

Many people have justly criticized the government for its failure to provide adequate information to draft registrants. It should be possible to go to a draft board and get a pamphlet fully explaining the current regulations on deferments for men with dependents, on conscientious objection, on student deferments, or on physical standards, but no such publications are provided by Selective Service. Therefore, if you want to know your choices and rights, you must turn elsewhere. This book is our contribution to that need.

Our object is to explore the alternatives open to the man faced by decisions about the draft. We have tried to describe the choices, whether popular or unpopular, which might interest more than a few people. Since this is not a book for lawyers or expert counselors, we have tried to explain the details of each choice in non-technical language.

The draft is a controversial subject, related to hotly debated questions of military and foreign policy, and ultimately to the subject of what kind of society Americans want. Those who advocate positions on these subjects offer an important social and political service. But that is not the purpose of this book.

All we advocate here is that you get the fullest possible information, consider your choices carefully in terms of your own values, and make your own decisions. If you don't, chance and your draft board will decide for you.

We believe that each man should try to control his own life, within the social realities that surround him, not allow a government agency or any other body to control him. Decisions about the draft involve questions of education, career, health, and marriage, of conscience and principle, of life and death. We believe each person to the extent possible should make such basic decisions for himself.

Making these decisions may not be easy. You may consult others —your parents, wife or girlfriend, a clergyman, teachers, or friends, and perhaps also a trained draft counselor or a lawyer—but ultimately, the decisions must be made in the loneliness of your own mind.

Our only hope is that your decisions will be right for you—and that you will still be glad you made them two or twenty years from now.

CONTENTS

Acknowledgments		iv
Preface		v
Introduction	The Alternatives	1

Part I General Principles

Chapter 1	The Need for Draft Counseling	11
Chapter 2	Basic Precautions and Rules	20
Chapter 3	The Selective Service System	25
Chapter 4	Registration, Classification, Reopening	32
Chapter 5	Personal Appearance and Appeal	61
Chapter 6	Examination and Induction	74
Chapter 7	Two Special Problems—Travel Abroad, Delinquency	93

Part II Military and Nonmilitary Service

Chapter 8	Military and Nonmilitary Service: I-C, I-D	101

Part III Deferment and Exemption

Chapter 9	Students: I-S(H), II-S, I-S(C)	113
Chapter 10	Occupational, Vocational Training, Agricultural, Government Officials: II-A, II-C, IV-B	130
Chapter 11	Fathers, and Others with Dependents: III-A	139

| Chapter 12 | Ministers, Men Preparing for the Ministry: IV-D Aliens: IV-C Veterans, Sole Surviving Sons: IV-A | 152 |
| Chapter 13 | Rejection for Physical, Mental, or Administrative Reasons: I-Y, IV-F | 161 |

Part IV Conscientious Objection

| Chapter 14 | Applying as a Conscientious Objector | 179 |
| Chapter 15 | Noncombatant Service and Civilian Alternative Service: I-A-O and I-C, I-O and I-W | 198 |

Part V Emigration

| Chapter 16 | Leaving to Avoid the Draft | 219 |
| Chapter 17 | Emigration to Canada | 225 |

Part VI Trial and Prison

Chapter 18	Two Kinds of Prisoner—the Noncooperator and the Unsuccessful Cooperator	235
Chapter 19	Legal Defense and Sentences	241
Chapter 20	Prison and After	248

Part VII Other Sources of Aid

| Chapter 21 | Draft Counseling and Legal Aid | 255 |

Appendix A	Addresses of Selective Service Directors	269
Appendix B	Birthdays and Lottery Numbers	272
	Index	274

LIST OF FORMS ILLUSTRATED

SS Form 100	Classification Questionnaire	36
SS Form 103	Graduate or Professional College Student Certificate	126
SS Form 104	Request for Undergraduate Student Deferment	116
SS Form 109	Student Certificate	118
SS Form 110	Notice of Classification	52
SS Form 118	Dependency Questionnaire	142
SS Form 127	Current Information Questionnaire	56
SS Form 130	Application by Alien for Relief from Training and Service in the Armed Forces	156
SS Form 150	Special Form for Conscientious Objector	186
SS Form 151	Application of Volunteer for Civilian Work	202
SS Form 152	Special Report for Class I-O Registrants	204
SS Form 153	Order to Report for Civilian Work and Statement of Employer	214
SS Form 171	Apprentice Deferment Request	134
SS Form 219	Notice to Registrant to Appear for Medical Interview	164
SS Form 223	Order to Report for Armed Forces Physical Examination	76
SS Form 252	Order to Report for Induction	90
SS Form 254	Application for Voluntary Induction	104
SS Form 300	Permit for Registrant to Depart from the United States	94
DD Form 62	Statement of Acceptability	80
Standard Form 89	Report of Medical History	168
	Draft Counselee Record Form	14

INTRODUCTION

The Alternatives

In the final analysis there are only six alternatives open to you after you are registered with a draft board:

1. Military service—by enlisting in active service or reserves, volunteering for induction, or being drafted (discussed in Part II).

2. Deferment or exemption until past draft age—by qualifying for one or more of 12 classifications. If these postpone induction until you reach age 26, you are usually safe from being drafted under present Regulations (discussed in Part III).

3. Conscientious objection—by applying for and getting one of two classifications, making you eligible to be drafted into noncombatant military service (usually in the Army Medical Corps) or into civilian alternative service (discussed in Part IV).

4. Emigration—by leaving the United States for another country which will let you stay, with the likelihood that you will never be able to return (discussed in Part V).

5. Prison or probation—for being convicted of refusing to obey Selective Service orders, because you aren't given the classification you believe you should have or because you refuse to cooperate with the Selective Service System at all (discussed in Part VI).

6. Exposure to the draft lottery without being called during your year of prime eligibility—by remaining in the I-A, I-A-O, or I-O classification until the end of the calendar year without your number being reached, after which you are unlikely to be drafted under present conditions (discussed in Chapter 6).

The first alternative is discussed only briefly in this book because information about military service (including reserves) is available in books and from recruiters. The other five alternatives are discussed in great detail here.

There are a few alternatives which don't fit easily into one of these six categories. A relative few men don't register and are never caught; many nonregistrants are eventually found and offered their choice between military service and prosecution (see page 33). A few men refuse orders and are never prosecuted. A few "go underground" by changing their identities and are never caught, but they may need to conceal their true identities for the rest of their lives, and for most this is neither possible nor attractive.

In addition, some men register while living outside the United States and are assigned to a special draft board for "foreign" registrants, which doesn't induct them as long as they don't return to the U.S. before they are 26 (see page 34). Men who are rejected for physical, mental, or "administrative" reasons receive a type of deferment (see Chapter 13).

ABBREVIATIONS AND REFERENCES

Four abbreviations occur in square brackets [ ] throughout this book:

MSSA refers to the Military Selective Service Act of 1967, the law passed and amended by Congress which is the basis of the present draft. Example: [MSSA 6(j)].

REG refers to the Selective Service Regulations, the rules issued by the President and the national director of Selective Service under authority of the law. Example: [REG 1622.25].

LBM refers to the Local Board Memorandums issued by the director of Selective Service to advise draft boards on interpretations of the law and Regulations. Example: [LBM 17].

AR refers to Army Regulations, some of which affect Selective Service decisions. Example: [AR 40-501, 2-10b(5)]. The two-part number (40-501) identifies the Regulation; the numbers and letters after the comma (2-10b(5)) identify the particular section within the Regulation.

All of these may be consulted at any draft board, and at many college and public libraries (especially "Federal Depository" libraries). The references are for those who want more detailed information than can be put into a handbook of this length or who need to point out these rules to their draft boards. All except some Army Regulations can be ordered from the Superintendent of Documents, Government Printing Office, Washington, D.C. 20402, by those who want their own copies.

They are also reprinted, along with important court decisions, in the *Selective Service Law Reporter* (abbreviated SSLR in citations of court decisions in this book), a subscription service for lawyers available from Selective Service Law Reporter, Dupont Circle Building, Suite 620, 1346 Connecticut Avenue, N.W., Washington, D.C. 20036.

Copies of other publications mentioned in this book can be ordered from the addresses given, and consulted or bought at many of the draft counseling services listed in Chapter 21.

On the following four pages is a list of all Selective Service classifications with a brief description of each and a short summary of your rights. Page numbers refer to the places in this book where fuller discussions may be found.

SELECTIVE SERVICE CLASSIFICATIONS

A draft board is required by law to place you in the lowest classification for which it considers you eligible. To the extent possible, you should supply your draft board with full information concerning *all* classifications, and notify it within 10 days of any change that might affect your classification. The classifications are listed in order below, starting with the highest [REG 1623.2].

Available for Service

		See page
I-A	Available for military duty.	79, 101
I-A-O	Conscientious objector opposed to combatant duty and available for noncombatant duty only (usually Medical Corps).	198
I-O	Conscientious objector opposed to both combatant and noncombatant military duty and available for assignment to civilian alternative service.	200
Note: Conscientious objection (I-O or I-A-O), under the present law, is based upon (1) "religious training and belief," formal or personal, defined as a deeply held belief or value which leads one to (2) opposition to "participation in war in any form," if (3) Selective Service believes he sincerely attempts to live in a manner consistent with his beliefs.		179

Deferred or Exempt

			See page
I-S	Deferment required by law for:		
	a)	Student who attends high school full time and is under 20 years of age: **I-S(H)**.	114
	b)	Undergraduate student (and an occasional graduate student) who has received an induction order while attending college full time; cancels induction order and defers until end of his academic year: **I-S(C)**. Not renewable and may be received only once.	125
I-Y	Deferment for man qualified for service only in time of war or new declaration of national emergency, for physical, mental, or administrative reasons.		161
II-A	a)	Deferment required by Regulation for a trades apprentice or full-time student in "approved" trade, business, or vocational school, or junior college.	136

	b)	If requested before April 23, 1970, deferred at discretion of draft board for necessary employment.	131
II-C		If requested before April 23, 1970, deferred at discretion of draft board for essential agricultural employment.	133
II-S		Deferred for full-time college study:	
	a)	Required by law for undergraduate if all the following conditions are met: (1) student has requested deferment by letter or Form 104, (2) school has sent Student Certificate (Form 109), (3) student is receiving credit for his courses toward a degree, (4) student is taking a full-time course load (as defined by his school), (5) student is making satisfactory progress toward finishing his degree in the usual number of years, and (6) student has not reached his 24th birthday.	115
	b)	Required by law for a student of medicine, dentistry, veterinary medicine, osteopathy, or optometry.	124
	c)	At discretion of draft board for a full-time graduate student in a nonmedical field who entered his *second or subsequent* year of continuous study toward a doctoral degree in October, 1967—for up to a total of five years of continuous graduate study.	124
I-D		Deferment for man in reserves, including National Guard and advanced R.O.T.C.	106
III-A		Deferred because of dependents:	
	a)	Required by Regulation if registrant notified local board before April 23, 1970, of child (born or conceived) regularly living in his home and had not requested and re-	139

		ceived II-S student deferment after June 30, 1967.	
	b)	At discretion of draft board if evidence is provided that induction would cause "extreme hardship" to dependents; student deferments do *not* affect qualification.	140
IV-B		Judge or elected official of state or federal government deferred by law.	131
IV-C		Exemption for alien not on immigration visa if he has been in U.S. less than one year or has given up right to future U.S. citizenship, or alien registrant outside the U.S.	154
IV-D		Exemption for a minister of religion, divinity student, or full-time student pre-enrolled in seminary.	152
IV-F		Deferment for man not qualified for any service for physical, mental, or administrative reasons.	161
IV-A		Exemption for man who has completed military duty, or is sole surviving son in family of which father, brother, or sister died as a result of military service.	159
V-A		Exemption for man over draft age (26 and over for those never deferred; 35 and over for those with "extended liability").	84

Performing Service

I-W	Conscientious objector (I-O) performing civilian alternative service; **I-W(Rel.)**: conscientious objector who has completed alternative service but is not yet over age.	200
I-C	Member of the active armed forces, or commissioned officer in Public Health Service or Environmental Science Services Administration.	101

Notes

1. No classification is permanent; all may be reviewed and, if evidence warrants, changed upward or downward. Furthermore, rules are subject to change by the President, and at this writing Congress has been asked to allow ending of most II-S, II-A, and I-S(C) deferments for college and vocational study and apprenticeship. — 54

2. When you receive any classification by a local board, you have a right to a *personal appearance with your local board* if you make written request within 30 days of the date on the classification card. When you receive a classification card after a personal appearance, you have a right to *appeal to a state appeal board* if you make written request within 30 days of the date on that classification card. — 61

3. For a personal appearance or appeal to be successful, it is important that you provide all available evidence in support of your request. — 22

4. All communications with the local board should be in writing, sent by *certified mail, return receipt requested*. These receipts and copies of all correspondence should be saved as important personal records. — 21, 22

5. Under present Regulations, men classified I-A, I-A-O, and I-O who have been ordered to pre-induction physical examinations may be drafted only in the order of their lottery numbers, unless they volunteer. — 79

PART I

GENERAL PRINCIPLES

"If a registrant or any other person concerned fails to claim and exercise any right or privilege within the required time, he shall be deemed to have waived the right or privilege."

[REG 1641.2(b)]

CHAPTER ONE

THE NEED FOR DRAFT COUNSELING

No book can include enough information about the draft law and the actual practices of 4,100 draft boards to provide a complete guide for everyone. This book is intended as a concise, handy, and reliable guide for most registrants. It does not cover every problem.

Problems arise for a number of reasons. You may make mistakes and pass up your rights. Draft boards also may make mistakes and violate the Regulations. Little-known or confusing rules may cause you to go astray. Situations may arise in which you can choose among several alternatives, or claim several rights at the same time, and you may be unsure what to do and in what order.

Help is available. In most parts of the United States, especially in larger cities and on larger college campuses, there are experienced draft counselors.

WHAT A DRAFT COUNSELOR IS

Draft counselors can offer you help, usually free, if you want to know what your rights are, what choices are open to you, and how to deal with your draft board in the most effective way.

A good counselor will try to stimulate you to do your own thinking—to consider all the choices, not just the most obvious or popular ones, and to make decisions on the basis of your own long-range interests and the beliefs and values by which you live. Naturally he has his own views, but he should not try to impose them on you.

Draft counselors have no connection with Selective Service. They are answerable only to the men they counsel and to their own ethical standards.

HOW TO FIND A DRAFT COUNSELOR

Independent draft counseling centers exist in a number of cities. Other draft counselors are associated with local or national organizations. In some areas, organizations like the American Friends Service Committee (Quakers), the War Resisters League, the Fellowship of Reconciliation, and the World Without War Council provide draft counseling. So do some draft resistance groups.

Ministers, priests, and rabbis, especially those who work with students, are increasingly getting training as draft counselors and offering aid to members of their religions and others. Some high schools, colleges, and universities recognize an obligation to provide students with reliable information and guidance, and see that teachers or counselors are trained as draft counselors. At many schools, student organizations provide draft counseling.

If you want to see a good draft counselor, you can usually find one by asking around your community or school. Chapter 21 of this book lists the addresses of some organizations which can refer you to a local counselor or provide information by mail or telephone.

HOW TO RECOGNIZE A GOOD DRAFT COUNSELOR

As in every other field, draft counseling has good and bad practitioners. You will have to make your own judgment of the quality of the counseling you get.

Before he offers advice, a good draft counselor will ask many questions, either with a written questionnaire like the one on the following pages, or in discussion. He needs to learn what the draft board has done, what you have done, and what classifications you may qualify for.

A good counselor finds out what you want to do, and why. He asks enough questions to be sure you know all the possibilities open to you. If he finds that you aren't fully informed, he explains all the choices and their probable effects. He asks questions about your beliefs and values. He doesn't tell you what you should do; he encourages you to make your own decision.

No draft counselor knows the answer to every question. The

good counselor never guesses. If he doesn't know an answer, he will say so, and if the information is important he will look it up or ask another counselor, an attorney, or one of the national service organizations which train and advise draft counselors.

A good counselor encourages you to stay in touch with him. Good draft counseling is rarely a one-shot affair. It may take weeks, months, or years for your decisions to be made and acted upon. The good counselor will remain available and encourage you to come back to see him as new questions come up, or he will make sure another counselor knows about the situation and that he will be available for return visits.

Last Name_____, First Name_____

DRAFT COUNSELEE RECORD FORM

Name_____ Age_____ Date_____

Address_____ Phone_____

_____ Zip code_____ Date of birth_____

Selective Service Number_____ Lottery number_____

Present   Date   Did you request a   Date of marriage_____
classification____ issued____   personal appearance?____ Appeal?____

What do you want from your draft board? Is there a particular reason why you do not want to be drafted? (To continue school or job, help family, object to war, etc.)

Draft history: Please list all contacts you have had with Selective Service, such as when you registered, forms or letters submitted, classifications received, personal appearance or appeals, delinquency, etc.; give dates. Describe what happened.

_____

_____

_____

14

Counselor _____

_____ _____

If you have ever been in the Reserves, ROTC, National Guard or other military unit:
Dates of Service   Type of Discharge   Reason and Authority for Discharge (on DD 214)

_____ _____ _____

Armed Forces Physical Examination: Transferred,   Date of Statement of
Date   City and State   Accepted or Rejected   Acceptability (DD 62)

_____ _____ _____

If you were examined by a psychiatrist or other
specialist at the examining station, give details: _____

Is there any reason why you think you should not have passed the physical? _____

Induction Order: Have you ever received an order to report for induction?
                                                              Transferred, Postponed,
Date Issued   Date to report   City and State   Canceled or Refused?

_____ _____ _____

15

DEFERMENTS AND EXEMPTIONS   What letters and documents have you sent in to support your claims for deferment or exemption?

```
┌─────────────────┐
│ Physical, Mental,│    List injuries, illnesses, allergies, and other health problems.
│ or Administrative│   Any physical limitations, emotional problems, tests, X-rays,
│ I-Y or IV-F     │    treatment, hospitalization? Give approximate dates or state
└─────────────────┘    how recently.
```

Have you ever been charged with or convicted of a crime? _____ Charge, trial date, sentence:

Student I-S, II-S, II-A, IV-D	Record of student deferments:	Which classification?	Form 109 or 103 sent?	Date requested	Date received	Expiration date

Are you now a full-time student? _____ Toward what degree? _____

Month and year you began this program _____ When do you expect to finish? _____

Hours or credits required for degree _____ Hours or credits completed _____

Name of school(s) _____ Have you had a I-S(C)? _____

| Occupational
I-A, II-C,
IV-D | What type of work do you do? _____ Are you an apprentice? _____
Did you have or request a II-A or II-C before April 23, 1970? _____
When did you start this job or sign a contract? _____
Would it be hard for your employer to replace you? _____ Will he request deferment? _____ |

| Dependency
III-A | Is anyone dependent on you for physical, emotional, or financial reasons? _____

Are there any children living with you? _____ Do you soon expect to be a father? _____
Did you notify the board of the child or pregnancy before April 23, 1970? _____ |

| Sole Surviving Son
IV-A | Did any member of your family die   Relation
as a result of military service? _____ to you _____
How many brothers do you have now living? _____ |

| Alien
IV-C | Are you a U.S. citizen? _____ If not, what nationality? _____
Do you have a permanent residence visa? _____ Other visa? _____ |

Objection
I-A-O, I-O

Do you object to military service? _____

If so, briefly state your objection: _____

Which possibilities would you consider? (circle)
  non-combatant service (probably as a medic)
  alternative service as a civilian
  prison
  emigration
  other _____

If you will not cooperate with Selective Service, please give details:

_____

Church or religious background, if any _____

Did you claim to be a conscientious objector by signing
Series VIII on the Classification Questionnaire (SSS Form 100)? _____

Have you ever requested the Special Form for Conscientious Objector (SSS Form 150)? _____

Date issued _____ Date returned _____

Do you request I-A-O (non-combatant)
or I-O (civilian alternative service)? _____

Are there family, vocational, or other pressures which complicate your decisions?
_____

How did you learn about this draft counseling service? _____

If you have been counseled before, by whom and where? _____

This form is designed to help counselors ask and record important questions. Many counselors prefer to fill out the form themselves; others ask their counselees to do it.
MCDC, AL, 7/70

CHAPTER TWO

BASIC PRECAUTIONS AND RULES

If you have decided to allow yourself to be drafted as soon as possible, or to leave the United States to avoid the draft, or to disobey the draft law and risk prison, you will have little use for this chapter.

But if you want to qualify for any of the deferments or exemptions, hope to be recognized as a conscientious objector, or prefer to pick your own time to perform military service, you will be wise to follow the suggestions in this chapter. They are designed to insure that you don't lose your rights by accident.

1. *Plan ahead.* Deferments end, sometimes sooner than expected. No one knows what lottery numbers will be reached in any given year. Learn the choices and think about them. Think about what you will do before you're actually faced with the decision. Talk with a draft counselor if that seems desirable, and with trusted family members and friends.

2. *Observe deadlines.* Forms must be returned within 10 days (30 days for Form 150) after the date they were mailed or given to you. A personal appearance or an appeal must be requested in writing within 30 days after the date the last classification card was mailed to you (longer if you are abroad). The 10 or 30 days start the day *after* the board mailed the item to you [REG 1641.6]. If your envelope is *postmarked* by the last day, you have acted within the deadline, regardless of when it is actually received by the board [LBM 72]. But postmarks are sometimes hard to read, so don't rely on them unless you have to. Don't wait till the very last minute.

3. *See a counselor before you act.* Every draft counselor dreads the interview in which he learns that the registrant has already

written to his draft board or taken some other action—and has done something which will harm rather than achieve his objective—but the time limits have already passed. The counselor wants to help, but there isn't very much he can do. The best time to talk with a counselor is within or before the time allowed to take action, but before action has been taken. If you're going to send a letter or form to the draft board, write a rough draft and take it with you when you see the counselor; he can tell you whether it will be the best thing to send. This applies equally to conversations with lawyers.

4. *Keep a complete file.* Never throw away anything you receive from Selective Service. Save letters, forms, old draft cards. Always make carbon copies of letters you send and photocopies of forms you fill out. Get copies of any letters and forms sent by others on your behalf; the easiest way is for them to give the letter or form to you so you can make a copy, then send the original to the draft board. Keep at least one copy, and several if possible; some lawyers and counselors suggest having five or six. If you haven't kept copies in the past, you can go to your draft board to examine your file and copy anything in it, or send someone else with your written permission (see page 51 for details). Your draft board will also have photocopies made for you if you pay the cost, but it's expensive. Save all of these items in a safe place, together, where you can find them quickly when needed. When you see a draft counselor or attorney, take your entire Selective Service file with you.

5. *Put everything in writing.* Any request to the draft board for a personal appearance, appeal, postponement, or the like, must be in writing. Immediately after a personal appearance, write as complete, detailed, and objective a summary of it as your memory allows, discuss it with your draft counselor, and promptly send it to the local board for your file. Do the same after any discussion, by telephone or in person, with the government appeal agent or the draft board clerk. If you appeal or protest, only the written information will reach the appeal board or higher official. If you ever end up in court, only the evidence in your file will usually be considered. Put the date, your full name, your current address, and your Selective Service number on everything you send your board.

6. *Get proof that your letters and forms were received.* The best way is to mail them by certified mail, return receipt requested (any post office offers this service for a 45¢ fee, in addition to postage). Save the certified slip and the return receipt in your file, attached to your copy of the item you mailed. Another way is to take the letter or form to the draft board in person, and ask the clerk to give you a receipt for it or to sign and date your own copy to acknowledge receipt of the original, but some clerks refuse to do this.

7. *Send evidence.* Don't count on the draft board to investigate your claims, write to your references, or verify the information you submit. It can, but usually it doesn't. Collect the most convincing evidence you can get and send it to the board. Sections of this book on particular classifications suggest the sorts of evidence you need. Try to take a witness to your personal appearances.

8. *Use all your procedural rights.* You have a right to both a personal appearance with the local board and an appeal to a state appeal board *every* time the local board reclassifies you. You may sometimes have a right to a Presidential appeal after the state appeal. If you are unable to consult a draft counselor quickly enough, simply write, "I request a personal appearance and an appeal," and date and sign it, including your Selective Service number; send this to the local board before the 30 days are over. Use appeal rights even if it seems useless; it may not be. Read Chapter 5 for full details about your appeal rights.

9. *See the government appeal agent.* He's usually a lawyer, he's likely to be sympathetic to the draft board's view, and he may or may not be well informed about Selective Service rules. But he may know how the draft board functions, what its attitudes and prejudices are, what kind of evidence it is impressed by. If you convince him your request is reasonable, he may help convince the board. If the board is doing something wrong, he may straighten it out. He is by no means a substitute for an independent draft counselor, but he can do some things a counselor can't (for details, see Chapter 3). Write a summary of the conversation with him immediately after your meeting and send it to the local board for your file. If he gives

good advice, he may help you. If he is ignorant of the law, prejudiced against you, or misleading, your summary of the interview might help you convince a higher official to act favorably, or might even help you win in court if you end up there. Talk over his suggestions with an independent draft counselor before you act on them.

10. *Send address changes.* The Regulations require you to send changes of mailing address to your local board within 10 days. This is important because the Regulations don't require that draft board letters and forms actually reach you—only that they be mailed to your last known address. If they don't get to you promptly, you may lose important rights, or be prosecuted for violating the Regulations. If you are studying or working away from home, you may be wise to have your draft board send mail to your current address rather than rely on family members to forward it, unless you are moving frequently and fear the mail would be lost. Pick the most reliable address.

11. *Have your mail opened if you're away.* When you're traveling, vacationing, or for any other reason away from home for more than a week, be sure a family member, neighbor, or friend will check your mail for Selective Service items. If something arrives that must be taken care of before your return, be sure he can reach you by telephone or telegraph so you can act to protect your rights. If you will be completely unreachable while traveling, notify your local board by letter before you leave, telling them when you will return or have a new address.

12. *Keep your draft board informed.* The Regulations require you to notify the local board of any change that could affect draft status, within 10 days after you learn of it. You should report marriage, your wife's pregnancy, adoption of a child, separation or divorce, support of any other dependents; entering or leaving school; beginning or leaving a job that might be deferrable; realization that your beliefs make you a conscientious objector; discovery of physical conditions that might affect draft eligibility. This will not only enable you to receive deferments you are entitled to, but may keep you from being prosecuted for breaking the law.

13. *Don't believe everything you hear*. There is a lot of misinformation around. The stories you hear in the neighborhood and at school are often inaccurate, as are some of those in newspapers. And remember that board members, appeal agents, and other Selective Service officials receive virtually no training. The same is true of local board clerks, who may misinform you unintentionally. If you read this book carefully, you will probably know more than most draft board members, and at least as much as most draft board clerks. Don't assume you know everything, but don't believe something is true just because somebody at a draft board said so. Check it with a draft counselor if you can.

CHAPTER THREE

THE SELECTIVE SERVICE SYSTEM

The Selective Service System is a separate federal agency, directly under the President. Unlike any other part of the government, it is run mainly by military officers and unpaid civilian volunteers, with the important exception of the local board clerks.

This chapter describes the structure of the system, the principal officials who operate it, and the powers they have.

THE LOCAL LEVEL

Local Boards

There were 4,098 draft boards in the United States and its territories at the end of fiscal year 1969. Every county has at least one, except for some rural areas where one local board may serve up to five counties. In heavily populated areas, a local board may serve only a part of a city. In general, a local board is supposed to serve an area with a total population of no more than 100,000 people.

In practice, the number of draft-age men in a local board area varies considerably. In 1966, three local boards had more than 50,000 registrants each; 147 local boards had fewer than 1,000 registrants each (*Report of the National Advisory Commission on Selective Service*).

Each local board must have three or more members. Typically a board has three to five members, and under the 1967 law, women as well as men may serve (242 were serving in mid-1970). Members are nominated by the governor of the state, usually on the advice of the state director of Selective Service, and appointed by the President of the United States. They must be at least 30 years old, and may not serve after they reach 75 or have been on a board for

25 years. They serve without pay and may not be members of the armed forces or reserves. Anyone should be able to find out who the local board members are because their names must be posted in the public part of the office [REG 1606.62(b)].

Local board members must live in the county served by the board and, if the board serves only part of a county, should "if at all practicable" live in the area served by the board [REG 1604.52(c)]. Research efforts and several court cases suggest that this requirement is often violated, but few men know it because the Selective Service System tries to keep the addresses of board members secret.

Minority groups, particularly Negroes, are underrepresented on draft boards. The director of Selective Service reported in mid-1970 that 1,257 local board members, or 6.6% of the total of 18,941, were Negroes, compared with 278 at the end of 1966, 623 at the end of 1967, and 1,091 in mid-1969. At that time he also reported that "588 Spanish-speaking Americans, 82 Oriental Americans, and 64 American Indians" serve on local boards (*U.S. News and World Report,* July 6, 1970). According to the National Advisory Commission report, most board members are business, professional, and other white-collar workers, except in rural areas, where many farmers serve on boards. About two-thirds of draft board members have served in the armed forces.

The members of the local board have sole authority to classify and induct registrants. Legal decisions can be made only at meetings attended by a majority of the members. Most boards meet once a month for a few hours; some meet more often.

Although a local board can ask you to come to a meeting, this is rarely done, except for conscientious objector applicants (see page following 196). Otherwise, the only time you are likely to meet your local board is when you request a personal appearance as part of the appeal process (discussed in Chapter 5).

Clerks

Since the average registrant accepts whatever classification he is given, he seldom or never meets the draft board members themselves. If you go to the draft board office, you will meet not board members but the full-time, paid clerks.

The principal clerk is the executive secretary, who may be assisted by additional clerks. In larger cities, a single office may contain a number of local boards and have a very large clerical staff.

The clerks have no legal authority to make decisions for the board, but their influence is great. Because the board members meet infrequently, most of the decisions are in fact made by the clerks and merely approved at board meetings. As full-time staff members, the clerks may be the only local Selective Service officials who take the time to become familiar with the details of the Regulations, and their advice is usually accepted by the board.

They may also be the best source of information if you want to know the actual practices of your board so you can present a convincing case for the classification you want. But you should be aware that clerks are often too busy to give full information, and sometimes don't know the rules themselves, so you should check what they say with an independent draft counselor.

Government Appeal Agents

Another source of information and help is the government appeal agent or his associate. He is usually a lawyer, appointed by the President on the recommendation of the governor of the state. His name must be posted in the public area of the draft board office.

In practice, his principal role is as advisor. You are notified of your right to see the appeal agent each time the local board classifies you I-A, I-A-O, or I-O so you may get information about your appeal rights. On your request, the local board clerk must arrange a meeting for you with the appeal agent or a suitable substitute [LBM 82].

The appeal agent is not an independent counselor, however. He is required "to be equally diligent in protecting the interests of the Government and the rights of the registrant in all matters" [REG 1604.71(d)(5)]. Some appeal agents file reports of their meetings with registrants and some may reveal to the board any unfavorable information they have learned.

In his dual role as advisor to the registrant and legal advisor and informant to the draft board, the appeal agent cannot necessarily be trusted to represent your interests adequately. Nor, as an unpaid, part-time volunteer, does the appeal agent always know very much about Selective Service rules. But he may be useful anyway, and you are wise to consult him.

First, the appeal agent may be able to tell you what kind of evidence the board expects to see, whether it will allow witnesses at personal appearances, whether it is generous or tight with the classification you are hoping to get. Second, if the appeal agent is convinced that your request is reasonable, he may be willing to help convince the board. On the board's invitation, the appeal agent can attend any meeting [REG 1604.71(d)(2)]. Third, if the board has acted illegally, the agent may help to get the error corrected. And if you want the board to reopen your classification so you may have another opportunity to meet with the local board and appeal to a state board, the appeal agent can recommend reopening [REG 1604.71(d)(3)].

He also has several other powers. He can appeal a classification to the state appeal board at any time before an induction order is issued, while you can usually appeal only during a 30-day period [REG 1626.2(b)]. If the state appeal board has ruled unfavorably, as long as no induction order has been issued, the appeal agent has the power to recommend to the state director that it be required to reconsider, or that a Presidential appeal be allowed even if the state appeal board vote was unanimous [REG 1626.61(b)].

Some local boards also have "advisors to registrants" who have no specific powers except to give information.

Medical Advisors

An unpaid local physician appointed by the President on the nomination of the state governor may serve as medical advisor to a local board. His principal role is to give "medical interviews" to registrants who claim to have physical conditions which may disqualify them for military service. On his advice, you may be classified I-Y or IV-F without the bother and expense of a complete armed forces physical examination (for details, see Chapter 13). Since the state director can authorize any medical advisor in the state to advise any local board [REG 1604.61], no local board should deny the right to a medical interview because it does not have a medical advisor available.

THE STATE LEVEL

State Appeal Boards

There are 96 state appeal boards, at least one in each state or territory and, within each state, one in every federal court district. Many of them are divided into two or more panels.

Each state appeal board or panel consists of five members nominated by the governor and appointed by the President. They must meet the same qualifications as members of local boards. They must live in the federal court district served by the appeal board. The members of the appeal board are supposed to be "representative of the activities of its area" and therefore "should include one member from labor, one member from industry, one physician, one lawyer, and, where applicable, one member from agriculture" [REG 1604.22].

No registrant can appear in person before an appeal board. When you appeal the local board classification, your complete Selective Service file is sent to a state appeal board. Without meeting you or performing any investigation, the appeal board members review the file and classify you as they think suitable. A 1970 Minnesota court decision reveals that the appeal board members often do not even see the file but act on the basis of a "brief" prepared by a clerk (*U.S. v. Wallen,* No. 4-70 CR 34, D. Minn., July 2, 1970). Then they send the file, their decision, and their vote back to the local board. Except in the rare cases when the appeal board is required to reconsider its decision or when a Presidential appeal is possible, this is a final decision. In fiscal year 1969 there were 165,054 appeals to state appeal boards, compared with 117,835 in 1968, 119,167 in 1967, 49,718 in 1966, and 9,741 in 1965.

State Directors

There is a state director of Selective Service for each of the 50 states and also for Puerto Rico, the Canal Zone, Guam, the Virgin Islands, the District of Columbia, and New York City (the director for New York State has no authority in New York City), for a total of 56 state directors. Each is a salaried employee appointed by the President on the recommendation of the governor of the state.

About five out of every six state directors are military officers or retired officers, as are many of the members of their state headquarters staffs who make most of the day-to-day decisions.

The state directors have very great power. Among other things, they can order a local board to reopen a classification, and can appeal a classification to the state appeal board or order the appeal board to reconsider its decision. They can appeal a classification to the Presidential appeal board regardless of the vote of the state appeal board, and can postpone or cancel an induction order. They can use any of these powers at any time, even after an induction order has been issued, or after a refusal of induction.

In addition, most state directors send memorandums to local boards interpreting the Regulations and advising on deferment and other policies. You can read and copy these at local boards or state headquarters. And a local board generally asks the advice of its state director when it is unsure what to do about a difficult case. The advice is not binding on the local boards, but local boards usually follow it as though it were the law.

The addresses of the 56 state directors are listed on page 269.

THE NATIONAL LEVEL

Presidential Appeal Board

The Selective Service Act provides for an appeal to the President of the United States as the final level of appeal. These appeals are in fact considered by a three-member board appointed by the President. Its formal name is National Selective Service Appeal Board, but it is usually called the Presidential appeal board. Its members, unlike the members of local and state boards, are paid for their time. One member is Negro.

Although many registrants are dissatisfied with the decisions of state appeal boards, very few are able to appeal them to the Presidential appeal board. In fiscal year 1969 there were 3,084 Presidential appeals, compared with 2,171 in 1968, 2,175 in 1967, 798 in 1966, and 163 in 1965. See Chapter 5 for the conditions under which a Presidential appeal is possible.

Director of Selective Service

The head of the Selective Service System is Dr. Curtis W. Tarr, appointed March 20, 1970, to succeed General Lewis B. Hershey. His powers include all of those held by the state directors, and others as well. He has authority, as does the President, to issue Selective Service Regulations, which have almost the same power as the law passed by Congress. He also issues several types of advisory memorandums—principal among them the Local Board Memorandums and the Operations Bulletins—to guide local and appeal boards and state headquarters in setting policies and interpreting the Act and Regulations. These have no legal status but are generally followed as faithfully as the law itself. His office publishes an informative monthly newsletter, called *Selective Service News* (formerly *Selective Service*), available at $1.00 per year from the Superintendent of Documents, Government Printing Office, Washington, D.C. 20402, and a *Semi-Annual Report to Congress,* 25¢ from the same address.

The director is assisted by a large staff in Selective Service National Headquarters, 1724 F Street, N.W., Washington, D.C. 20435.

FOR FURTHER INFORMATION

Two books contain fairly recent information about the structure, personnel, and attitudes of the Selective Service System: *In Pursuit of Equity: Who Serves When Not All Serve? Report of the National Advisory Commission on Selective Service* (Washington: Government Printing Office, 1967, $1.50); and James W. Davis, Jr., and Kenneth M. Dolbeare, *Little Groups of Neighbors: The Selective Service System* (Chicago: Markham Publishing Co., 1968, $3.95).

CHAPTER FOUR

REGISTRATION, CLASSIFICATION, REOPENING

In this chapter and the next one, we will describe the official procedures and offer suggestions for making use of them.

These procedures should be followed very carefully if you are trying to get the classification you believe you deserve. A mistake may cost you important rights.

You should also watch closely to be sure your draft board obeys the Regulations and gives you all the rights you are entitled to. A draft board will generally correct its mistakes when they are pointed out by a registrant, though sometimes the help of the appeal agent, state director, or national director, or even a Congressman, is needed. But only you, aided by your draft counselor (or lawyer), are likely to discover the procedural errors.

Many court cases have been won by registrants because draft boards didn't follow the right procedures, and many have been lost because registrants didn't follow them.

REGISTRATION

In the U.S.

The law requires men of draft age, including nearly all American citizens, and most noncitizens living in the United States and its territories, to register for the draft [MSSA 3]. By order of the President (Proclamation 2799, July 20, 1948), a man subject to registration must go to the nearest draft board within 5 days after his 18th birthday, although no one is drafted before he is 19.

The only citizens exempt from registration are those in the armed forces, including the reserves and military academies, in the Environmental Science Services Administration, and most of those in the Public Health Service. If they leave these services, they must register with Selective Service within 30 days [REG 1611.2(a), 1611.4].

A number of categories of aliens are exempt from draft registration. Those admitted as permanent residents must register just as citizens do. But those admitted on temporary visas may be exempt from registration if they are representatives or employees of foreign governments, workers admitted for seasonal labor, students, reporters for foreign newspapers, or members of the immediate families of any of these [REG 1611.2].

In addition, treaties make all temporary aliens from 15 countries exempt from registration: Argentina, Austria, Costa Rica, China, Estonia, Honduras, Ireland, Italy, Latvia, Liberia, Norway, Paraguay, Spain, Switzerland, Yugoslavia. All aliens living in the Canal Zone, whether on permanent or temporary visas, are exempt from registration [LBM 16]; aliens in other U.S. territories must register unless they are exempted for one of the reasons listed here.

Noncitizens living in the U.S. who don't fall into one of these exempt categories must register with a draft board just as citizens must, within 5 days after they turn 18. If they arrive in the U.S. after they become 18, but before they reach age 26 (35 for medical specialists), they must register within six months after their arrival [REG 1611.1, 1611.5]. Those who are exempt but later change their status to a category required to register must do so immediately. (See Chapter 12 for special rules on the classification of aliens.)

Men in asylums, jails, or similar institutions at the age of registration are registered by the institution when they leave it [REG 1611.6, 1613.41]. Ironically, this includes men sent to prison for refusing to register for the draft.

What happens to those who don't register at the required time? Draft boards usually overlook a short delay. It is usual for a board to classify in the normal way a man who registers voluntarily days, weeks, and sometimes many months after his 18th birthday, though a man who is very late is sometimes threatened with prosecution unless he "volunteers" for military service.

When a man who hasn't registered is discovered by the Selective

Service System (typically because of a police inquiry when he is arrested for something else, or because a neighbor notifies the draft board), he is often given the choice between arrest and immediately entering the armed forces. Sometimes he is simply allowed to register and is subject to the draft only if his lottery number is reached. A Supreme Court decision (*Toussie v. U.S.,* 397 U.S. 112, 2 SSLR 3451, 1970) allows prosecution of those who refuse to register only if charges are filed within five years after registration was required (in other words, by the time the man is 23 years and 5 days old); after that he can't be punished, provided he lived openly in the United States during the five years.

At the time of registration, you are required to give only general information, such as personal identification, address, age. The permanent address you give is important because it will determine which local board you are assigned to. If you live at several addresses at different times of the year, you have a right to decide which you regard as your permanent address for draft board purposes [REG 1613.12(a)].

If you register at a draft board which doesn't have jurisdiction over your address, it will transfer the records to the proper local board.

The local board which is assigned at the time of registration is permanent; you can never transfer to another after you are classified. (For the one exception, see "Registration Abroad," below.) However, if you are living far from your local board at the time you return your Classification Questionnaire (discussed below), on written request you can have a local board near you decide your initial classification and can have your personal appearance there; this limited transfer is allowed only for the first classification [REG 1623.9(a)].

Shortly after registration, the local board mails you a Registration Certificate, one of the two draft cards you are required to keep.

Registration Abroad

If you are an American citizen living outside the United States and its territories when you turn 18, you are required to go to an American consulate or embassy as soon as possible. There you will be registered for the draft and assigned to a local board at your permanent address in the United States.

However, if you don't give any address in the United States, you join 28,000 other men registered with the District of Columbia Local Board No. 100 (Foreign). As long as you don't enter the United States, present Selective Service policy is not to order you for physical examination or induction [LBM 73]. If you return to the United States and settle in a community, your registration is transferred to the local board there and you are subject to the draft like any other registrant of that local board [LBM 62]. Or Local Board 100 may draft you when it learns of your return, even if you didn't settle in the U.S. Of course, if you have remained abroad until your 26th birthday and are not in a medical profession, you will not be drafted even if you are transferred to an ordinary local board. This loophole in the draft rules seems intended primarily for the children of American diplomats and career military men abroad. If larger numbers of men tried to take advantage of this policy, it probably would be changed.

Another policy which affects only a tiny number of Selective Service registrants forbids sending any mail to, or ordering physical examination or induction of, a registrant while he is in Cuba [LBM 73].

CLASSIFICATION

Classification Questionnaire (Form 100)

Shortly after registration, the local board to which you are permanently assigned will send you a Classification Questionnaire (Form 100). The form is reproduced on the following pages. The form in use as this book is completed asks a number of questions relating to classifications that can no longer be given, and it is likely that Selective Service will issue a revised form.

You have 10 days to complete and mail back the Form 100. Since it is important to fill it in correctly if you hope to receive the most favorable classification you are entitled to, you need this time. Sometimes the clerk will give it to you at the time you register and ask you to fill it out on the spot. This is improper, and you should explain that you need the 10 days you are entitled to, and will take

SELECTIVE SERVICE SYSTEM

Form approved.
Budget Bureau No. 33-R102.13.

CLASSIFICATION QUESTIONNAIRE

DATE QUESTIONNAIRE RECEIVED AT LOCAL BOARD

Date of Mailing _____

COMPLETE AND RETURN BEFORE _____   2. Selective Service No.

(Local Board Stamp)

1. Name of Registrant (First)   (Middle)   (Last)

3. Mailing address (Number and street, city, county and State, and Zip code)

(The above items, except the date received back at local board, are to be filled in at the local board before the questionnaire is mailed.)

INSTRUCTIONS

The law requires you to fill out and return this questionnaire on or before the date shown to the right above in order that your local board will have information to enable it to classify you. A notice of your classification will be mailed to you. When a question or statement in any series does not apply, enter "DOES NOT APPLY," or "NONE," otherwise complete all series.

36

The law also requires you to notify your local board in writing, within ten days after it occurs, of (1) every change in your address, physical condition and occupational, marital, family, dependency and military status, and (2) any other fact which might change your classification.

Fill out with typewriter or print in ink.

....
Member, Executive Secretary, or Clerk of local board

STATEMENTS OF THE REGISTRANT

Confidential as Prescribed in the Selective Service Regulations

Series I.—IDENTIFICATION

1. Name	2. Date of birth
(Last) (First) (Middle)	
3. Other names used (If none, enter "None")	4. Place of birth
5. (a) Color eyes	(b) Color hair	(c) Height	(d) Weight	6. Citizen or subject of (country)
7. If naturalized citizen, give date, place, court of jurisdiction and naturalization number
8. Current mailing address
(Number and street or R.F.D. route) (City, town, or village) (County) (State) (Zip code)
9. Telephone No. (If none, enter "None")	10. Social Security No. (If none, enter "None")
11. Name and address of person other than a member of my household who will always know my address
(Name) (Address)

SSS Form 100   (Revised 10-8-68)   Supplies of previous printings shall be used until exhausted.

(1)

Series II.—MILITARY RECORD
(Use Page 6, if necessary)

1. If you are now on or have been separated from active military service enter: (*a*) Armed Force ....
   (*b*) Service number .... (*c*) Date of entry ....
   (*d*) Date of separation .... (*e*) Character of service ....
   (*f*) Type of transfer or discharge ....
2. If you are now a member of a Reserve component (including the National Guard) give: (*a*) Name and address of unit ....
   (*b*) Service number .... (*c*) Date of enlistment or appointment ....
3. If you are now a member of a Reserve Officer Training Corps or any other officer procurement program, state the program, the Armed Force, date of entry, and any identifying number ....

(Enter on page 6 military service other than in Armed Forces of the United States.)

Series III.—MARITAL STATUS AND DEPENDENTS
(Use Page 6, if necessary)

1. (*a*) I (check one): ☐ have never been married; ☐ am a widower; ☐ am divorced; ☐ am married.
   (*b*) I (check one if applicable): ☐ DO ☐ DO NOT live with my wife; if not, her address is ....
   (*c*) We were married at ...., on ....
                           (Place)   (Date)
2. I have .... children under 18 years of age of whom .... live with me in my home.
          (Number)   (Number)
3. If you have no child, other than an unborn child, attach a statement from a physician showing the basis for his diagnosis of pregnancy and the expected date of birth.
4. The following other persons are wholly or partially dependent upon me for support:

38

Dependent	Relationship	Age	Approximate Income (Annual)	Amount Contributed by Me
Name Address			$	$
Name Address			$	$
Name Address			$	$
Name Address			$	$

Series IV.—REGISTRANT'S FAMILY
(Use Page 6, if necessary)

List below all the living members of your immediate family who are 14 years of age or over (except those shown in Series III) including your father, mother, brothers, sisters, father-in-law, and mother-in-law.

Relatives	Relationship	Age	Can This Relative Contribute to Support of Claimed Dependents [1]
Name Address			☐ Yes ☐ No
Name Address			☐ Yes ☐ No
Name Address			☐ Yes ☐ No
Name Address			☐ Yes ☐ No
Name Address			☐ Yes ☐ No
Name Address			☐ Yes ☐ No

[1] If your answer is "Yes," state extent of ability to contribute in detail on page 6.

(2)

Series V.—OCCUPATION

(Use Page 6, if necessary)

If Engaged in Agriculture, Also Fill in Series VI

1. I am now employed as a (Give full title, for example: bricklayer, farmer, teacher, auto mechanic, steelworker. If not employed, so state.) ....

2. I do the following kind of work (Give a brief statement of your duties. Be specific.)
   ....
   ....

3. My employer is ....
   (Name of organization or proprietor, not foreman or supervisor. Enter "Self" if self-employed.)

   ....
   (Address of place of employment—Street, or R.F.D. Route, City, and State)

   whose business is ....
   (Nature of business, service rendered, or chief product)

4. (a) I have been employed by my present employer since ....
   (Month and year)

   (b) I am paid at the rate of $.................... ☐ Per Hour ☐ Day ☐ Week ☐ Month.
   (c) I work an average of .... hours per week.

5. Other business or work in which I am now engaged is ....
   (Nature of business, if none, enter "NONE")

6. Other occupational qualifications, including hobbies, I possess are ....
   ....

7. My work experience prior to that described in items 1 and 2, this series, is ....

8. I speak fluently the following foreign languages or dialects ....
9. I read and write well the following foreign languages or dialects ....

Series VI.—AGRICULTURAL OCCUPATION
(Use Page 6, if necessary)

1. I have been engaged continuously in farmwork since .... (Month and year)

2. I am (check appropriate box): ☐ Sole owner-operator of a farm ☐ Joint owner-operator with another ☐ Hired manager ☐ Cash tenant or renter ☐ Standing rent tenant ☐ Sharecropper ☐ Share tenant ☐ Wage hand (hired man) ☐ Unpaid family worker.

3. I (check one): ☐ AM ☐ AM NOT personally responsible for the operation of the farm where I work.

4. The principal crops and livestock of the farm I operate or work on are:

Names of Crops	Acres Devoted to Each	Kinds of Livestock	Number of Each Now on Farm

5. Principal products marketed during the last 2 years ....

6. Total value of products sold from this farm during the last crop year $..................

7. The number of year-round workers on this farm is .... of whom .... are hired hands.
   (Number) (Number)

8. Other farm experience ....

Series VII.—MINISTER OR STUDENT PREPARING FOR THE MINISTRY
(Use Page 6, if necessary)

1. I have been a minister of the .... since ....
   (Name of sect or denomination)   (Month) (Day) (Year)
   and (check one): ☐ HAVE ☐ HAVE NOT been formally ordained.
2. I was formally ordained at .... by ....
   on (date) ....
3. I am a student preparing for the ministry pursuing a full-time course of instruction at the ....
   .... under the direction of ....
   (Name and address of theological or divinity school)   (Name of church or religious organization)
4. I am a student preparing for the ministry under the direction of ....
                                                                                    (Name of church or religious organization)
   pursuing a full-time course of instruction at the ....
                                                                                    (Name and address of school)
   leading to my entrance into ....
                                                                                    (Name and address of theological or divinity school)
   in which I have been pre-enrolled.

Series VIII.—CONSCIENTIOUS OBJECTOR

(DO NOT SIGN THIS SERIES UNLESS YOU CLAIM TO BE A CONSCIENTIOUS OBJECTOR)

I claim to be a conscientious objector by reason of my religious training and belief and therefore request the local board to furnish me a Special Form for Conscientious Objector (SSS Form 150).

....
(Signature)

Series IX.—EDUCATION

(Use Page 6, if necessary)

GRADE OR YEAR COMPLETED (Line through all grades or years successfully completed) (Exclude trade or business schools)	NONE	ELEMENTARY AND HIGH SCHOOL												COLLEGE				POST GRADUATE			
		1	2	3	4	5	6	7	8	9	10	11	12	1	2	3	4	1	2	3	4	5

1. (*a*)

   (*b*) I graduated from high school in (month) .... (year) ....

2. (*a*) I am a full-time student in (check one): ☐ High school ☐ Trade school ☐ Business school ☐ College

   .... majoring in ....
   (Name and address of institution)

   preparing for .... and expect to (check one):
   (Occupation or profession)

   ☐ Finish course on .... ☐ Complete degree requirements on ....
   (Date)   (Date)

   (*b*) I will be a full-time student next semester at ....
   (Name and address of institution)

3. (*a*) I have completed .... years of college, majoring in .... and (check one): ☐ HAVE ☐ HAVE NOT

   at .... received a degree.
   (Name and address of institution)

   (*b*) I have received the degree(s) of ....

Series X.—STATEMENT OF ALIEN

1. I was admitted to the United States for (check one): ☐ PERMANENT RESIDENCE ☐ TEMPORARY RESIDENCE on ....
   (Date of entry)

2. My Alien Registration Number is ....
   If you have not been admitted to the United States for permanent residence, enter on page 6 a supplemental statement setting out the date you first entered the United States, with the dates of each subsequent departure and reentry when applicable. Attach copies of documentary evidence in your possession verifying your claimed alien status.

(4)

43

Series XI.—PHYSICAL CONDITION
(Use Page 6, if necessary)

1. If you were ever found not qualified for service in the Armed Forces state (*a*) when .... (*b*) where ....

2. If you have any physical or mental condition which, in your opinion, will disqualify you for service in the Armed Forces, state the condition and submit a physician's statement, if you have one, with this form or submit such a statement at a later date.

....

3. If you have ever been an inmate or a patient in a mental or tuberculosis hospital or institution, give the name and address of each hospital or institution, and the period of hospitalization.

....

Series XII.—COURT RECORD
(Use Page 6, if necessary)

1. I (check one): ☐ HAVE ☐ HAVE NOT been convicted or adjudicated of a criminal offense or offenses, other than minor traffic violations. (If "HAVE" box is checked, complete this series.)

Offense (other than minor traffic violations)	Date of Conviction (Month, Day, Year)	Court (Name and Location)	Sentence

2. I (check one): ☐ AM ☐ AM NOT now being retained in the custody of a court of criminal jurisdiction, or other civil authority. Specify ....
(Awaiting trial, on probation, on parole, etc.)

Series XIII.—SOLE SURVIVING SON

I (check one): ☐ AM ☐ AM NOT the sole surviving son of a family of which the father or one or more sons or daughters were killed in action or died in line of duty while serving in the Armed Forces of the United States or subsequently died as a result of injuries received or disease incurred during such service.

REGISTRANT'S CERTIFICATE

INSTRUCTIONS.—You are required to make the registrant's certificate. If you cannot read, the questions and your answers shall be read to you by the person who assists you in completing this certificate. If you are unable to sign your name, you shall make your mark in the space provided for your signature in the presence of a person who shall sign as witness.

NOTICE.—Imprisonment for not more than 5 years or a fine of not more than $10,000, or both such fine and imprisonment, is provided by law as a penalty for knowingly making or being a party to the making of any false statement or certificate regarding or bearing upon a classification. (Military Selective Service Act of 1967.)

I CERTIFY that I am the registrant named and described in the foregoing statements in this questionnaire; that I have read (or have had read to me) the statements made by and about me, and that each and every such statement is true and complete to the best of my knowledge, information, and belief.

....   Registrant   ....
(Date)   sign here   (Signature or mark of registrant)

....
(Date)   (Signature of witness to mark of registrant)

If anyone has assisted you in completing this questionnaire, such person shall sign the following statement: I have assisted the registrant herein named in completing this questionnaire because ....

....
(For example—registrant unable to read and write English, etc.)

....
(Signature of person who has assisted)

....
(Number and Street or R.F.D. Route)

Date ....
               (City)   (State)   (Zip code)

(5)

Series XIV.—STATEMENT OF REGISTRANT
(Refer to Series Number)
(Use additional sheets if necessary)

_____
(Signature of Registrant)

_____
(Date)

(6)

(Registrant Will Make No Entries on This Page)

Dates	Minutes of Actions by Local Board and Appeal Board and on Appeal to the President (Continued from Page 8)	Vote	
		Yes	No

(7)

(Registrant Will Make No Entries on This Page)

Dates	Minutes of Actions by Local Board and Appeal Board and on Appeal to the President	Vote	
		Yes	No

(Continue on Page 7)

(8)

U.S. GOVERNMENT PRINTING OFFICE

the form home and return it when it is due. Normally, however, the form is mailed to you a few weeks or months after you register. If you have a good reason, the board can extend the 10-day limit for returning it [REG 1621.10(b)].

The Form 100 should be filled out very carefully. The answers to it will determine your classification and perhaps how soon you may be drafted, if at all. If you need more space for any answer, you should use the blank lines on page 6 of the form or attach your own extra pages. You should also get letters, forms, or other evidence from members of your family, your employer, your school, your minister, your doctor, or others as needed to prove answers which may make you eligible for certain classifications, and this evidence should be sent with the Form 100 (or as soon afterwards as possible). As with all Selective Service papers, you should make photocopies of the completed form and all related papers, and keep them together safely where they can be found if needed later.

Series I of the Form 100 asks for information about identification and address. Since it is important that you get mail from the draft board promptly to protect your rights, you should give the address where you actually get your mail.

Series II asks about your past or present military service. If you have served enough time in the armed forces of the United States or an allied country, you may be exempt from the draft in classification IV-A (see Chapter 12 for details). If you are in a reserve unit, the National Guard, or advanced college R.O.T.C., you probably are eligible for a I-D classification (see Chapter 8 for details). You should provide full information if you think you qualify for either of these.

Series III and IV ask about marriage and family relationships. If you provided evidence before April 23, 1970, that you had children or that your wife was pregnant, you would probably have qualified automatically for classification III-A. Now you must show that your child or other family members or other dependents would suffer "extreme hardship" if you were drafted to qualify for III-A, and this type of deferment is hard to get and takes careful proof. If you think you may qualify for the "extreme hardship" deferment, you should answer Series III and IV only after reading Chapter 11 of this book, and if possible talking with a draft counselor.

Series V asks about work and occupational skills. Before April 23, 1970, the answers could be used to give a II-A occupational deferment, but this can now be given only to men who applied before that date. Apprentices are still able to get this deferment, and so are some full-time vocational school and junior college students (see Chapter 10 for details). Evidence, usually a letter from the employer or school requesting this deferment, is essential.

Series VI asks about farm work and was the basis for giving the II-C deferment (discussed in Chapter 10) before April 23, 1970, but it, like other occupational deferments, is now restricted to those who had applied before that date.

Series VII should be filled out carefully if you are eligible for the IV-D exemption as a minister or while preparing for the ministry (details in Chapter 12). You must receive this exemption if you are a minister as your "regular and customary vocation," whether or not you are ordained. You are also classified IV-D while a full-time student in a seminary or in a preparatory program leading to a seminary in which you are pre-enrolled, provided your studies are sponsored by a church or religious organization.

Series VIII should be signed if your beliefs make you opposed to participating in war. Signing it will cause the board to send the Special Form for Conscientious Objector (Form 150), to apply for the I-O or I-A-O classification, so you should be prepared to fill this out too. See Chapters 14 and 15 for a discussion of this subject; most conscientious objectors need the help of a draft counselor. If you are a conscientious objector and also are eligible for a deferment (as a college student, for example), you should sign Series VIII and file Form 150 as soon as possible to get your claim on record. Doing so should not have any effect on deferments; the board shouldn't consider the conscientious objector claim while you are eligible for any deferments.

Series IX asks about education and is the basis for giving I-S(H) and II-S deferments, and sometimes II-A. If you are under 20 and a student in high school, you should get a I-S(H) deferment without difficulty, but you may be asked for a letter from the high school saying you are a full-time student. If you are a student in college, you will receive the II-S deferment only if you request it in writing (separately from this form) and have the school send its form to the draft board. The date you expect to graduate (question 2(a)) may be important; it might be difficult to get further deferments if you need more time than you estimated to complete school, so the *latest* probable date should be entered. If you are a full-time student in a trade, vocational, or business school and are not working for a college degree, you should get a II-A deferment and need to have the school send a form or letter to the draft board. If you are entering college or other school next term, you should specify where (question 2(b)) and attach a copy of your admission letter, receipt for a tuition deposit, or other evidence. The President proposed changes in the law and Regulations on April 23, 1970, which would deny new II-S and II-A educational deferments to those who first qualified for them after that date, but at this writing Congress has not acted on the request. See Chapters 9 and 10 for details of these deferments.

Series X must be completed if you are not a U.S. citizen but are required to register for the draft. The calculation of time spent in the U.S. is important because the IV-C classification is given only during the first one year in this country, whether in a single visit or several visits added together. See Chapter 12 for details.

Series XI asks about physical and mental conditions which might disqualify you from military service. Classifications I-Y and IV-F (discussed in Chapter 13) may be based on your answer to this question and the doctors' letters and other evidence which you should send with the form or as soon as possible afterwards. In most cases, however, the information isn't used until a medical interview or examination is ordered by the draft board. Although Selective Service files are supposed to be confidential, this isn't always true, and information about physical and mental conditions sent to Selective Service may be seen at some time by other government agencies.

Series XII asks about criminal convictions and court custody. If you have been convicted of a felony (a crime that can be punished by more than a year in prison), you may sometimes, but not always, be classified IV-F. If you have a long record of minor convictions, you may possibly be classified I-Y or IV-F. If you are awaiting trial or are on probation or parole, you cannot be drafted until you are out of the custody of the court. Copies of records to prove this status should be attached to the form if possible. See Chapter 13 for details.

Series XIII asks about eligibility for the IV-A exemption (discussed in Chapter 12) as the only living son in a family of which at least one member died as a result of service in the U.S. armed forces. Evidence should be attached; the Veterans Administration may be the best source of evidence and advice.

You must sign and date the Form 100 on page 5. If someone else has written the answers, he must sign at the bottom of this page, but a lawyer or draft counselor who merely advises or gives information should not sign here.

The completed Form 100 becomes the basis for future draft classifications. The last two pages (the back cover and inside back cover) contain spaces where the draft board members or clerks will record actions taken, including letters and forms sent and sometimes also those received, classifications and the votes by which they were given, and appeals. Since you have the right to examine and copy your file [REG 1606.32, 1670.8, LBM 97], this is the first place you would look to learn what has been done and when. (Clerks record some actions by form numbers, so you may need to copy the list and take it to a draft counselor to figure out what the numbers mean.)

Initial Classification

Soon after you return the Form 100, often at the next monthly meeting, the local board should classify you in the lowest classification it believes you are qualified for (considering I-A highest, and continuing in the order of the list on pages 4–6). For information on transferring the initial classification if you live far from your local board, see page 34.

The board must consider all the information in the file, including any letters or forms you have sent with the Form 100 or later.

If you have indicated that you might be eligible for a lower classification than I-A, but haven't given enough information for the board to be sure whether you qualify, the board can ask you or others (employer, school, etc.) for more information. The board can also ask governmental and welfare organizations for information about you. And the board can ask you to come to a board

SELECTIVE SERVICE SYSTEM

This is your Notice of Classification, advising you of the determination of your selective service local board that you have been classified in accordance with Selective Service Regulations. The various classifications are described on the reverse side of this communication. You are required to have a Notice of Classification in your personal possession.

When a subsequent Notice of Classification is received you should destroy the one previously received, retaining only the latest.

FOR INFORMATION AND ADVICE
GO TO ANY LOCAL BOARD

SELECTIVE SERVICE SYSTEM
NOTICE OF CLASSIFICATION
This is to certify that

_____
(First name) (Middle initial) (Last name)

Selective Service No. _____

Is classified in Class _____

until _____
by Local Board unless otherwise checked below:
☐ by Appeal Board vote of ___ to ___
☐ by President

_____
(Date of mailing)

_____
(Member, Executive Secretary, or clerk of local board)

_____
(Registrant's signature)
(Sign here)

SSS Form 110 (Rev. 5-25-67)
(Previous printings are obsolete)
(Approval not required)

DETACH ALONG THIS LINE

(Fold along this line)

The law requires you to have this Notice in addition to your Registration Certificate, in your personal possession at all times and to surrender it upon entering active duty in the Armed Forces.

The law requires you to notify your local board in writing within 10 days after it occurs, (1) of every change in your address, physical condition and occupational (including student), marital, family, dependency and military status, and (2) of any other fact which might change your classification.

Any person who alters, forges, knowingly destroys, knowingly mutilates or in any manner changes this certificate or who, for the purpose of false identification or representation, has in his possession a certificate of another or who delivers his certificate to another to be used for such purpose, may be fined not to exceed $10,000 or imprisoned for not more than 5 years, or both.

(LOCAL BOARD STAMP)
SEE OTHER SIDE

SELECTIVE SERVICE CLASSIFICATIONS

CLASS I

Class I-A: Registrant available for military service.
Class I-A-O: Conscientious objector registrant available for noncombatant military service only.
Class I-C: Member of the Armed Forces of the United States, the Environmental Science Services Administration, or the Public Health Service.
Class I-D: Qualified member of reserve component, or student taking military training, including ROTC and accepted aviation cadet applicant.
Class I-O: Conscientious objector available for civilian work contributing to the maintenance of the national health, safety, or interest.
Class I-S: Student deferred by law until graduation from high school or until attainment of age of 20, or until end of his academic year at a college or university.
Class I-W: Conscientious objector performing civilian work contributing to the maintenance of the national health, safety, or interest, or who has completed such work.
Class I-Y: Registrant qualified for military service only in time of war or national emergency.

CLASS II

Class II-A: Occupational deferment (other than agricultural and student).
Class II-C: Agricultural deferment.
Class II-S: Student deferment.

CLASS III

Class III-A: Extreme hardship deferment, or registrant with a child or children.

CLASS IV

Class IV-A: Registrant with sufficient prior active service or who is a sole surviving son.
Class IV-B: Official deferred by law.
Class IV-C: Alien not currently liable for military service.
Class IV-D: Minister of religion or divinity student.
Class IV-F: Registrant not qualified for any military service.

CLASS V

Class V-A: Registrant over the age of liability for military service.

SPECIAL NOTICE

A registrant who was deferred on or before his 26th birthday should ascertain from his local board if his liability has been extended to his 28th or 35th birthday. (See other side.)

NOTICE OF RIGHT TO PERSONAL APPEARANCE AND APPEAL

If this classification is by a local board, you may, within 30 days after the mailing of this notice, file a written request for a personal appearance before the local board (unless this classification has been determined upon such personal appearance). Following such personal appearance you may file a written notice of appeal from the local board's classification within the applicable period mentioned in the next paragraph after the class of mailing of the new notice of classification. If you do not wish a personal appearance but do want to appeal your case, you may do so by making such an appeal in writing, to your local board, within the specified time.

Appeal from classification by local board may be taken by filing written notice of appeal with your local board within one of the following periods after the date of mailing of this notice:
(1) 30 days if the registrant is located in the United States, its territories, possessions, Canada, Cuba, or Mexico OR;
(2) 60 days if the registrant is located in a foreign country other than Canada, Cuba, or Mexico.

You may file with your local board a written request that the appeal be submitted to the appeal board having jurisdiction over the area in which your principal place of employment or current place of residence is located.

If an appeal has been taken, and one or more members of the appeal board dissented from such classification, you may file a written notice of appeal to the President with your local board within 30 DAYS after the mailing of this notice.

Your Government Appeal Agent, attached to your selective service local board, is available to advise you regarding your rights and liabilities under the selective service law.

Your Selective Service Number, shown on the reverse side, should appear on all communications with your local board. Sign this form immediately upon receipt.

FOR INFORMATION AND ADVICE, GO TO ANY LOCAL BOARD

GPO : 1967 O - 284 -141

meeting so it can ask you for more information before classifying you. But these things are not usually done. Most boards don't go out of their way to get information, leaving it up to you to send it if you want a lower classification.

When you have been put into a classification, the local board sends you a Notice of Classification (Form 110), usually called a classification card, the second card (along with the Registration Certificate) which you are required to keep. It shows the classification and the date on which it was mailed (an important date for appeal purposes), and sometimes the "expiration" date of the classification, the date on which the board plans to reconsider your classification. The Notice of Classification is illustrated on pages 52 and 53.

REOPENING

The first classification you get isn't necessarily permanent, even if you don't appeal or if you use up all your appeal rights and are still left in that classification. The local board sometimes must "reopen" the classification—that is, start the classification process all over again, consider all the evidence in the file, and place you in the lowest classification it considers you eligible for, thus giving you the right to personal appearance and appeal.

When a deferment expires, the local board reopens your classification and either renews your deferment or puts you in a different classification. The local board will often send a Current Information Questionnaire (Form 127), before it reopens your classification or issues an induction order, to learn of new circumstances; this form is illustrated on the following pages. If you send in new information, as you are required to do within 10 days after any change in your circumstances which might affect your classification, the local board should look it over. If your evidence is for a *higher* classification, the board shouldn't reopen your classification as long as you qualify for the lower classification. For example, if you send in a claim as a I-O conscientious objector or evidence of a temporary medical disqualification while you are a college student classified II-S, the evidence would just be put into your file for later use. But if you send information about a *lower* classification than your present one, the board should reopen your classification at its next meeting and consider giving you the lower classification.

The Regulations say a local board "may" reopen the classification on request "if such request is accompanied by written information presenting facts not considered when the registrant was classified, which, if true, would justify a change in the registrant's classification" [REG 1625.2]. Although the Regulations say the board "may" reopen when new facts supporting a reclassification are first presented, the Supreme Court has ruled that it *must* reopen, provided no induction order is outstanding (*Mulloy v. U.S.,* ... U.S. ..., 3 SSLR 3011, 1970).

You may make a request for reopening at any time. It may also be made by anyone who claims to be your dependent, or by the government appeal agent who serves the local board. When requesting a reopening (or reclassification), it is sometimes helpful to ask for a meeting with the board to discuss your reasons. This is especially important if you claim to be a conscientious objector, in which case the local board should give you an interview before it can turn down your claim [LBM 41]; see Chapter 14 for details.

When the local board reopens your classification, it mails a new Notice of Classification to you—and a Classification Advice (Form 111) to a dependent or employer who requested a deferment for you—showing your classification. Sometimes the classification will be the same as before, but the reopening is still desirable, for it gives you a new chance to get a personal appearance and appeal.

The Regulations do not allow reopening a classification after an induction order has been issued, "unless the local board first specifically finds there has been a change in the registrant's status resulting from circumstances over which the registrant had no control" [REG 1625.2(b)]. Therefore, it is important to submit all evidence and make all claims before an induction order is issued. However, a few claims may be recognized after issuance of an induction order—for example, a hardship deferment if your father has suddenly died and you must support the family. If you are seeking reopening after issuance of an induction order, it may be especially useful to ask for a meeting with your local board (often called a "courtesy hearing" or "interview").

Form Approved.
Budget Bureau No. 33-R178.11

SELECTIVE SERVICE SYSTEM
CURRENT INFORMATION QUESTIONNAIRE

(Local Board Stamp)

TO:

DATE QUESTIONNAIRE RECEIVED BY LOCAL BOARD

Selective Service No.	Date of birth	Class
	(Month) (Day)	

Date of Mailing

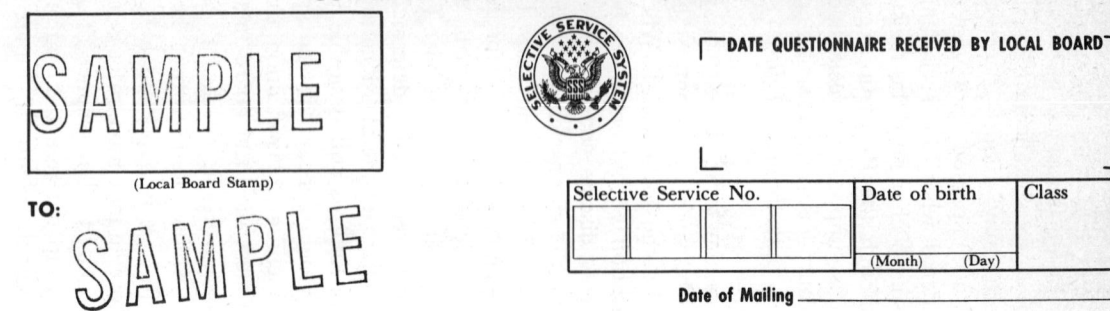

COMPLETE AND RETURN BEFORE

(The above items, except the date questionnaire returned, are to be filled in by the local board clerk before questionnaire is mailed)

The law requires you to fill out and return this questionnaire on or before the date shown to the right above in order that your local board will have current information to enable it to classify you. When a question or statement in any series does not apply, enter "DOES NOT APPLY", or "NONE"; otherwise complete all series. You may attach any additional information you believe should be brought to the attention of the local board. After completing the statements be sure to date the form and sign your name. FILL OUT WITH TYPEWRITER, OR PRINT IN INK.

_____
(Member, Executive Secretary, or Clerk of Local Board)

STATEMENTS OF THE REGISTRANT
CONFIDENTIAL AS PRESCRIBED IN THE SELECTIVE SERVICE REGULATIONS

SERIES I.—MAILING ADDRESS

1. Name(s) and address(es) of person(s) other than a member of your household who will always know your address _____

2. My current mailing address is _____

3. My telephone number (home or business) is _____ (ZIP code) _____

Series II.—MARITAL STATUS AND DEPENDENTS

1. (a) I (Check one) ☐ HAVE NEVER BEEN MARRIED ☐ AM A WIDOWER
                      ☐ AM MARRIED   ☐ AM DIVORCED
   (b) I (Check one) ☐ DO ☐ DO NOT live with my wife; if not, her address is _____
   (c) We were married at _____ (Place) _____ on _____ (Date)

2. (a) I have the following children under 18 years of age who live with me in my home:
   Name _____ Age _____ Name _____ Age _____
   Name _____ Age _____ Name _____ Age _____
   (b) If you have no child other than an unborn child, attach a statement from a physician showing the basis for his diagnosis of pregnancy and the expected date of birth.

3. I (Check one) ☐ DO ☐ DO NOT have dependents other than those listed above.

Series III.—MILITARY RECORD

1. If you are now on or have been separated from active military service enter (a) Armed Force _____
   (b) Service number _____ (c) Date of entry _____
   (d) Date of separation _____ (e) Type of separation _____

2. If you are now a member of a reserve component (including the National Guard) give (a) Name and address of unit _____
   (b) Service number _____ (c) Date of enlistment, transfer, or appointment _____

3. If you are now a member of a Reserve Officer Training Corps or any other officer procurement program describe fully _____

SSS FORM 127 (Revised 4-22-69)
(Previous printings may be used)

(CONTINUED ON REVERSE SIDE)

Series IV.—PRESENT OCCUPATION

1. I am now employed as a (give full title: for example, bricklayer, farmer, teacher, auto mechanic, steel worker. If not employed, so state) _____
2. I do the following kind of work. (Give a brief statement of your duties. Be specific) _____
3. My employer is _____
   (Name of organization or proprietor, not foreman or supervisor; enter "Self" if self-employed)
   _____
   (Address of place of employment—Street, or R.F.D. Route, City, and State)
   whose business is _____
   (Nature of business, service rendered, or chief product)
4. I have been employed by my present employer since _____ (Month and year)
5. Other occupational qualifications, including hobbies, I possess are _____
6. I speak fluently the following foreign languages or dialects _____
7. I read and write well the following foreign languages or dialects _____

Series V.—EDUCATION

1. (a) Grade or year completed

	Elementary and High School	College	Post Graduate
None	1 2 3 4 5 6 7 8 9 10 11 12	1 2 3 4	1 2 3 4 5

(Line through all grades or years successfully completed) (Exclude trade or business schools)

(b) I graduated from high school in (month) _____ (year) _____.

2. (a) I am a full-time student in (check one) ☐ High School ☐ Trade School ☐ Business School ☐ College
   at _____
   (Name and address of institution)
   preparing for _____
   majoring in _____
   and expect to (check one) ☐ finish course on ☐ complete degree requirements on _____ (Occupation or profession) (Date)

   (b) I will be a full-time student next semester at _____

3. (a) I have completed _____ years of college, majoring in _____ and (check one) ☐ HAVE ☐ HAVE NOT received a degree.
   at _____ Date _____
   (Name and address of institution)
   (b) I have received the degree(s) of _____ Date _____, _____ Date _____

Series VI.—Court Record

1. If you have been convicted or adjudicated of a crime or crimes other than minor traffic violations complete this series. If none enter "NONE."

Offense (other than minor traffic violations)	Date of Conviction (Month, Day, Year)	Court (Name and Location)	Sentence

2. I (Check one) ☐ AM ☐ AM NOT now being retained in the custody of a court of criminal jurisdiction, or other civil authority. Specify _____
(Awaiting trial, on parole, etc.)

Series VII.—Physical Condition

1. If you were ever rejected for service in the Armed Forces state (a) when _____ (b) where _____

2. If you have any physical or mental condition which, in your opinion, will disqualify you for service in the Armed Forces, state the condition and submit a physician's statement, if you have one, with this form or submit such a statement at a later date. _____

3. If you have ever been an inmate or a patient in a mental or tuberculosis hospital or institution, give the name and address of each _____

Series VIII.—Sole Surviving Son

I (Check one) ☐ AM ☐ AM NOT the sole surviving son of a family of which the father or one or more sons or daughters were killed in action or died in line of duty while serving in the Armed Forces of the United States or subsequently died as a result of injuries received or disease incurred during such service.

REGISTRANT MUST DATE AND SIGN BELOW

NOTICE.—Imprisonment for not more than 5 years or a fine of not more than $10,000, or both such fine and imprisonment, is provided by law as a penalty for knowingly making or being a party to the making of any false statement or certificate regarding or bearing upon a classification.

_____   _____
(Date)   (Registrant's signature)

U.S. GOVERNMENT PRINTING OFFICE : 1969 OF—348-294

(For conscientious objection claimed after issuance of an induction order, see page 185; for college students who receive induction orders during the school year, see page 125.)

If a reopening is allowed, the induction order is automatically canceled, except in a few unusual cases [REG 1625.14].

CHAPTER FIVE

PERSONAL APPEARANCE AND APPEAL

Every time you are classified by the local board, whether it is your first classification or not, you have at least two rights: a personal appearance with your local board and an appeal to a state appeal board. This is true even if the new classification card has the same classification as the old one. And it is true every time the local board changes the classification, as when a deferment runs out and the board issues a I-A.

There is one exception. If the new classification card is issued as a result of a personal appearance, you have only the right to appeal to a state appeal board; you can't ordinarily get another personal appearance immediately. (If the classification is a state appeal board decision, the box on the card marked "by Appeal Board" is checked and the vote is shown. In that case you can't have a personal appearance or a state appeal, but you can sometimes get reconsideration by the state appeal board or a Presidential appeal. While there is no further appeal possible after a Presidential appeal, other steps may be possible.)

You must have the personal appearance before the appeal. There is no need to choose between them; you have a right to both, and except in unusual circumstances it is a good idea to use both. This is true even if you have no convincing grounds for a lower classification. You have the right to these procedures, and at the least you may gain three to six months or more during which no induction order can be issued. By the end of that time your circumstances may have changed. If so, you may be eligible for a different classification and should send in the new information and request a reopening (discussed on page 54). However, under the rules of the draft lottery, delaying until you reach your 26th birthday by use of these procedures will not necessarily enable you to escape the draft (see Chapter 6).

PERSONAL APPEARANCE

Request

If you want to meet with your local board, to try to convince it to give you the classification you want, you must request a personal appearance in writing within 30 days after the date your classification card was mailed to you (this deadline applies even if you are outside the country). No one but the registrant can request this right.

Your request does not have to be in any particular form. A letter saying, "I request a personal appearance" would do. You should include your Selective Service number, the date, and your signature. Of course it is better if you also explain in this letter why you think your classification should be changed, and include evidence you want the board to consider. Sometimes the board will give the desired classification without a personal appearance, on the basis of the letter and evidence, but the personal appearance should be requested anyway so the right won't be lost.

All Selective Service deadlines should be taken seriously, but the 30 days allowed to request a personal appearance should be considered especially important because the Regulations discourage the board from granting late requests [REG 1624.1(a)]. Despite this, some boards *have* granted late requests when good reasons were given, so there is no harm in trying if the deadline has already passed. The 30-day period begins on the day *after* the board mails the classification card. If your letter is postmarked on or before the 30th day, your request must be granted, even though the letter was received after the 30 days ended [LBM 72].

The personal appearance can't ordinarily be transferred. This may mean inconvenience and travel expense if you live far from the local board, but the effort may impress the board with your sincerity. If you are having difficulty getting the classification you want by corresponding with the board, you should usually consider it worth the trouble and cost to present your arguments in person, and to answer their questions. Unless you are applying for CO status, personal appearance is the *only* chance you ever have to meet the Selective Service officials who are making the decisions about you. Where the classification you want is a matter of judgment rather than an automatic right, the personal appearance is the most important part of the process, far more likely to succeed than the state appeal.

If you have applied for recognition as a conscientious objector, you should also receive a preclassification interview with the local board, and you then have the right also to a personal appearance if still dissatisfied (see Chapter 14).

For additional suggestions for a personal appearance (some of them in disagreement with the advice in this book), see Allan Blackman's *Face to Face with Your Draft Board* (Berkeley: World Without War Council, 2nd edition, 1970, 95¢).

If it is impossible to travel immediately to a personal appearance, the board will sometimes agree to a reasonable delay—until a school vacation, for example.

If there is no time when you can travel to a personal appearance, as a last resort you can ask your local board to allow you to appear before a board where you are then living. This courtesy is sometimes allowed in place of a personal appearance. The nearby board meets with you and sends your local board a report. Your local board then makes its decision without meeting personally with you.

If even this isn't allowed, you will have little choice but to pass up your right to a personal appearance and just appeal to a state appeal board.

If you aren't sure you will get to the personal appearance, but want to keep the possibility open while making sure you will have the right to appeal to a state appeal board, you may want to request both rights in the same letter. This letter might begin, "I request a personal appearance and will appeal if necessary." If you miss the personal appearance, write to remind the board (preferably within 30 days) of your earlier request for an appeal.

Preparation

There are several things you can do to prepare for a personal appearance. First, you may want to talk with a draft counselor.

Second, you may want to talk with the government appeal agent or the local board clerk, or both of them, to ask what sort of evidence the board requires, why the board didn't give the desired classification, how much time you should expect to have, whether the board usually admits witnesses, and what its attitudes are toward the classification you requested. (The clerk should arrange an appointment with the appeal agent on request.) Third, you should go over the evidence you have submitted to be sure nothing helpful, or essential, has been forgotten and that you have attempted to explain any obvious weaknesses in your case; the draft counselor may help with this. Fourth, you should prepare a very simple outline, perhaps on an index card, of the things you want to say at the meeting; you should take this with you as a reminder, look at it occasionally during the meeting, and be sure you mention everything you intend to.

If you are applying for one of the harder classifications to get (I-A-O, I-O, III-A because of extreme hardship, and sometimes IV-D), you will probably want to take a witness to the personal appearance. The Regulations allow a local board to admit witnesses but don't require it to [REG 1624.1(b)], so you and your witness should be prepared for the possibility of refusal. But even if you know in advance that your board doesn't usually admit witnesses, if you think a witness would supply needed information and strengthen your case, you should ask the witness to attend with you. The board may admit him, or a refusal to hear the witness may show prejudice or unfairness on appeal or if the case ever gets to court.

If you plan to take a witness, select him carefully. If you are having trouble getting renewal of an occupational deferment, you will probably take your employer or supervisor. If you want a hardship-to-dependents deferment, you may want to take your dependent, a doctor who can testify about disability or family circumstances, a clergyman, social worker, employer, family friend, or neighbor. If you are a conscientious objector, you would take witnesses who know your character and sincerity, preferably from long acquaintance, and who may also know your religious beliefs and your feelings about war. In general, the best witness would be older than you and respected in the community—someone the board members would trust. Some boards have been willing to hear two or three, or even more, witnesses, but this is rare.

Once the best witness has been selected and has agreed to attend, you and your witness should spend some time together talking about the process. Only the witness can decide what he will say, but you can help him understand what you are applying for and why, the purpose of the meeting, and the kind of information he will need to supply.

Any specific information the witness has should be put into letter form in advance and given to the board at the personal appearance. But the presence of the witness may still be valuable, for it gives the board members a chance to ask him questions and to evaluate his honesty and reliability. One of the Regulations on personal appearances states, "The registrant may present such further information as he believes will assist the local board in determining his proper classification" [REG 1624.2(b)]. It can be argued that the presence of the witness is the only way to show the board members that he is trustworthy, and therefore that refusing to allow witnesses would violate this provision of the Regulations.

The Regulations do not allow you to be represented or advised by a lawyer at the personal appearance [REG 1624.1(b)]. Most courts have upheld this limitation, but the Supreme Court has agreed to review it during its 1970–71 term (*U.S. v. Weller*). Meanwhile, if you have an attorney and he and you believe his presence at your personal appearance (or a preclassification interview or courtesy hearing, at which the Regulations do not forbid participation by an attorney) would be valuable, make a written request for him to be admitted, then take him with you even if the board makes him wait outside, but avoid argument about his right to advise you. There is nothing to stop a lawyer from being admitted as a witness.

You may find it helpful to arrange for a group of friends to act as a "draft board" and put you through an advance "personal appearance." Some draft counselors will arrange for this role-play preparation because they believe it lets you experience some of the emotions of the actual personal appearance while you practice explaining your position.

At the Personal Appearance

It isn't possible to know how soon after your request the personal appearance will actually take place. Usually the clerk will send you a letter asking you to come to the board's next monthly meeting, but sometimes it may be several months before a board will schedule it. Some boards prefer to delay the personal appearance until after you have received your pre-induction physical examination. However long it takes, no induction order can be issued to you during the time allowed to request a personal appearance or appeal or while you are waiting for either [REG 1624.3]. For this reason, if you want to gain as much time as possible, you may mail your request for the personal appearance toward the end of your 30-day period.

If transportation problems or a personal emergency keep you from attending your personal appearance, you should write to the board as quickly as possible explaining what happened and asking for a new appointment. If the reason is good, the local board should schedule a new personal appearance.

Or if you find you cannot go at all, submit whatever additional information you can in writing for the board's reconsideration, and state that if they cannot give you the classification you want, you hereby appeal to the state appeal board.

When the personal appearance actually takes place, you may meet with the entire board, some of its members, or only one member [REG 1624.2(a)]. The clerk is usually present. Of course, if a majority of the members isn't present, no decision can legally be made at that time [REG 1604.56], but those present can talk with you and report to the others at a later meeting. Some lawyers question the legitimacy of the Regulation that allows a minority of the board members to hold a personal appearance, and advise clients whose claims are turned down after such hearings to request a new appearance before the entire board in addition to appealing; such requests are sometimes granted.

Sometimes the clerk or one of the board members takes notes of the meeting; you may be asked to sign these "official" notes to acknowledge that they are accurate. If they are, there is no harm in your signing if you wish to, but otherwise you should politely decline and promise to send your own summary.

You and all witnesses are required to swear (or affirm) that you will tell the truth [REG 1604.57].

The personal appearance may last only a few minutes or may continue for half an hour or in rare cases even an hour. Some boards ask many questions; others merely allow you to make a statement. You should be prepared for anything. If you have brought the brief outline of your arguments suggested above, it will help you give a concise statement explaining why you should get the classification you want. If the board controls the discussion with questions, you may want to check off on your outline each of your arguments as you get the chance to make it. If you find the meeting is ending before you have said everything you consider important, you should ask permission to add a final statement. Some boards ask you if you have additional comments to make before they end the personal appearance.

It is sometimes useful to ask the board members some questions, if you can do so in a diplomatic way. "Have you read the letter from Mr.———?" may tell you how well they know your claim; if they haven't, you should summarize its contents. This may cause them to read your file more closely. "What would you consider sufficient evidence—or a suitable situation—to give the——— classification?" may tell you on what basis the board grants the classification you want, and perhaps enable you to provide the needed information. It may even reveal whether the board is making decisions on an illegal basis.

Following the personal appearance, the local board must consider all the evidence and place you in the lowest classification it believes you qualify for (using the order shown on page 3).

Some boards vote immediately and tell you the result before you leave. Others dismiss you and vote in private.

In either case, the local board *must* send you a new classification card after the personal appearance [REG 1624.2(d)]. This gives you official notice of the decision and starts a new 30-day period during which you can appeal.

After the Personal Appearance

Immediately after the personal appearance, you should write down everything that happened there, in dialogue form if possible. Your witness, if one was admitted, can help you remember, and can write about the part in which he participated. This summary should be as complete as memory allows, written in an objective, factual way. If your rights seem to have been violated by anything the board did or said, or failed to do, this should be included. At the end of the summary, or in a cover letter, you should ask the board to notify you if the summary has any inaccuracies. You should send your summary, and any prepared by witnesses, to the local board for your permanent file. In this way, although no transcript of the meeting is made, you can create a record which may aid you if you later need to complain of unfairness to the appeal board or state director, or to defend yourself in court. And at the same time you fulfill your obligation to summarize in writing any new information you give at the personal appearance [REG 1624.2(b), LBM 52].

APPEAL

You have the right to appeal within 30 days after the board mails you a new classification card following the personal appearance (60 days if you are in a foreign country, other than Canada or Mexico). Or, if you can't use your right to a personal appearance, you can appeal within the same period after you receive the original classification or reclassification. All that is necessary is a letter to the local board saying, "I request an appeal," with your Selective Service number, the date, and your signature; usually the letter should go on to explain why you feel you should receive the classification you want and to point out any ways in which you feel your local board gave inadequate or unfair consideration to your claim.

If you miss the 30-day deadline, a late request can be granted if you have a good excuse or didn't understand your rights [REG 1626.2(d)], and any letter you send should be interpreted in your favor to allow an appeal even if you weren't very specific [REG 1626.11(a)].

You aren't the only one with the right to appeal your classification. An employer who has requested an occupational deferment for you must be notified of the board's decision at the same time as you are, and he has the right to appeal whether you do or not. Similarly, anyone who claims to be your dependent has the right to appeal for a III-A. Three officials of the Selective Service System also have this power—the government appeal agent for the local board, the state director, and the national director—and they may sometimes appeal when the local board gives you a classification which you want but which they disagree with.

It may be a good idea to try to find out why your previous efforts have been unsuccessful. Check your file at the draft board, to learn the board's vote and see if anything was written to explain the decision. A few local boards will answer a letter asking why the requested classification wasn't given, but most will not. Sometimes the clerk knows. This is a good time to see the government appeal agent again, for he may be able to find out why the local board didn't give the desired classification in response to the written request and the personal appearance.

If these efforts give clues to the evidence needed, it should be obtained if possible and mailed to the local board with your request for an appeal. If you are submitting important new evidence with your request for an appeal, ask the local board to review the file before sending it to the appeal board; the board may decide to give you the classification you want on the basis of the new evidence.

Even if you have written to request an appeal early in the 30-day period, the Regulations seem to require that your file be kept at the local board until this period is over, then sent to the appeal board within five days [REG 1626.14], but boards often don't wait. Thus you should have 30 days to try to get evidence that will convince the appeal board, but you would be wise to act as quickly as possible.

Unlike personal appearances, some appeals can be transferred. If you are working or living in a different appeal board area, your appeal letter or that of your employer or dependent may ask that the appeal be sent to the appeal board there instead of the one in your local board area. This seems especially useful if you are seeking renewal of an occupational deferment given by an out-of-state appeal board, or if you believe you will be the victim of prejudice in your home area. The transfer must be allowed on request if you work in a different area and are applying for occupational deferment, or if you live in a different area regardless of the classification you want [REG 1626.11(b) and (c)].

According to the Regulations, the appeal board considers only the written information in your file and its own knowledge of "economic, industrial, and social conditions" in the area. It does not allow you to appear before it, nor does it do any investigation of its own. If it feels more information is needed, however, it can send the file back to the local board to get the information and then return it [REG 1626.23], but this is not often done. The appeal board is supposed to consider all the information in the file, then place you in the lowest classification it believes you are eligible for (using the order on page 3).

In reality, the Presidential appeal board and many state appeal boards rarely read registrants' files but rely on résumés or summaries prepared by clerks. Therefore, in your letter to the local board requesting an appeal, it may be helpful to ask whether a résumé will be prepared. If one is, request that you be allowed to see a copy so you can correct any errors before it goes to the appeal board to use in deciding your classification. Your request probably will not be granted, but it may provide a defense if you end up in court.

After it classifies you, the appeal board sends its decision, including its vote, to the local board, which mails a new classification card to you. Thus you know the appeal board's decision and whether you can appeal further, for only a split vote in the appeal board allows you the right to a Presidential appeal, and split votes are rare.

AFTER AN UNSUCCESSFUL APPEAL

Reconsideration by Appeal Board

In cases where the state appeal board vote is unanimous, you don't have the right to appeal to the Presidential board, but there are several steps open to you.

The first of these is to try to get the state appeal board to reconsider its decision. The Regulations provide that it must reconsider on request of the state or national director of Selective Service, and they give the government appeal agent for the local board specific power to ask the state director to issue such a request [REG 1626.61].

Presidential Appeal

Those few registrants who receive split votes at the state appeal board level have a right to a Presidential appeal. You must request it in writing within 30 days after the local board mails the classification card with the result of the state appeal (no longer period is allowed for those who are in foreign countries), although the local board may allow the appeal after 30 days if it is convinced you didn't understand your right to appeal or that your delay was due to a cause beyond your control [REG 1627.3].

But there is also another way the Presidential appeal can be obtained. The state and national directors have the right to order it at any time regardless of the vote of the appeal board [REG 1627.1], and the government appeal agent has the right to ask the state director to use this power, provided no induction order has been issued [REG 1626.61]. Therefore, if your request was denied by unanimous vote of the appeal board, but you want a Presidential appeal because you feel the decision was unjust, you should ask these officials to use these powers. This advice applies equally if reconsideration by the state appeal board is not granted, or if the appeal board has reconsidered but still denies the request unanimously.

Since the local board is free to issue an induction order as soon as a unanimous state appeal board decision has been mailed to you, provided you have already passed (or failed to attend) a pre-induction physical examination and your lottery number has been reached, great haste is sometimes necessary at this point. The following steps may be taken:

1. Write to the state director (addresses are on page 269) asking him to request that the appeal board reconsider its decision or to make a Presidential appeal, and enclose copies of

a few of your most convincing items of evidence. If your local board is in one state and your appeal was transferred to another, write to both state directors.

2. At the same time, see the government appeal agent and ask him to make both requests of the state director.

3. At the same time, send the national director a carbon copy of the letter to the state director and the evidence, along with a cover letter telling him that he is being kept informed in case his help is needed later. If the state director refuses to act, ask the national director to allow appeal board reconsideration or Presidential appeal.

4. If neither director will act, write directly to the President (The White House, Washington, D.C. 20500), sending him copies of your correspondence with the directors and your most convincing evidence. Send a copy of your letter and the same enclosures to Chairman, National Selective Service Appeal Board, 1724 F Street, N.W., Washington, D.C. 20435. Ask that you be granted a Presidential appeal. The Presidential appeal board has the power to accept appeals on its own authority [MSSA 10(b)(3), REG 1604.6(b)].

5. Send the local board copies of all letters as they are sent and ask it by letter to postpone issuance of an induction order until the directors or the President decides whether to act.

Even if an induction order is issued during this period, it will automatically be canceled if one of them agrees to allow a reconsideration or a Presidential appeal.

If a Presidential appeal is allowed, the file is reviewed by the three-member National Selective Service Appeal Board, which does not meet you. Like the lower boards, the Presidential board must put you in the lowest classification it believes you qualify for. It returns the file to your local board, which mails you a classification card showing the decision of the Presidential board.

There is, of course, no further appeal possible after the Presidential appeal, but even so you may not have reached the end of the process. If you can provide evidence that you qualify for a different classification, or get very significant and entirely new evidence for the classification you were denied, you may be able to get the local board to reopen your classification, which would allow you to start the entire process over again.

If your rights seem to have been violated or strong evidence has been unreasonably ignored, and if no Selective Service official will act to correct the situation, as a final resort you may wish to write to your Congressman and Senators.

Sometimes an experienced draft counselor or an attorney familiar with Selective Service can see possibilities you may have overlooked.

CHAPTER SIX

EXAMINATION AND INDUCTION

There are two final steps by which you are drafted into military service: an examination to determine whether you are eligible, and induction into the armed forces. (Chapter 15 deals with alternative service for conscientious objectors.)

ARMED FORCES PHYSICAL EXAMINATION

You may not be ordered into military service by your draft board unless you have taken, passed, and been officially notified of passing an armed forces physical examination.

There are only two exceptions. If you have been ordered to take a pre-induction examination but have "refused or otherwise failed to comply" [REG 1631.7], or if you have volunteered for induction (discussed in Chapter 8) [REG 1628.10], you may be ordered for induction without the examination, but you must be given it at the time of induction and will be rejected if you fail it.

Except for those classified I-O, men who don't report for examination when ordered to do so can be prosecuted for breaking the law; however, the current policy is not to do so but to induct them in their normal turn.

Most men are examined shortly before the board expects to draft them. A local board may order registrants to take their physical examinations whenever they are classified as eligible for service (I-A, I-A-O, or I-O), regardless of whether an appeal is pending, starting with those closest to being drafted [REG 1628.11(b)]. A board may also order a man in any other classification to take this examination "if it determines that his induction may shortly occur" [REG 1628.11(c)].

Under a 1970 change, you may request a pre-induction examination if you have never been given one, in which case your local board must schedule it within 60 days (unless the national director rules that the local board or the examining station is too overburdened to meet all requests). You must request the examination in writing, visiting or sending a letter to your own local board. If you want to take the examination in a different place from the local board area, the transfer should be requested and the reasons explained when the examination is requested, and your local board (unless it turns down the transfer) will arrange for a local board near you to order an examination within 60 days after the nearby board gets the notice. You must receive at least 15 days' notice of the time of an examination given at your request [REG 1628.11 (e), LBM 105].

The Regulations do not state how much time you must ordinarily be given from the time the Order to Report for Armed Forces Physical Examination is mailed until the date set for the examination, but it seems logical to assume that at least the same notice should be allowed. In practice, the order is usually mailed two to four weeks before the date of the examination.

When an Order to Report for Armed Forces Physical Examination (Form 223) is issued, you are required to obey it unless you get it postponed or canceled, or transferred to a different city.

The conscientious objector classified I-O is the only exception. He may take the physical examination if he wishes, but he will be ordered to perform civilian work anyway if he doesn't take it. The I-O registrant who fails the examination isn't required to do civilian work.

A local board is allowed to postpone your examination for up to 60 days in case of a death in your family, extreme family emergency, serious illness, or other emergency, and one additional 60-day postponement is possible if the emergency makes it necessary. In addition, the state and national directors of Selective Service have unlimited authority to allow postponements for any reason [REG 1628.12].

The Regulations don't provide for or prohibit canceling an order to take a physical examination, but both logic and the national director [LBM 66, for example] suggest that it can be canceled by

SELECTIVE SERVICE SYSTEM

ORDER TO REPORT FOR ARMED FORCES PHYSICAL EXAMINATION

Approval Not Required.

(LOCAL BOARD STAMP)

---------- (Date of mailing)

SELECTIVE SERVICE NO.

To _____

at: _____

You are hereby directed to present yourself for Armed Forces Physical Examination by reporting at: _____ (Place of reporting)

on _____ (Date) at _____ (Hour)

_____
(Member, Executive Secretary, or clerk of Local Board)

☆ U.S. GOVERNMENT PRINTING OFFICE: 1969—357-419

IMPORTANT NOTICE
(Read Each Paragraph Carefully)

TO ALL REGISTRANTS:

If you are so far from your own Local Board that reporting in compliance with this Order will be a hardship and you desire to report to the Local Board in the area in which you are now located, take this Order and go immediately to that Local Board and make written request for transfer for examination.

When you report pursuant to this order you will be forwarded to an Armed Forces Examining Station where it will be determined whether you are qualified for military service under current standards. Upon completion of your examination, you will be returned to the place of reporting designated above. It is possible that you may be retained at the Examining Station more than 1 day for the purpose of further processing. You will be furnished transportation, and meals and lodging when necessary, from the place of reporting designated above to the Examining Station and return. Following your examination your local board will mail you a statement issued by the commanding officer of the station showing whether you are qualified for military service under current standards.

If you are employed, you should inform your employer of this order and that the examination is merely to determine whether you are qualified for military service. To protect your right to return to your job, you must report for work as soon as possible after the completion of your examination. You may jeopardize your reemployment rights if you do not report for work at the beginning of your next regularly scheduled working period after you have returned to your place of employment.

IF YOU HAVE HAD PREVIOUS MILITARY SERVICE, OR ARE NOW A MEMBER OF THE NATIONAL GUARD OR A RESERVE COMPONENT OF THE ARMED FORCES, BRING EVIDENCE WITH YOU. IF YOU WEAR GLASSES, BRING THEM. IF YOU HAVE ANY PHYSICAL OR MENTAL CONDITION WHICH, IN YOUR OPINION, MAY DISQUALIFY YOU FOR SERVICE IN THE ARMED FORCES, BRING A PHYSICIAN'S CERTIFICATE DESCRIBING THAT CONDITION, IF NOT ALREADY FURNISHED TO YOUR LOCAL BOARD.

TO CLASS 1-A and 1-A-O REGISTRANTS:

If you fail to report for examination as directed, you may be declared delinquent and ordered to report for induction into the Armed Forces. You will also be subject to fine and imprisonment under the provisions of the Military Selective Service Act of 1967.

TO CLASS 1-O REGISTRANTS:

This examination is given for the purpose of determining whether you are qualified for military service. If you are found qualified, you will be available, in lieu of induction, to be ordered to perform civilian work contributing to the maintenance of the national health, safety or interest. If you fail to report for or to submit to this examination, you will be subject to be ordered to perform civilian work in the same manner as if you had taken the examination and had been found qualified for military service.

SSS Form 223 (Revised 7-9-69) (Previous printings may be used until exhausted.)

the local board which issued it, especially if it seems to have been issued in error, as when the local board has ordered you examined while you are deferred and there is no likelihood that your deferment will end soon.

Transfer

Any physical examination may be transferred to where you are, but the procedure is different when you haven't requested the examination. Simply take the order to a nearby local board and fill out a transfer form, indicating why you are in that area. The Regulations require you to do this "immediately" [REG 1628.14(b)], but in practice, transfers seem to be allowed without dispute up to the date set for reporting, and sometimes even later. The local board to which you go is supposed to allow the transfer only if you have a "good reason" and if returning would be a real hardship [REG 1628.14(c) and (d)]. In practice, transfers are routinely allowed.

To transfer the examination the nearby board must get your papers from your own local board and then order you to report the next time it sends men for examination. Most boards do so once a month. As a result, a delay may occur, sometimes of three to six weeks, before your examination takes place.

The Examination

Physical examinations are given by the Army, not the Selective Service System. They take place at Armed Forces Examining and Entrance Stations (AFEES), generally buildings in the centers of major cities but occasionally on Army bases. Transportation is provided or paid for, as well as meals and lodging if the examination takes long enough to require any.

Since the AFEES examines large numbers of men each day, and since the doctors, orderlies, and clerks assigned there often don't know the Army Regulations and must process men in assembly-line fashion as quickly as possible, the examinations are often careless (see the American Medical Association publication *Today's Health,* April 1970). If you believe you have a medical or other condition which should disqualify you, bring letters and other evidence from your own doctors and insist that they be read and that your condition be carefully evaluated. Chapter 13 gives detailed suggestions for insuring full consideration of medical and other grounds for rejection.

In rare cases, when extended examination is necessary, the AFEES may require you to stay there or go to a military hospital for up to three days, or to return at a later time.

You should be told before you leave the AFEES whether or not you have been found acceptable for military service [AR 601-270, 4-20h(12)]. If they don't tell you, you may wish to ask. However, you must also receive an official notification from your local board. Usually about 10 days later, it sends you a Statement of Acceptability (DD Form 62) indicating whether you were found acceptable or unacceptable. As soon as this form is mailed to you, an induction order may be issued if you are liable, though the day of induction must be at least 21 days after the form was mailed [REG 1631.7(a)].

There is no official provision for appealing the decision that you are acceptable, unless it results in a change of classification—as from I-Y to I-A—in which case you have the usual personal appearance and appeal rights described in Chapter 5. Unofficial appeal procedures are discussed in Chapter 13.

INDUCTION

An induction order requires you to report for military service. It can be issued by the local board only when *all* of these requirements are met:

1. You are classified I-A or I-A-O.
2. You have no further right to appeal. (It can't be issued during the 30-day period after a classification is given by a local board, or while an appeal is in process.)
3. The file is at the local board. (Thus if the government appeal agent has sent the file to the state director, or the state or national director has sent for it for any reason, no induction order can be issued.)
4. You have taken and passed a pre-induction physical examination and have been notified officially on the Statement of

☆ U.S. GOVERNMENT PRINTING OFFICE: 1966—222-921

STATEMENT OF ACCEPTABILITY

LAST NAME - FIRST NAME - MIDDLE NAME		PRESENT HOME ADDRESS
SELECTIVE SERVICE NUMBER	LOCAL BOARD ADDRESS	

THE QUALIFICATIONS OF THE ABOVE-NAMED REGISTRANT HAVE BEEN CONSIDERED IN ACCORDANCE WITH THE CURRENT REGU-
LATIONS GOVERNING ACCEPTANCE OF SELECTIVE SERVICE REGISTRANTS AND HE WAS THIS DATE:
- ☐ 1. FOUND FULLY ACCEPTABLE FOR INDUCTION INTO THE ARMED FORCES.
- ☐ 2. FOUND NOT ACCEPTABLE FOR INDUCTION UNDER CURRENT STANDARDS.

DATE	PLACE	TYPED OR STAMPED NAME AND GRADE OF JOINT EXAMINING AND INDUCTION STATION COMMANDER	SIGNATURE

DD FORM 62
1 MAR 59

PREVIOUS EDITIONS OF THIS FORM ARE OBSOLETE.

REGISTRANT COPY 2

Any inquiry relative to personal status should be referred to your Local Board

Acceptability (except for volunteers and men ordered to pre-induction examinations who do not take them, discussed at the beginning of this chapter).

5. The local board cannot meet its current quota with registrants who are higher than you in draft eligibility. (A proposal now before Congress would change this to a national instead of a local quota, so men with the same lottery numbers would be called at the same time everywhere; if this is approved, substitute "National Selective Service" for "local board" in the preceding sentence and the following discussion.)

Order of Call—The Draft Lottery

In determining draft eligibility for the fifth requirement above, local boards must use the following "order of call" [REG 1631.7 (a)]:

1. Delinquents (under a 1970 Supreme Court decision, Selective Service can no longer draft delinquents first, though the Regulations have not yet been revised [LBM 101]; see Chapter 7).
2. Volunteers, 17 through 25 years old, in order of volunteering.
3. Men whose lottery numbers are reached before they are 26 years old:
   In 1970—men 19 through 25 years old, in order of lottery numbers.
   In 1971 and later years—
      1st priority: men who became 19 during the previous calendar year, along with men 19 through 25 whose deferments end and who were not exposed to the lottery previously, in order of lottery numbers.
      2nd and lower priorities: men not drafted in an earlier year because their numbers were not reached.
   In each of these groups, "Kennedy husbands" (men married on or before August 26, 1965, and still living with their wives) can be drafted only after that group's eligible unmarried men and men married after this date.

4. Men who turn 19 during the year, not yet eligible for lottery, oldest first.
5. Men 26 through 34 years old with "extended liability" because they have received deferments, youngest first.
6. Men 18½ to 19 years old, oldest first.

If your local board didn't follow this order of call, your induction order would be illegal. Under predicted draft calls, men in groups 4, 5, and 6 are very unlikely to be drafted; not all of those in the 1st priority within group 3 are expected to be taken, so men in the 2nd priority (in years after 1970) and "Kennedy husbands" should also be safe. But this safety is only relative. If draft calls rise because of new, massive military expansion, draft boards will go farther through the lottery numbers of the 1st priority in group 3, then to 1st-priority "Kennedy husbands," then to 2nd-priority men. Similarly, continued reduction of the size of the armed forces and further limitations of draft deferments would insure that men below the 1st priority in group 3 are not drafted and would reduce the number of men called by lottery numbers in this group.

The 2nd priority in group 3 will first be formed at the beginning of 1971, made up of men subject to the lottery in 1970 but whose lottery numbers were not reached. In 1972 and later years, group 3 will include 3rd and lower priorities made up of men previously in the 2nd priority but not drafted; each year these men move to a less eligible position, leaving group 3 entirely if they are not needed before they turn 26, when they move to group 5.

But probably in 1970, and fairly certainly after 1970, only by being "exposed" to the draft lottery by having a I-A, I-A-O, or I-O classification can a man move to a lower priority. Those who have deferments enter the 1st priority when they lose them, staying there until the end of the year. If their numbers aren't reached by December 31, they move to the 2nd priority the following year, while a new group of men enter the 1st priority—those who turned 19 the previous year and those whose deferments have expired during the new year.

Men who start the year in I-A but get deferments before their numbers are reached have not been exposed; they will enter the 1st priority the year their deferments end. But those who lose deferments during the year and who finish the year in a draftable classification have been exposed, even if they were eligible for only a small part of the year; if their numbers aren't reached they will move to the 2nd priority the following January 1. This is because each month the draft board fills its quota by starting over at lottery number 1, going as far into the numbers as necessary to fill the quota. Therefore, a man whose number was passed earlier in the year while he was deferred might be close to the top of the order of call when he loses his deferment.

Or he might not be called, even though his number was reached earlier. Here's an example: Suppose you have lottery number 210 and your draft board took men with numbers up to 212 in September, while you were deferred. You lost your deferment in October and remained in a draftable classification until after December 31, but so did other men who finished school or had other changes in circumstances, and some of them had lower lottery numbers. As a result, your board reaches only as high as 200 during October, November, and December. Regardless of whether you were using your personal appearance and appeal rights, or whether you had completed your physical examination, it appears to us that as of January 1 you move down to the 2nd priority because your number was not called while you were in a draftable classification. However, this interpretation is far from certain; the "or otherwise" clause in the Regulation quoted below has raised doubt about it which only an official Selective Service interpretation or a court decision may settle.

Let's make another assumption. Suppose again that you have number 210 and that your deferment was changed to I-A in October. You begin using the personal appearance and appeal rights described in Chapter 5, and these are still in process when the year ends. Of course, you can't be drafted while your appeals are under way, or even in the 30-day periods you are allowed to request appeals. Now assume that your local board reached your lottery number in November, but because you and the others who were appealing couldn't be drafted, it went on to draft men with numbers 211 and 212. When your appeals are over, if you are still I-A or I-A-O, you will be drafted ahead of the men in the current 1st priority, under a provision of the Regulation which reads:

> ... any registrant classified in Class I-A or Class I-A-O who is subject to random selection as herein provided, whose random sequence number has been reached, and who would have been ordered to report for induction except for delays due to a pending personal appearance, appeal, preinduction examination, reclassification, or otherwise, shall if and when found acceptable and when such delay is concluded, be ordered to report for induction next after delinquents and volunteers even if the year in which he otherwise would have been ordered to report has ended and even if (in cases of extended liability) he has attained his twenty-sixth birthday ... [REG 1631.7(a)].

So you would still be drafted even if your year of exposure ended during the appeal, and perhaps even if you turned 26, provided your lottery number was reached and the only thing that kept you from being drafted during your year in the 1st priority was the unsuccessful appeal. It is unclear whether the 30-day safe period allowed for requesting an appeal counts as a "delay" for a man who doesn't use his appeal rights.

The classification list beginning on page 3 indicates which classifications are deferments and which exemptions. The difference may be significant to some men who turn 26 while using appeal rights because only those who have at some time received a deferment have "extended liability" past their 26th birthdays [LBM 38].

Of course, if your appeal succeeded, you would not have finished your year in the 1st priority; you would go back into it the year your deferment or exemption ended, if you were still under 26. And if you turned 26 while deferred or exempt, you would go directly to group 5 in the order of call and be relatively safe from induction even if you lost your deferment later.

Some of these interpretations are in dispute, both within Selective Service and among draft counselors and lawyers, and it is difficult now to say which men will fall into the 2nd priority on January 1, 1971. By the time you read this book, an official interpretation probably will have been publicly announced. These were the possibilities at the time of writing:

1. Whether a man's lottery number was reached would probably be decided on the basis of the numbers reached by his local board rather than the cut-off numbers announced by Selective Service National Headquarters, but the significance of these national cut-offs (discussed below) isn't clear. Whichever applied, only those with higher numbers would fall into the 2nd priority.

2. In the cases of men who lost deferments during the year and remained available to December 31, will eligibility for the 2nd priority be determined by the highest number reached at any time during the year (by one of the methods in paragraph 1 above—local or national) or the highest number reached after his deferment ended and he was in a draftable classification? The authors believe the second interpretation should prevail, but perhaps the courts will have to decide.

3. It is unclear whether all men who end the year in draftable classifications—I-A, I-A-O, and I-O—and whose numbers weren't reached (by one of the methods in paragraphs 1 and 2 above) will move into the 2nd priority, or only those not involved at year's end in administrative procedures which make them temporarily undraftable but don't result in deferment. Will the mere fact of administrative delay (discussed above) keep one from the 2nd priority, or will this apply only to men whose lottery numbers were reached and who would have been drafted except for the delay? The authors lean toward the second interpretation, especially in the light of the 1970 Selective Service decision not to order examinations for men with lottery numbers over 215; if only fully available men could move into the 2nd priority, this would keep men without examinations indefinitely in the 1st priority.

4. Because of unclear wording in the Regulations, there is some conjecture that *all* men with lottery numbers in 1970 whose numbers aren't reached (by one of the methods in paragraph 1 above) by the end of 1970 will move into the 2nd priority on January 1, 1971, even those with deferments. It seems fairly certain for years after 1970 that only those without

deferments at year's end will move to the 2nd priority and that men protected by deferments will enter the 1st priority when their deferments end.

This system was established by changes in the law and Regulations on November 26, 1969. On December 1, 1969, the first drawing was held to give lottery numbers to all men, regardless of their draft classifications, who were born from January 1, 1944, through December 31, 1950—those aged 19 through 25 at the end of 1969. Men who turned 19 during 1970, who were born in 1951, received lottery numbers in another drawing, held July 1, 1970. The numbers assigned in these two drawings are given in Appendix B. As long as these Regulations remain in effect, additional drawings will be held annually for men who turn 19 that year.

At the time the draft lottery went into effect, the newspapers reported that it had three purposes: to enable most draft-age men to know how likely they were to be drafted so they could make educational, career, and family plans; to reduce the period of uncertainty from seven years to one; and to draft men shortly after they turn 19 or as soon as their deferments end. These goals are still far from reached.

When the lottery plan was started, the White House predicted that in 1970 those with the most eligible one-third of the numbers (1–122) would certainly be drafted, those in the next one-third (123–244) must wait to see, and those in the least eligible one-third (245–366) would almost certainly not be drafted. This expectation was soon contradicted by Selective Service officials, some of whom predicted that all 366 numbers would be called in some states. Therefore reliable predictions about "safe" lottery numbers were impossible.

To reduce the uncertainty even at the cost of not meeting quotas, local boards received instructions to limit induction each month to men within designated lottery numbers—up to 30 in January 1970, to 60 in February, to 90 in March, and so on, reaching 195 in August and September, with the likelihood that 195 will be the limit for the rest of 1970. To achieve this goal of national uniformity in a more permanent way, the President has asked Congress for permission to use a "direct national call" by lottery numbers, drafting all available men with the same lottery numbers at the same time, to prevent one local board from calling a higher number while another is meeting quotas with lower numbers. Until such a system is in effect, you can learn where you stand in the lottery, if your number is at the national cut-off or lower, only by asking your own local board what lottery number it has reached.

The President also put new Regulations limiting occupational and fatherhood deferments into effect on April 23, 1970, and he asked Congress for limitations on college and vocational training deferments (for details see Chapters 9, 10, and 11). By increasing the number of men eligible for the draft, these changes are expected in time to make the lottery more acceptable by enabling draft boards to meet their quotas with fewer lottery numbers. Since men who lost deferments were likely to delay induction for three to six months or longer by use of their personal appearance and appeal rights (described in Chapter 5), the results of these changes were just slightly visible as this book was completed.

If at 19 you were deferred for any reason—because you were going to college, because you failed a physical examination for a condition subject to change or re-evaluation, or because you have dependents, for example—you will re-enter the draft pool as a member of that year's 1st priority if you run out of deferments before you are 26. So the years of uncertainty remain for many men.

And despite references to the lottery system as a "19-year-old draft," it most frequently takes men at age 20 or older. Although your lottery number is assigned during the year you turn 19, you aren't eligible to be drafted until sometime in the next calendar year. Therefore, of those who aren't deferred, at least half would be drafted at age 20, a few at nearly 21. And those who receive deferments may be as old as 25 when they become subject to the draft.

In view of the unpredictability referred to above, choosing a time in 1971 and later years to be exposed to the lottery is nearly impossible. If you have a very eligible number, you have nothing to gain except the certainty of being drafted if you give up a deferment; if you wish not to serve, the odds favor holding onto deferments as long as possible on the chance the Indo-China war may end or the draft be phased out. If you have a relatively safe number (perhaps 250 and over), you stand a good chance of escaping if you remain undeferred, though this isn't certain and conditions could change. If you are somewhere in the middle, you hold no winning cards in this lottery. You might try to hold onto your deferment until late in the year, then try to give it up if it looks as though your number will be safe, but for at least two reasons this may not work.

First, your local board may not reclassify you soon enough. You might drop enough college courses to become ineligible for II-S, quit a job that qualifies for II-A or have your employer write that he no longer considers your availability necessary to the national interest, inform your local board that your dependents are now otherwise provided for, or correct a disqualifying medical condition, to name a few of the steps available to the man who wants to give up a deferment. When your local board receives word of this change in your circumstances, it may reclassify you immediately, exposing you to that year's lottery, or in the press of other work it may not get to your file for months, perhaps not until after December 31. In that case, you have exposed yourself to a new year's lottery and totally unknown conditions. On the other hand, if you give up your deferment early enough to be sure of reclassification that year (that may mean July or August with some local boards), you may not be able to judge whether your lottery number will be reached.

Second, it may be hard to predict how far the lottery will go even late in a given year, since draft calls are subject to last-minute changes and since there is apparently no way to learn how many eligible men have any given lottery number in one local board or in the whole country. If you guess wrong and your "safe" number is reached, you will be drafted even if you use the personal appearance and appeal process to delay into the next year or past your 26th birthday, as explained above.

For these reasons, today it seems nearly impossible to choose on any rational basis a year to be exposed to the draft lottery. Observation of the trends of American military activity throughout the world and several years' experience with the lottery system may eventually make rough predictions possible. If you are uncertain whether your lottery number will be reached in a given year, the best advice if you wish not to be drafted is to hold onto deferments as long as possible.

Those whose deferments continue to their 26th birthdays are virtually certain of safety from the draft under present Regulations. The only exceptions are physicians, dentists, and other medical specialists subject to the Doctors' Draft; they are drafted in the same order as other men under special calls for their specializations. Usually there aren't enough qualified men under 26 to fill the calls, so doctors 26 and over are drafted. In the fiscal year ending June 30, 1971, however, the Defense Department expects to draft no medical specialists except optometrists because enough doctors have enlisted in reserve programs to meet expected needs.

Induction Order

When you are near enough to the top of your local board's eligibility list to be needed for its current draft quota, you are issued an Order to Report for Induction (Form 252). As mentioned above, the date to report must be at least 21 days after the mailing of your Statement of Acceptability. In addition, the order must be mailed at least 10 days before the date you are to report.

An induction order can be postponed or transferred under exactly the same conditions as an order to report for a pre-induction physical examination, discussed at the beginning of this chapter. In addition, recent professional school graduates may get their induction dates postponed to allow them to take the examination to qualify for state licensing, and pharmacy graduates may also receive postponements for up to a year to complete their pre-examination internships [LBM 44]. For students who receive induction orders during a school year, see page 125.

When the local board issues the induction order, you no longer have the right to have your classification reopened because of changed circumstances or new information (except in the cases discussed on page 55), nor can the government appeal agent take formal action to get your classification considered further. However, the state and national directors have the right to reopen or appeal a classification at any time, and any induction order would automatically be canceled if this power were used. And presumably

Approval Not Required.

SELECTIVE SERVICE SYSTEM
ORDER TO REPORT FOR INDUCTION

(LOCAL BOARD STAMP)

....
(Date of mailing)

SELECTIVE SERVICE NO.

The President of the United States,

To

GREETING:

You are hereby ordered for induction into the Armed Forces of the United States, and to report

at ....
(Place of reporting)

on .... at ....
(Date)   (Hour)

for forwarding to an Armed Forces Induction Station.

....
(Member, Executive Secretary, or clerk of Local Board

IMPORTANT NOTICE
(Read Each Paragraph Carefully)

IF YOU HAVE HAD PREVIOUS MILITARY SERVICE, OR ARE NOW A MEMBER OF THE NATIONAL GUARD OR A RESERVE COMPONENT OF THE ARMED FORCES, BRING EVIDENCE WITH YOU. IF YOU WEAR GLASSES, BRING THEM. IF MARRIED, BRING PROOF OF YOUR MARRIAGE. IF YOU HAVE ANY PHYSICAL OR MENTAL CONDITION WHICH, IN YOUR OPINION, MAY DISQUALIFY YOU FOR SERVICE IN THE ARMED FORCES, BRING A PHYSICIAN'S CERTIFICATE DESCRIBING THAT CONDITION, IF NOT ALREADY FURNISHED TO YOUR LOCAL BOARD.

Valid documents are required to substantiate dependency claims in order to receive basic allowance for quarters. Be sure to take the following with you when reporting to the induction station. The documents will be returned to you. (a) FOR LAWFUL WIFE OR LEGITIMATE CHILD UNDER 21 YEARS OF AGE—original, certified copy or photostat of a certified copy of marriage certificate, child's birth certificate, or a public or church record of marriage issued over the signature and seal of the custodian of the church or public records; (b) FOR LEGALLY ADOPTED CHILD—certified court order of adoption; (c) FOR CHILD OF DIVORCED SERVICE MEMBER (Child in custody of person other than claimant)—(1) Certified or photostatic copies of receipts from custodian of child evidencing serviceman's contributions for support, and (2) Divorce decree, court support order or separation order; (d) FOR DEPENDENT PARENT—affidavits establishing that dependency.

Bring your Social Security Account Number Card. If you do not have one, apply at nearest Social Security Administration Office. If you have life insurance, bring a record of the insurance company's address and your policy number. Bring enough clean clothes for 3 days. Bring enough money to last 1 month for personal purchases.

This Local Board will furnish transportation, and meals and lodging when necessary, from the place of reporting to the induction station where you will be examined. If found qualified, you will be inducted into the Armed Forces. If found not qualified, return transportation and meals and lodging when necessary, will be furnished to the place of reporting.

You may be found not qualified for induction. Keep this in mind in arranging your affairs, to prevent any undue hardship if you are not inducted. If employed, inform your employer of this possibility. Your employer can then be prepared to continue your employment if you are not inducted. To protect your right to return to your job if you are not inducted, you must report for work as soon as possible after the completion of your induction examination. You may jeopardize your reemployment rights if you do not report for work at the beginning of your next regularly scheduled working period after you have returned to your place of employment.

Willful failure to report at the place and hour of the day named in this Order subjects the violator to fine and imprisonment. Bring this Order with you when you report.

If you are so far from your own local board that reporting in compliance with this Order will be a serious hardship, go immediately to any local board and make written request for transfer of your delivery for induction, taking this Order with you.

SSS Form 252 (Revised 4-28-45)   (Previous printings may be used until exhausted.)

the local board which issued an induction order has the power to cancel it if it was improperly issued, as when the wrong order of eligibility was followed, although the Regulations do not deal with this question.

If your pre-induction physical examination was more than a year before the date of induction, you must receive another complete examination at the time of induction; if it was more recent, you receive a far less complete "physical inspection" at the time of induction [AR 601-270, 4-20a and 4-21a]. If the examination or inspection reveals a disqualifying condition, you will be rejected and sent home, and later be reclassified by your local board.

If you are found still qualified, you are immediately inducted into the armed forces—usually the Army, but occasionally the Marines. The other services rarely use draftees.

The actual induction consists of a brief ceremony in which you are told that you are about to enter military service and that you must take one step forward when your name and branch of service are announced. If you take the step forward, you are in the armed forces and subject to military law, whether or not you take the oath of allegiance, which is given later [AR 601-270, 3-22 and 3-23].

If you refuse to take the step forward, even after warnings and repeated chances, you are considered to have refused induction and are reported to Selective Service for prosecution [AR 601-270, 3-31c]. You are asked to sign papers acknowledging that you have refused induction, but you are not required to sign them. In most cases you are allowed to leave to await later arrest, but in Chicago and a few other cities you will probably be arrested immediately, then released on bond within hours. If you wish to challenge your classification in court by refusing induction, you will be advised by your attorney to cooperate with the process up to the point of stepping forward. If you hope for a successful court test, you should consult an attorney experienced in Selective Service cases before refusing induction, and preferably much earlier, as soon as it becomes likely that a court trial will take place.

CHAPTER SEVEN

TWO SPECIAL PROBLEMS—
TRAVEL ABROAD, DELINQUENCY

This chapter discusses two unrelated Selective Service provisions that affect relatively few registrants but that often create confusion and problems when they arise.

TRAVEL ABROAD

There is a provision for a local board—or the state or national director—to issue a Permit for Registrant to Depart from the United States (Form 300) [REG 1621.16]. Many registrants and some draft boards believe it is illegal for a registrant to go abroad without this permit, but this is not true.

While called a "permit," it is more like an insurance policy against being bothered by your draft board while you are abroad for a specified period of time. It is a formal promise from Selective Service that your deferment will continue for the period for which the permit is used; or if you are not deferred, that no induction order will be issued for this period. It enables you to travel, work, or study abroad for a limited time with reasonable certainty that your draft board won't do anything that will force you to return early.

Most draft boards will issue the permit only if you don't need it, because they intend to take no action that would affect you during that period anyway. But some boards refuse to grant permits even then.

If you are deferred, it may be best simply to inform your board in writing, just before your departure, telling it where you are going, when you will leave, and when you will return. Give an address or

Form approved
Budget Bureau No. 33.R106.4.

_____
(Date)

(LOCAL BOARD STAMP)

SELECTIVE SERVICE SYSTEM

PERMIT FOR REGISTRANT TO DEPART FROM THE UNITED STATES

1. NAME OF REGISTRANT
   (First) (Middle) (Last)

2. SELECTIVE SERVICE NO.

3. PRESENT ADDRESS
   (Number and Street) (City or town) (State) (Zip Code)

4. CLASSIFICATION

5. PLACE OF BIRTH
   (City or town) (State) (Country)

6. DATE OF BIRTH

7. IF NONCITIZEN, ALIEN REGISTRATION NUMBER _____

8. IN HIS APPLICATION THE REGISTRANT GAVE THE FOLLOWING INFORMATION:

   A. COUNTRIES TO BE VISITED

B. ORGANIZATIONS OR INDIVIDUALS REPRESENTED

C. NATURE OF BUSINESS

The above-named registrant is hereby authorized to depart from the United States and to remain absent therefrom until _____
(Date)

_____
(Signature)

_____
(Title)

NOTICE: Before leaving the United States, if an alien, secure a reentry permit, if necessary, from the Immigration and Naturalization Service, Department of Justice.

SSS Form 300 (Revised 1-29-65) (Previous printings are obsolete)

U.S. GOVERNMENT PRINTING OFFICE 1965 OF—742-886

addresses abroad if you can, so the board will send any correspondence directly to you, and so you will have 60 days instead of 30 to appeal an unexpected reclassification (only 30 days if you are in Canada or Mexico).

If you request the permit and your request is denied, you can still leave the country and return perfectly legally even though your board may be annoyed with you.

Many students go abroad for the summer without informing their boards, relying upon parents to forward any mail promptly. Sometimes they leave signed letters requesting a personal appearance and appeal for their parents to mail to the board in case of a reclassification. So long as your board has a mailing address, this is perfectly legal, but we advise sending the board your overseas address. Your parents may forget, or a personal appearance may be scheduled before you can return.

If you are I-A, I-A-O, or I-O, and therefore in a position to be ordered to a pre-induction physical, or to induction or civilian work, it is best to apply for the permit. Physicals can sometimes be taken abroad [LBM 69], but this may be difficult to arrange and you may have to pay for your own transportation to an Army base. Boards have been known to delay the processing of registrants who have an opportunity to travel abroad for several weeks, and yours might be that kind of board. The same applies if you are awaiting a personal appearance, or the results of an appeal.

Undergraduate exchange students should receive the II-S deferment if their year abroad gives them full credit toward their degree.

The permit is not relevant to registrants who emigrate (see Chapters 16 and 17).

DRAFT DELINQUENCY

At this writing, the Regulations still contain a section allowing a local board to punish a man who "fails or neglects to perform any duty required of him under the provisions of the selective service law" by declaring him delinquent, removing any deferment he may hold, and issuing him an induction order ahead of all others even if he could not otherwise be drafted. However, two Supreme Court decisions early in 1970 ruled these uses of the delinquency regulations illegal (*U.S. v. Gutknecht,* 396 U.S. 295, 2 SSLR 3367; *Breen v. Selective Service Local Board No. 16,* 396 U.S. 460, 2 SSLR 3373). The Selective Service System responded to these decisions by instructing local boards to "suspend all processing of delinquents" [LBM 101]. If you believe your local board is violating this instruction, you would be wise to consult a draft counselor or an attorney experienced in Selective Service law immediately.

PART II

MILITARY AND NONMILITARY SERVICE

"The Congress further declares that in a free society the obligations and privileges of serving in the armed forces and the reserve components thereof shall be shared generally, in accordance with a system of selection which is fair and just, and which is consistent with the maintenance of an effective national economy."

[MSSA 1(c)]

CHAPTER EIGHT

MILITARY AND NONMILITARY SERVICE: I-C, I-D

If you perform military service, you will enter it in one of three ways (in addition to the noncombatant service for conscientious objectors discussed in Chapters 14 and 15):

1. Enlisting or applying for a commission—by volunteering directly for one of the branches of the armed forces.
2. Being inducted through Selective Service—by waiting until you are drafted in the normal order (discussed in Chapter 6), or volunteering for earlier induction.
3. Joining the reserves of one of the armed forces, including the National Guard and Coast Guard.

We will not try to explain all the choices open to you if you decide to serve in the armed forces. There are many choices, and they are constantly changing. A publication which gives recent information is *Basic Facts about Military Service,* distributed without charge by the Department of Defense High School News Service, Building 1-B, Great Lakes, Illinois 60088. A revised edition is published in limited quantities each September for distribution to high school counselors; it is sent to others on request while supplies last.

For a dissenting view, read *GI Rights and Army Justice: The Draftee's Guide to Military Life and Law,* by Robert S. Rivkin (New York: Grove Press, 1970, $1.75).

While on active duty, you are classified I-C by your draft board, though it does not send you a classification card. After active duty is completed, if you have served the required time, you are classified IV-A (discussed in Chapter 12).

ENLISTING

More than three out of every four men in the armed forces enter by voluntary enlistment or commissioning. Most of the openings in the Army are filled by enlistment, and the Marine Corps, Navy, Air Force, and Coast Guard seldom or never take draftees. All of the branches prefer volunteers because the man who enlists is generally more strongly motivated to serve in the armed forces and is more likely to re-enlist, so the military gets more return for its investment in training.

Therefore, the military branches offer various incentives for enlisting. Recruiters may promise training in the field you are interested in, or assignment overseas in the area of your choice, but these promises may not be kept if the program is closed or you don't meet the qualifications for it. Ordinarily you must sign up for three, four, or more years, although the Army and the Marines have accepted a limited number of two-year volunteers. In general, the longer you agree to serve, the more training you will receive.

Another advantage of enlisting is the chance to choose which branch of the armed forces you will enter.

The man who enlists, like the man who is drafted, must spend a total of six years in military service. Only part of the six years is on full-time, uniformed, active duty. The remainder is spent in the reserves. In general, unless you serve on active duty for five years or longer, you enter the Ready Reserve of your branch of service when you finish your active duty and remain in it until the last year or two years, when you are transferred to the Standby Reserve. In the Ready Reserve, you will probably have to attend weekly or monthly drill meetings, and often two weeks of summer camp. You can be called into active service with your unit in case of need. Thus you will probably not be free of a military obligation when you finish the number of years you volunteered for. Ready Reserve units have been called to active duty during the Vietnam buildup. Once you are transferred to the Standby Reserve, it is extremely unlikely that you will be called to active duty, and there are no training requirements.

If you enlist you will get the same pay (based on rank and number of dependents) and benefits as those who are drafted, and you will receive the same educational and other veterans' benefits after you finish active duty, including the right to get your job back if you are still qualified for it.

There are basically three ways you can get a commission as an officer:

1. By graduating from one of the military academies.
2. By taking advanced R.O.T.C. in college.
3. By qualifying for Officer Candidate School. This possibility may be open to you after you have entered the armed forces, but it often means extending your length of service.

INDUCTION THROUGH SELECTIVE SERVICE

If you volunteer for induction, you are in precisely the same situation as the man who is drafted. You are required to serve two years in the Army, and you have no choices of training and location. You will have a reserve obligation after your two years of active duty, but you will not ordinarily be required to join a Ready Reserve unit unless you wish to. The only advantage of volunteering for induction is getting it over with, ending the wait to be drafted.

To volunteer for induction, you apply through your local board (with parents' written permission if you are under 18). Usually the board will issue an induction order as soon as possible, whether or not you have taken a pre-induction physical examination; if you haven't, you will get a complete examination at the time of induction. Sometimes you are first sent for a pre-induction examination, then inducted if you pass it.

Any man 17 years old through 25 can volunteer for induction through his local board. However, you may be turned down if your board considers you eligible for deferment in II-A (occupational), II-C (agricultural), III-A (fathers and hardship-to-dependents), or IV-B (elected officials and judges).

Some men wait to be drafted, instead of enlisting or volunteering for induction, to delay military service as long as possible. Others hope their lottery numbers won't be reached. Your circumstances may change while you are waiting, and you may qualify for a

SELECTIVE SERVICE SYSTEM

Form Approved.
Budget Bureau No. 33-R122.5.

APPLICATION FOR VOLUNTARY INDUCTION

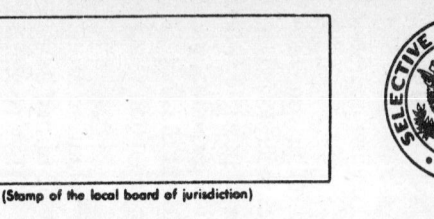

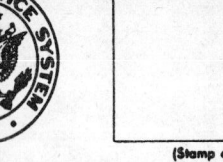

(Stamp of the local board of jurisdiction)

(Stamp of local board at which application is filed if other than local board of jurisdiction)

I hereby apply for voluntary induction into the Armed Forces of the United States under the provisions of the Military Selective Service Act of 1967. For this purpose, I waive all rights of personal appearance and appeal if I am classified as available for service, and I consent to my induction at any time convenient to the Government. I understand that I may not be ordered to report for a preinduction armed forces physical examination, but that I may be ordered to report to an Armed Forces Induction Station for immediate induction. I am also aware of the possibility that I may be found not qualified for induction into the Armed Forces.

....
(Applicant's Signature)

....
(Date of Application)

DESCRIPTION OF APPLICANT

1. Name of applicant

....
(First)   (Middle)   (Last)

2. Selective Service No.

3. Present mailing address

(Number and street or R.F.D. Route) | (City, Town, or Village) | (County) | (State) | (Zip Code)

4. Number and address of local board where registered

5. Date of birth | 6. Place of birth

7. If you were ever found not qualified for service in the Armed Forces, state (a) when _____
   (b) where _____

CONSENT WHEN APPLICANT IS UNDER 18 YEARS OF AGE

I/we hereby certify that the above applicant has no other legal guardian than me/us and I/we do hereby consent to his induction into the Armed Forces of the United States under the provisions of the Military Selective Service Act of 1967. I/we understand that he may be assigned to overseas duty immediately upon completion of the required period of training.

_____
(Other Parent, when required)   (Strike out one)   Parent or Legal Guardian

_____   _____
(Address)   (Address)

_____   _____
(Date)   (Date)

All entries must be typewritten or printed except signatures. The consent must be signed by both parents if living or by the surviving parent except that when another person is the legal guardian the consent must be signed by such guardian.

SSS Form 254 (Revised 10-29-64) (Previous printings may be used.)   GPO 927-836 classification which will allow you to avoid military service entirely, if that is your desire. On the other hand, delay may be a disadvantage, for it may mean interrupting your career, education, or family life at a much less convenient time.

JOINING THE RESERVES

Each branch of the armed forces has a variety of programs which allow you to spend most of your six-year period in the Ready Reserve except for a few months spent in full-time training or a longer period on active duty, usually soon after you enlist. Each state has National Guard programs with similar requirements.

The full-time active duty lasts from four months to three years, depending on your branch of service and the specialization you are trained for. When it is over, you may be required to spend the remainder of the six years in the Ready Reserve, usually training once a week or one weekend a month and for two weeks each summer. You remain subject to call-up to active duty at the order of the President. National Guard members can be called up by the governor of the state as well.

Many men think getting into the reserves will keep them from having to be away from home and job once the training period is finished. This is often true, and it is the reason most reserve units have long waiting lists. But, as mentioned above, reserve units were called to active duty during 1968. In some cases they remained in the United States to replace military units being sent overseas, and in other cases they were sent overseas, either as a unit or divided up, with members assigned individually.

The attraction of the reserve programs is the chance of a short active-duty period and relative safety from being sent into combat. But you should consider the disadvantages as well. Your unit may be activated at any time, and in the case of the National Guard it may be called into service to deal with a natural disaster or to put down a riot. You will probably have to spend evenings or weekends for years in regular drill meetings and up to five summer vacations in training camp. And there is a widespread feeling among reservists that their training is both militarily worthless and of no value in civilian life, and that the time is therefore wasted.

Your draft board will classify you I-D during the time you are in the reserves or National Guard, including time spent in "active duty for training." When you have completed the required time, you are classified IV-A (discussed in Chapter 12). If your participation is considered unsatisfactory, you may be called to punitive active duty for 45 days; this usually applies only to those who have completed at least two years of active duty. Ordinarily, if you haven't served on active duty for two years, you will be removed from the reserve unit and assigned to active duty for two years, less time already served. Or you may be turned over to your draft board for immediate induction and then must spend a full two years in the Army. One of these steps is often taken if you miss more than 10% of the required drill meetings.

You will also be classified I-D while you are in certain military training programs. These include the senior divisions (normally the last two years) of the Army's college R.O.T.C. program and equivalent programs of the other services, provided you have agreed to accept a commission as an officer and to perform active duty when you graduate. This classification also is given to students in military colleges approved by the Secretary of Defense [listed in LBM 45], and to aviation cadets.

Few draft counselors have detailed information about the military alternatives. For this type of advice, you can often get current information from recruiters, though they will tend to try to sell their own branches of service. Naturally, as salesmen they will emphasize the advantages and challenges but say little about the frustrations and problems. Most of them know much more about active duty than about the reserves. Usually the best way to get information about reserve units is to visit those in your area and talk with men in them.

DISCHARGES AND TRANSFERS

In general, if you enter military service in any of these ways, you must stay in until your term is over. However, each branch of the armed forces allows earlier discharges and transfers under certain conditions—subject to its judgment and convenience.

If your family circumstances change while you are on active

duty and you are able to show that your dependents will suffer extreme hardship if you remain on active duty, you may be able to get a discharge or a transfer to duty near your home. The Red Cross may be able to help you verify the facts and apply for discharge.

If you develop a physical or mental disability, you may be eligible for a medical discharge. The conditions serious enough to warrant medical discharge from the armed forces are listed in Chapter 3 of Army Regulation 40-501. It may be helpful to get letters from civilian doctors in addition to seeing military doctors.

If you are in the Ready Reserve and you are working in a field considered vital to the civilian economy, or are a college senior or graduate student preparing to enter such a field [listed in LBM 79], you may be transferred to the Standby Reserve, provided you are not judged to have a "critical military skill." You may also be transferred to the Standby Reserve if recalling you to active duty would cause your family extreme hardship.

If, while on active or reserve duty, you become conscientiously opposed to participation in war, you may be transferred to noncombatant duty, often medical service. If you are opposed even to this, you may be discharged. The requirements for transfer and discharge as a conscientious objector (CO) are the same as for Selective Service classifications I-A-O and I-O, discussed in Chapters 14 and 15. However, there are two important differences. First, your conscientious objection must have crystallized *after* you entered military service. A man classified I-A-O may apply for discharge as a CO, however, if his conscientious position has clearly changed. And second, it is hard to achieve recognition as a CO within the armed forces. After two years during which nearly all CO discharge applications were turned down, an estimated 25% to 30% have been approved since the spring of 1968 by the Army, with somewhat higher approval rates in the other services. Applications for transfer to noncombatant duty are more often approved.

Applications for discharge are decided by the military authorities. However, if a legitimate claim has been turned down, you can sometimes apply again with new information, or go to a federal court for a writ of habeas corpus, a court order requiring that the armed forces release you. If you believe you were illegally inducted, or that your conscientious objection claim was improperly turned down by Selective Service, you may decide not to refuse induction and face criminal trial and the risk of prison. In that case, immediately after being inducted into the armed forces, your attorney can request a writ of habeas corpus from a federal court (discussed in Chapter 19). You certainly should not accept induction on the assumption that such action would be successful, since courts seldom grant these requests. You should act only on the advice of a lawyer experienced in this field.

If you are unsuccessful in your application for discharge or for a writ of habeas corpus, you will of course remain in the armed forces. If your conscience forces you to disobey legal orders, you will be subject to court-martial. You may receive a sentence of up to five years in military prison, followed ordinarily by a less-than-honorable discharge.

CCCO can provide information and aid and can refer you to a counselor or lawyer; it also publishes *Advice for Conscientious Objectors in the Armed Forces* ($1.00) (see Chapter 21 for addresses).

PUBLIC HEALTH SERVICE

Other than the civilian work for conscientious objectors discussed in Chapters 14 and 15, there are only two nonmilitary services that fulfill the draft requirements. Both of them are open only to trained professionals.

The Public Health Service provides commissions to doctors, dentists, and other medical specialists, pharmacists, social workers, male nurses, trained therapists, hospital administrators, engineers, scientists, and others whose special skills are related to health. By serving for two years as a commissioned officer doing hospital, research, or public health work, either assigned to work for the Public Health Service (including the National Institutes of Health) or assigned through it to serve the Coast Guard, the Bureau of Prisons, or the Environmental Science Services Administration, you fulfill the requirements of the Selective Service System. Doctors in the PHS are often assigned to the Coast Guard for six months. No reserve obligations apply to PHS officers, unless they wish to join the PHS Reserve Corps.

While on active duty, commissioned officers in the PHS are classified I-C by their draft boards. After serving the required time, they are classified IV-A.

You can get information by writing to U.S. Public Health Service, Office of Personnel (OSG), 9000 Rockville Pike (NBOC #2), Bethesda, Maryland 20014.

ENVIRONMENTAL SCIENCE SERVICES ADMINISTRATION

Two years as a commissioned officer in ESSA will also complete the draft obligation, without reserve commitment, but ESSA requires that you serve for at least three years. This agency is a combination of the Coast and Geodetic Survey, the U.S. Weather Bureau, and the Central Radio Propagation Laboratories of the National Bureau of Standards. Its work involves scientific research and service. You must have at least a bachelor's degree with a major in science or technology to qualify for a commission.

While on active duty, your draft classification is I-C. You receive a IV-A classification when you complete ESSA service.

Information is available from Chief, Commissioned Personnel Branch, Environmental Science Services Administration, Washington Science Center, Rockville, Maryland 20852.

It should be noted that officers of both PHS and ESSA may be transferred to the armed forces in time of war or national emergency, so these are not options for most conscientious objectors. While this is unlikely, if you adopt one of these alternatives you must accept the possibility that it may not keep you from serving in the armed forces.

PART III

DEFERMENT AND EXEMPTION

"The Congress further declares that adequate provision for national security requires maximum effort in the fields of scientific research and development, and the fullest possible utilization of the Nation's technological, scientific, and other critical manpower resources."

[MSSA 1(e)]

CHAPTER NINE

STUDENTS: I-S(H), II-S, I-S(C)

Although people often speak of a "student deferment," there isn't just one classification for students. Actually there are five:

1. I-S(H)—high school students
2. II-S—college and some graduate students
3. I-S(C)—college students (and rarely, graduate students) who have received induction orders, got them canceled, and who are deferred until the end of the academic year
4. II-A—students in nondegree vocational training programs, including trade and business schools, as well as trades apprentices
5. IV-D—most students in seminaries or pre-enrolled in seminaries

The last two are discussed in other chapters—the II-A in Chapter 10, and the IV-D in Chapter 12. The first three are fully discussed in this chapter.

You should keep in mind, however, that this chapter, like the rest of this book, describes the rules as they were at the time the book went to press. On April 23, 1970, the President asked Congress for authority to end II-S deferments for undergraduates who began college on or after that date, as well as I-S(C) deferments, and stated that if this were done he would also end further II-A deferments for vocational students and apprentices. No Congressional action has been taken yet, and it is far from certain how or when Congress will change the law, if at all. If you are a student, you should watch the newspapers and stay in touch with your local draft counselor.

I-S(H)

Some draft boards don't classify registrants until they have finished high school. But if yours classifies you while you are still a full-time high school student, it must give you a I-S(H) deferment until you either reach age 20, leave full-time high school, or graduate [REG 1622.15(a)].

No proposals for changes in the law have been made concerning I-S(H) deferments for high school students.

The board will usually believe your statement in Series IX of the Classification Questionnaire (discussed in Chapter 4) that you are a high school student and give you the I-S(H). But sometimes you may receive a I-A even though you notified the board that you are in high school. In this case, if there is any risk that you may be reached by the lottery while you are still in high school (usually there is none), ask your school to give you (or send to the board) a letter saying you are a full-time student there. Send it to the board within 30 days with your own letter asking for a I-S(H) deferment and saying that you want a personal appearance and appeal if the board doubts that you qualify.

The Regulations don't require that your I-S(H) continue after your 20th birthday. Boards in some areas make a policy of not drafting you if you are 20 years old but need additional time to graduate from high school. Others will draft you if you turn 20 and your lottery number is reached, but will generally postpone your induction date until the end of the school year. If you need more time to finish high school after you are 20, you should write to your local board explaining how long you will need, asking that the board allow you to finish, and explaining any unusual circumstances. If you are reclassified anyway, the appeal procedures described in Chapter 5 may not get your deferment back but they will give you three to six months to complete your high school education.

If you expect to enter college or vacational school soon after you finish high school, be sure to notify your draft board of these plans. It is a good idea to send the board a copy of your college admission letter and other proof that you will continue your education, such as a copy of your receipt for a tuition deposit.

If you are 18 or younger when you graduate from high school, you are able to take a year off before going to college and remain classified I-A without danger of being drafted, since present rules don't allow drafting anyone younger than 19. This may be especially useful if you need to take some noncredit courses to make up deficiencies and be ready for college, if you need to work for a time to save money for college, or if you just need to take a year off. Once you enter college, you usually cannot drop out for a time without losing your II-S deferment forever.

II-S

Undergraduate Students

The 1967 draft law requires that all undergraduate college students receive the II-S deferment if they meet the qualifications for it [MSSA 6(h)(1)].

To receive the II-S for undergraduate study, you must meet six requirements [REG 1622.25]:

1. You must request the deferment in writing, either on a Request for Undergraduate Student Deferment (Form 104) or by letter. The form is available from your draft board and from most colleges.

2. You must make sure your college sends a Student Certificate (Form 109 or equivalent) to your draft board, stating that you meet the requirements for the deferment. At many colleges, this is not done automatically; you must ask the school to send it.

3. You must be receiving credit for your courses that can count toward a bachelor's degree. This means that at some colleges "nonmatriculated" or "special" students may not qualify for II-S deferments, though they may qualify for II-A (see Chapter 10).

4. You must be a full-time student. At many colleges this is defined as twelve or more credit hours, but standards vary from one school to another. Since the law and Regulations

APPROVAL NOT REQUIRED.

SELECTIVE SERVICE SYSTEM

REQUEST FOR UNDERGRADUATE STUDENT DEFERMENT

The Military Selective Service Act of 1967 provides in pertinent part as follows:

Section 6. "(h)(1) Except as otherwise provided in this paragraph, the President shall, under such rules and regulations as he may prescribe, provide for the deferment from training and service in the Armed Forces of persons satisfactorily pursuing a full-time course of instruction at a college, university, or similar institution of learning and who request such deferment. A deferment granted to any person under authority of the preceding sentence shall continue until such person completes the requirements for his baccalaureate degree, fails to pursue satisfactorily a full-time course of instruction, or attains the twenty-fourth anniversary of the date of his birth, whichever first occurs. * * * No person who has received a student deferment under the provisions of this paragraph shall thereafter be granted a deferment under this subsection, * * * except for extreme hardship to dependents (under regulations governing hardship deferments), or for graduate study, occupation, or employment necessary to the maintenance of the national health, safety, or interest. * * * Any person who requests and is granted a student deferment under this paragraph, shall, upon the termination of such deferred status or deferment, and if qualified, be liable for induction as a registrant within the prime age group irrespective of his actual age, unless he is otherwise deferred under one of the exceptions specified in the preceding sentence. As used in this subsection, the term prime age group' means the age group which has been designated by the President as the age group from which selections for induction into the Armed Forces are first to be made after delinquents and volunteers."

TO: Local Board No. ....

....
....

I have read and understand the preceding provisions of the Military Selective Service Act of 1967. I am pursuing a full-time course of instruction at a college, university, or similar institution of learning, and do hereby request that I be granted an undergraduate student deferment in Class II–S.

....
(Signature)

....
(Selective Service Number)   (Number and Street or RFD Route)

....
(Date)   (City and State)   (ZIP Code)

SSS Form 104 (6-29-67)   U.S. GOVERNMENT PRINTING OFFICE : 1967—O-265-614

FORM APPROVED
BUDGET BUREAU NO. 33-R 0124

SELECTIVE SERVICE SYSTEM
STUDENT CERTIFICATE
(Complete Appropriate Item or Items)

Date _____

Selective Service No. ☐ ☐ ☐

Student No. ☐

1. Name and Current Mailing Address of Student

   SAMPLE

2. The student identified above has been accepted for admission for a full-time course of instruction at the college, university or similar institution of learning shown below which will commence on or about
   _____
   (Date)

3. The student identified above has entered upon and is satisfactorily pursuing a full-time course of instruction at the college, university, or similar institution of learning shown below in the ☐ 1st ☐ 2nd ☐ 3rd ☐ 4th ☐ 5th year class, which commenced on _____, and is expected to receive a degree on or about _____
   (Date)   (Date)

4. The student identified above is (check one)   ☐ No longer enrolled full time
   ☐ Not eligible to continue   ☐ Graduated
                                                  _____
                                                  (Date)

5. Remarks

INSTRUCTIONS

Selective Service Regulations define a student's academic year as the twelve month period following the beginning of his course of study.

This form may be submitted when an individual has been accepted for admission as an undergraduate student in a college, university, or similar institution of learning (item 2) and will be submitted promptly (1) at the beginning of the student's academic year (item 3) or (2) when a student is no longer enrolled full time, is not eligible to continue, or has graduated (item 4). When graduation occurs, the date of graduation should be entered in the space following that caption. The original may be forwarded to the State Director of the State in which the institution is located, for distribution to local boards within the State, or to other State Directors of Selective Service, or direct to local boards. When the latter plan is followed the address of the registrant's local board should be in his possession on a Registration Certificate (SSS Form 2) or a Notice of Classification (SSS Form 110).

Submission of this form does not constitute a request for deferment.

Authentication of information on this form may be by any means evidencing that a responsible official of the institution has verified its preparation.

6. ADDRESS OF LOCAL BOARD	7. AUTHENTICATION
SAMPLE	SAMPLE
	Name and Address of Institution

S S S FORM 109 (REVISED) (6-9-69)

don't define "full time," it appears that each college can adopt any definition it considers appropriate.

5. You must be "satisfactorily pursuing a full-time course of instruction." According to the Regulations, this means that you must be completing enough course work each year to receive your degree in the normal number of years. Thus, if you are in a four-year program, you must complete about 25% of your credits by the beginning of your sophomore year, 50% by the beginning of your junior year, and 75% by the beginning of your senior year to continue to receive the deferment. If you are in a five-year program, you must complete about 20% of your credits each year.

6. You must be under 24 years old. If you turn 24, you are likely to lose your II-S deferment, even in the middle of a school year.

Class rank, grades, and test results are no longer used to determine eligibility for II-S.

The Regulations require that you receive the II-S deferment for an entire academic year at a time, unless you graduate or leave full-time study earlier, and your local board should not reclassify before that time [LBM 43]. Since the academic year is defined as "the 12-month period following the beginning of [your] course of study" [REG 1622.25(b)], you will have the summer to make up any credit you lose in the regular school year.

Your "academic year" doesn't necessarily start in September. If you began the year in September, you will have until the following September. But if you began your year in January or June, your "academic year" must continue until the following January or June.

Some colleges have defined "full time" to give their students the advantages of maximum flexibility in planning their educations. Since the Regulations require that the student take enough courses to be on schedule for graduation, they define "full time" in terms of this requirement: any student taking enough courses to graduate on schedule is considered full-time. Thus the student who has taken extra courses in his early years can take a reduced schedule later and still be full-time if he will graduate on schedule. And a student who takes a reduced schedule but agrees to make it up in summer school, or by taking a heavier schedule later, can be considered full-time if his college feels confident that he will still graduate on schedule. This is appropriate, since Selective Service says a favorable Student Certificate can be given to a student who has fallen somewhat behind schedule, if his college "is convinced that this deficiency will not delay the expected date of completion of his course of study . . . the intent [of the Regulations] is to indicate that a student should receive his degree in the normal and specified length of time" (*Selective Service,* September, 1967). However, only a few colleges have adopted this flexible definition; most still define "full time" in terms of a rigid number of credit hours.

Some colleges have also created five-year and longer degree programs for students with special academic needs, such as those with inadequate secondary school preparation who must take special remedial courses before beginning regular college work, and are therefore able to certify satisfactory progress even though the student has finished less than one-fourth of his degree requirements each year.

In a few states, the state director of Selective Service has defined "full time" as a stated number of credit hours. Since the Student Certificate form doesn't have a space for the number of credit hours you are taking, some state directors have designed questionnaires for local boards to send to students. However, there is no authority in the law or Regulations for the Selective Service System to impose its own definition of the length of a degree program or of "full-time" study. As indicated above, that power seems to belong to the school. It is proper that it should, for educational requirements vary from one college to another, and each should be free to establish standards suitable to its educational plan.

Despite the flexibility available under these rules, there are several ways you can lose your deferment. You may fall behind schedule. If you do, it is likely that most colleges will feel obligated to refuse to provide a Student Certificate (Form 109), or will add a note in the Remarks section indicating that you are not "satisfactorily pursuing" your degree.

Even if the school won't give you a favorable Student Certificate because you are too far behind to catch up, the local board may use its discretion in giving deferments "when the failure to earn the required credits was due to illness or some other reason which the board considers adequate" (*Selective Service,* September 1967). If you have made normal progress since July 1, 1967, you are eligible for the II-S deferment [LBM 43]. In practice, this is decided by your school, which indicates an estimated graduation date each time it sends in your Student Certificate (Form 109). If you were a college freshman in the fall of 1967, the probable graduation date your school put on the form then should normally decide how long you will be allowed. If you have earned enough course credits to remain on schedule toward that graduation date, you should be able to keep your II-S (provided, of course, that you meet all the other requirements), regardless of how long you had been in college before July 1, 1967. If you have fallen farther behind since then, you may lose your II-S.

In addition, if you have interrupted college to do other things, you may be able to return without having the interruption counted against you if while you were out of school you were classified II-A or IV-D [LBM 83]. Thus you are able to go back to college after time out for Peace Corps or VISTA service (if you received the II-A occupational deferment) or for theological study or missionary work (if you are given the IV-D minister's exemption).

You may also lose your deferment because you are taking fewer courses than your school defines as full-time, or because you start a semester as a full-time student but later find it necessary to drop a course or two. When this happens during a school year, many schools will notify your draft board immediately. They are not obligated to do this. The regulations place the responsibility on you to notify your board of changes, though they encourage others to report information about you [REG 1625.1(b), 1641.7(a)]. But state directors often ask colleges to inform draft boards when students drop out or change from full-time to part-time study, and many schools do so. This may take away your legal right to catch up by going to summer school.

The II-S deferment will usually be given if you are in a junior college taking courses which may be applied toward a bachelor's degree (although a II-A may also be available, and it may allow more flexibility than II-S). There may be greater leniency in continuing your II-S deferment if you are behind schedule as a result of junior college credits not being accepted by the senior college; your local board can give you a II-S deferment for the first year after the transfer, then evaluate your progress toward a degree [LBM 43]. Only if you are a junior college student in a vocational program, taking courses not transferable to a senior college, are you ineligible for II-S; then you are probably eligible for II-A, discussed in Chapter 10 [LBM 105].

After the 1967 law was passed, many draft counselors (and previous editions of this book) advised students to avoid requesting a II-S deferment as long as possible, primarily because that law denied future III-A fatherhood deferments to men who requested and received II-S student deferments after June 30, 1967. However, in view of the phasing out of III-A fatherhood deferments (discussed in Chapter 11), the major reason for this advice no longer exists. There are still some reasons why you may try to avoid a II-S if you can go to school without one. If you make a false start—begin college, soon leave, then later start over—it may be advantageous not to have applied for II-S the first time. If you first ask for II-S when you begin in earnest, you will be more likely to get the full four years to finish your degree. If you get a II-S the year of the false start, you may be required to finish in four years from then to keep the II-S, and that may be impossible. Of course, you have no need for a deferment until the year you are exposed to the lottery, when you will be at least 19, and a safe lottery number might decide you not to seek a deferment at all (discussed in Chapter 6).

The President's April 23, 1970, proposal, if passed by Congress, "would bar all undergraduate deferments, except for young men who are undergraduate students prior to today. These young men would continue to be eligible for deferment under present regulations during their undergraduate years." Those who began college on or after that date would lose their II-S deferments, but if they are drafted under the lottery rules, their induction will be postponed on request until the end of that semester. Those in R.O.T.C. and other military training programs who are obligated to perform military service would be allowed to complete their study before entering active duty, probably holding I-D deferments (see Chapter 8). Of course, until Congress acts on this request, local boards must continue to give II-S deferments under the rules described in this chapter.

Graduate and Professional Students

Under present rules, only two groups of graduate and professional students are eligible for II-S deferments.

If you enter graduate study in one of five medical fields—medicine, dentistry, osteopathy, optometry, or veterinary medicine—you must be given a II-S deferment as long as you are "satisfactorily pursuing" your degree [REG 1622.26(a)].

If you are a graduate student in any other field, you may be given a II-S deferment at your local board's discretion, provided you meet these very limiting requirements [REG 1622.26(b)]:

1. You must have begun your second year of "post-baccalaureate study" by October 1, 1967. Thus, in the fall of 1970, you probably were a fifth-year student.

2. You must request the deferment by letter (some states provide forms). This isn't required by the Regulations, but by a memorandum from the national director [LBM 84].

3. Your school must send a Graduate or Professional College Student Certificate (Form 103 or equivalent), certifying that you are a full-time student "satisfactorily pursuing" your degree.

4. You must be in "a course of study leading to a doctoral or professional degree or the equivalent (or a combination of master's and doctoral degrees)."

5. You must not have interrupted your graduate study (unless you returned to graduate school in the fall of 1967 after an interruption during all of which you were classified II-A or IV-D [LBM 83]).

The deferment is renewable for a maximum of five years, including time previously spent in graduate study.

The Regulations don't define "satisfactorily pursuing" in the case of graduate students, and the undergraduate definition seems not to apply. Nor is an academic year defined for graduate students.

The 1967 law permits the National Security Council and the Director of Selective Service to allow additional graduate school deferments, but this seems extremely unlikely to be done. At present, it appears that a local board lacks the legal power to grant a II-S deferment for graduate study except to the two groups discussed above, though a few boards have given them anyway.

I-S(C)

The I-S(C) is a curious deferment. It is the only one that you can't get until *after* you've received an induction order. It cancels the induction order and defers you until the end of that academic year, unless you leave school earlier.

Both the Act and the Regulations make it mandatory that a local board give you the I-S(C) deferment on request if you are a full-time student and receive an induction order while you are in school. But there are several important limitations.

First, according to the Regulations, it is available only if you are an undergraduate, or if you are one of the rare graduate or professional students who either have not received a bachelor's degree or have not received a II-S deferment since June 30, 1967 [REG 1622.15(b), LBM 87].

Second, the I-S(C) classification can be received only once, and it can't be renewed. However, if you had lost your undergraduate II-S because you were behind schedule, then received an induction order and qualified for a I-S(C), it is possible that you could use this period to make up enough work to qualify for a II-S again, or you might become eligible for some other classification. After your academic year is over (presumably the same 12-month academic year that applies to the undergraduate II-S deferment, though the Regulations aren't specific), you must be reclassified and have the right to submit new information and have full appeal rights before an induction order can again be issued.

Although the Regulations deny the I-S(C) to all graduate students who have received II-S deferments under the 1967 law and who have bachelor's degrees, the Act seems to deny it only to those who have been given II-S deferments for *undergraduate* study since June 30, 1967 [MSSA 6(h)(1), 6(i)(2)]. Following

Form Approved
Budget Bureau No. 33-R-0202

SELECTIVE SERVICE SYSTEM

GRADUATE OR PROFESSIONAL COLLEGE STUDENT CERTIFICATE

(Complete Appropriate Item or Items)

Date_____

Selective Service No. ☐☐☐☐

1. Name and Current Mailing Address of Student

PART I – GRADUATE STUDENTS

2 (a). The student identified above has been accepted for admission to graduate school for a full-time course of instruction leading to the degree of _____, in _____, in the class commencing _____ and being the first class commencing after he completed the requirements for admission.

2 (b). The student identified above has entered upon a full-time course of instruction as a candidate for a graduate degree, which commenced on _____, and currently is meeting degree requirements, and is expected to attain the degree of _____, in _____, on or about _____.

PART II – PROFESSIONAL STUDENTS

3 (a). The student identified above has been accepted for admission to _____ school in the first year class commencing _____ and being the first class commencing after he completed requirements for admission.

3 (b). The student identified above has entered upon, the _____ year of his professional studies, and is satisfactorily pursuing a full-time course of study leading to graduation with the degree of _____ on or about _____.

★ U.S. GOVERNMENT PRINTING OFFICE: 1967-279-764

126

PART III - GENERAL

4. The student identified above is (check one) ☐ Not eligible to continue ☐ No longer enrolled full time ☐ Graduated _____ (Date)

5. Remarks

INSTRUCTIONS

Selective Service Regulations define a student's academic year as the twelve month period following the beginning of his course of study.

This form should be submitted when an individual has been accepted for admission as a graduate or a professional student to a college, university, or similar institution of learning (Item 2(a) or 3(a), and will be submitted promptly (1) at the beginning of a student's academic year (Item 2(b) or 3(b), or (2) when a student is no longer enrolled, not eligible to continue, or graduated (Item 4). When graduation occurs Item 4 should be completed, entering the date of graduation after that caption.

The original may be forwarded to the State Director of the State in which the institution is located, for distribution to local boards within the State, or to other State Directors of Selective Service, or direct to local boards. When the latter plan is followed the address of the registrant's local board should be in his possession on a Registration Certificate (SSS Form 2 or 2-A) or a Notice of Classification (SSS Form 110). A copy may be furnished to the registrant and a copy returned.

Submission of this form does not constitute a request for deferment.

Authentication of information on this form may be by any means evidencing that a responsible official of the institution has verified its preparation.

6. ADDRESS OF LOCAL BOARD

7. AUTHENTICATION

Name and address of Institution

S S S Form 103 (Revised 10 - 11 - 67) (Previous printings are obsolete) this reasoning, several courts have ruled that graduate and professional students who have received II-S deferments only for graduate study since June 30, 1967, are still eligible for I-S(C) deferments when they receive induction orders during a school year, and these courts have even granted injunctions to stop draft boards from inducting them immediately (*Carey v. Local Board No. 2,* 412 F.2d 71, 2 SSLR 3106, 2nd Circuit, 1969; *Foley v. Hershey,* 409 F.2d 827, 1 SSLR 3376, 7th Circuit, 1969). If you are in this position, you should request a I-S(C) and consult a draft counselor or attorney about the current status of this dispute. Even if the I-S(C) deferment is denied, graduate students who receive induction orders should have them postponed to allow them to finish the current academic year (*Selective Service,* October 1969).

You will be eligible for a I-S(C) if your induction order is issued during a period when classes are actually in session and you are enrolled in them full-time. (Presumably if you get an induction order between semesters or quarters, or even during registration period but before classes start, you might not get the I-S(C), but this definition seems to have grown up in practice and isn't specified in the Regulations.)

If you receive an induction order while a student, write to your local board requesting a I-S(C) deferment and point out that you were a full-time student on the date the induction order was mailed. Also ask your school to send a new certificate (Form 109 for undergraduates, Form 103 for graduate and professional students), and be sure that two items of information are correctly entered: that you were a full-time student on the date the induction order was issued (this should go into the Remarks section of the form), and the correct date when you began your current academic year so you will receive the I-S(C) until the end of the proper period.

The President's request for a change in the Selective Service Act would end the I-S(C) deferment, but he announced on April 23, 1970, that if the change were approved by Congress, students who receive induction orders "will have their entry into service postponed until the end of the academic semester." A postponement of induction is less advantageous because it does not provide for reopening of classification and appeal rights when it ends as I-S(C) does, and of course the I-S(C) permits finishing the *year*, not just the semester.

If you are a conscientious objector classified I-O, you do not receive an induction order and are therefore not eligible for I-S(C) deferment. However, if you receive an order to find civilian work (Form 152) or to report for civilian work (Form 153) while you are in a student category that would normally entitle you to a I-S(C), you are entitled to a postponement until the end of the academic year [paragraph 11 of LBM 64]. This isn't a change of classification, so there are no appeal rights when the academic year is over and the postponement ends. To get the postponement, take the same steps suggested above for getting a I-S(C).

CHAPTER TEN

OCCUPATIONAL, VOCATIONAL TRAINING, AGRICULTURAL, GOVERNMENT OFFICIALS: II-A, II-C, IV-B

Regulations issued by the President on April 23, 1970, have ended new occupational deferments, though they liberalized deferment for vocational training. Under the revised rules, there are still three deferments for men engaged in work "found to be necessary to the maintenance of the national health, safety, or interest" [MSSA 6(h)(2)]:

1. II-A—any occupation except agriculture, including several types of vocational training
2. II-C—agriculture
3. IV-B—certain judges and elected government officials

This chapter describes the rules in effect as this book goes to press, but further changes may occur if Congress approves changes requested by the President for undergraduate college deferments (discussed in Chapter 9). If the President is allowed to end II-S deferments for men who began college on or after April 23, 1970, as he has proposed, he intends also to end further II-A deferments for men who began vocational training programs, junior college courses, and apprenticeships on or after that date. In this case, men called up under the lottery system "will have their entry into service postponed until the end of the academic semester, or for apprentices and trainees, until some appropriate breaking point in their programs" (Message to Congress, April 23, 1970). Congress has not yet acted on the President's request, and its response is unpredictable.

The IV-B deferment is provided by Congress for Congressmen and other elected officials at the federal and state levels, and for judges of courts of record. With only 85 men in it as of April 30, 1970, it is easily the most exclusive Selective Service classification. It will not be affected by recent or proposed changes.

OCCUPATIONAL DEFERMENT

A II-A or II-C deferment is given for a year or less at a time, but may be renewed as long as you are doing work judged essential by your draft board if you received it or applied for it before April 23, 1970, and continue in deferrable work, though not necessarily in the same field or for the same employer. In future years your draft board will have the power to give you an occupational deferment only if you have previously received one (you would be eligible even if you were later given some other classification and now seek to regain the occupational deferment), or if you sent a written request or some written evidence to your board which was received or postmarked *before* April 23, 1970, provided you were already doing the work (or had a firm contract before that date to begin work later) [REG 1622.22(a), LBM 105, Operations Bulletin No. 338].

If you work on a farm and want to renew a II-C deferment, or in some other occupation and want to renew a II-A deferment, and you meet these conditions, you should ask your employer or supervisor to write to your draft board asking that you be deferred again. He should emphasize the following points, taken from the Regulations [REG 1622.23(a)]:

1. That the work is "necessary to the maintenance of the national health, safety, or interest." The letter should explain why your product or service is essential to the national economy or defense, or to the community in which you work.

2. That you are actually performing the work, or would be except for a "seasonal or temporary interruption."

3. That without a qualified person in your job, your employer's organization would suffer "a material loss of effectiveness."

This is best shown by describing your job and explaining its contribution to the end product.

4. That another qualified person can't readily be found to take your place, because of a shortage in your field or because you have unique abilities. If possible, the letter should describe the unsuccessful efforts to find a replacement.

In addition to your employer, you should write requesting the deferment, making essentially the same points. Your letter alone may be enough to get you the deferment, but a letter by the employer is usually necessary as well.

An employer who has requested your deferment must be notified of the board's decision. He is sent a Classification Advice (Form 111) at the time you are sent a Notice of Classification (Form 110). He has the same right of appeal as you have, though only you can request a personal appearance. Before appealing, it is usually advisable to have the personal appearance, and if possible to take your employer or supervisor as a witness. If you appeal, you (or your employer) can have the appeal transferred to the state appeal board for the area where you work or live, if different from the one where your local board is, by requesting a transfer in the letter requesting the appeal. This is usually desirable if you are applying for an occupational deferment.

If you are self-employed, you will probably want to get letters from responsible people stating that they know your work and consider it essential, and perhaps to ask one of them to attend your personal appearance.

The comments so far in this chapter apply equally to II-A and II-C deferments. Specific information on each of them follows.

II-A

Draft boards are likely to continue II-A deferments for hard-to-replace men in industry, technology, scientific research and development, social service, and teaching. There are no job lists indicating which occupational deferments local boards should renew, and there is little uniformity among local boards, but a few courts have held that a draft board cannot arbitrarily refuse to renew an occupational deferment previously granted if the man's work is still the same.

There are advisory memorandums on several occupations, and if you are in one of these fields you may find it useful to read them and perhaps refer your local board to them: male nurses [LBM 33], doctors and other medical specialists [LBM 77], merchant marine officers [Operations Bulletin 299], skilled workers in the forging and machine tool industries [Operations Bulletin 303]. These can be read and copied at any local board office or state headquarters.

None of these memorandums are binding on your local board. It can do as the national director advises, or ignore his advice. However, not all boards know this, and most boards follow the director's suggestions.

Although there is no uniform policy, most local boards will allow continued II-A deferment during service in the Peace Corps and some other government volunteer programs to men who applied before April 23, 1970. A Peace Corps volunteer accepted for training during 1970 who requested deferment after April 23, 1970, cannot receive II-A, but if he gets an induction order, Selective Service National Headquarters will postpone the reporting date until the end of his initial tour of service in the Peace Corps. He will then be inducted "unless eligible for a deferment on other grounds" [LBM 105, Operations Bulletin 338].

II-C

Farm workers and owners may qualify for renewal of II-C deferment on the same basis as other workers qualify for II-A. However, two additional questions can be considered. First, your local board is supposed to consider whether your farm is at least as productive as others in your area. It will try to determine this by figuring "average annual production per farm worker" for your farm compared with the "local average farm of the type under consideration" [REG 1622.24(b)]. Only production for market is considered, not any used by the farm families.

In addition, the board can consider whether there is a surplus or a shortage of the commodities you produce. Presumably it should

SELECTIVE SERVICE SYSTEM

APPRENTICE DEFERMENT REQUEST

Form approved.
Budget Bureau No. 38-R180.

Date _____

1. Name of apprentice

   _____ _____ _____
   (Last)   (First)   (Middle)

2. Selective Service No.

3. Date of birth

   (Month) (Day) (Year)

4. Mailing address

   _____ _____ _____ _____
   (Number and street or R.F.D. route) (City, town, or village) (County) (State)

5. Number and address of local board where registered _____ (ZIP Code)

6. Name and address of sponsor

7. Name of apprentice training program and activity in which sponsor is engaged

8. Request is hereby made for the occupational deferment of the person identified in items 1 and 2 of this form as an apprentice in an apprentice training program. The criteria set forth in Selective Service Regulations, as indicated below, have been fulfilled, both as to the individual and the apprentice training program.

9. The apprentice training program identified in item 7 of this form has been accepted for the purpose of deferment by the (check one) ☐ State Director of Selective Service for _____ (State) ☐ Director of Selective Service.

9. ☐ The apprentice identified in items 1 and 2 of this form is currently meeting all the standards and requirements of the apprentice training program and is satisfactorily performing and progressing in his on-the-job training and related trade instructions as _____ (Trade or occupation)

10. ☐ The apprentice identified in items 1 and 2 of this form is engaged in and has completed _____ hours of a term of _____ hours of apprentice training in an activity necessary to the maintenance of the national health, safety, or interest.

11. ☐ The apprentice identified in items 1 and 2 of this form is engaged in and has completed _____ hours of related training. This related training is being conducted by _____

12. It is understood that if this deferment request is granted both the registrant and the sponsor are required to notify the local board immediately of any change in the registrant's status as an apprentice. This form must be signed by the registrant, and by the sponsor or his representative.

_____   _____
(Signature of registrant)   (Signature of sponsor or representative)

                             _____
                             (Title)

(SEE REVERSE SIDE FOR INSTRUCTIONS)

SSS Form 171 (Revised 12-28-68) Previous printings are obsolete.

INSTRUCTIONS

This form is to be prepared by sponsors of accepted apprentice training programs as a request to selective service local boards for the occupational deferment of registrants who are employed as apprentices in such programs and signed by both the registrant and his sponsor. This form is to be completed by filling in all appropriate blank spaces and placing an "X" in each appropriate box. When requested by the registrant a sponsor may submit the original of this form to the registrant's local board at the address shown in item 5. A copy may be furnished to the registrant and a copy may be retained for the sponsor's file.

To qualify for deferment, an apprentice must be engaged in a program which, in addition to on-the-job training, includes a minimum of 144 hours of organized and systematic related trade instructions *each* year.

When a request for deferment has been submitted and granted, both the registrant and the sponsor are required to notify the local board immediately of any change in the registrant's status as an apprentice.

This form will be completed annually for each apprentice where continued deferment is desired.

(Reverse of SSS Form 171)

---

be more willing to continue to defer you if your products are in short supply, though this isn't required.

Information about computing the productivity of your farm and other aid in renewing a II-C deferment may be available from your county agricultural agent. He, or the elected stabilization and conservation committee for your county, may also be consulted by the board [LBM 13], so it might be a good idea to see him before you apply for renewal.

VOCATIONAL TRAINING

Regulations issued April 23, 1970, require that

In Class II-A shall be placed any registrant satisfactorily pursuing an approved full-time course of instruction not leading to a baccalaureate degree in a junior college, community college or technical school, or engaged in an approved apprentice training program, such deferment to continue until such registrant fails to pursue satisfactorily such full-time course of instruction or training, or until the expiration of the period of time normally required to complete such course of full-time instruction or training [REG 1622.22(b)].

Therefore, boards must give the II-A deferment to full-time students in trade, technical, and business schools, to apprentices in recognized and organized apprenticeships, and to students in junior colleges not working toward bachelor's degrees, as long as they remain on schedule toward completion of their programs [LBM 105]. Sometimes these deferments can extend for the period of formal instruction and for an additional period of required on-the-job training.

Both the national and state directors of Selective Service keep lists of apprentice training programs which they have approved [REG 1622.23(b)(2), 1622.23a(e)], and employers, unions, and others involved in apprenticeship programs know whether they are on them. Only programs on these lists can make you eligible for II-A deferment as an apprentice. The best source of advice is the sponsor of the apprenticeship you are taking or considering taking. Form 171 is used to request deferment of an apprentice. Those deferred as apprentices on the basis of requests made before April 23, 1970, may be given later II-A occupational deferments as journeymen in the same trade if the local board considers their work essential [Operations Bulletin No. 338, May 20, 1970].

If you are a student in a technical, trade, business, or other vocational school, you should ask the school to send a letter to your draft board. It should say that you are a full-time student and indicate how long your program will last. In addition, you should write to your board and request the II-A deferment, pointing out that you are a full-time student in a program that does not lead to a college degree.

If you are a junior college or community college student, you may be eligible for II-A or II-S (see Chapter 9). If you are taking a full-time course which can't be transferred to a senior college and applied toward a bachelor's degree because it is essentially vocational training, you are eligible for II-A.

Unlike apprenticeships, there are no lists of "approved" vocational training schools or junior colleges, and no explanation of the meaning of this word in the Regulation.

If you go to college or junior college for a time and receive a II-S deferment, then leave to enter a vocational training program, you should be given a II-A deferment while you are in vocational school "where the change of program occurs early so that the overall period of deferment as a student will not exceed reasonable limits" [Operations Bulletin No. 338]. If you transfer the other way —out of a vocational program into an academic program leading to a college degree—you should qualify for II-S.

If you have a choice between II-S and II-A, as you may in some junior college programs, it may be slightly more advantageous to have your school notify your local board that you qualify for II-A, which does not have such a rigid definition of satisfactory progress and may therefore allow somewhat more educational flexibility to both you and your school.

CHAPTER ELEVEN

FATHERS, AND OTHERS WITH DEPENDENTS: III-A

There are actually two types of III-A deferment, one of which you can no longer apply for but can get renewed if you already have it. You *may* be given a III-A because the draft board believes that your dependents will suffer "extreme hardship" if you are drafted. You *must* be allowed to keep a III-A if you sent your local board evidence of your fatherhood before April 23, 1970, unless you are disqualified for one of the reasons discussed below.

FATHERHOOD III-A

If you sent proof to your local board received or postmarked before April 23, 1970, that you were a father and that your child lived with you, the board had to give you the III-A deferment and continue it as long as the child lives with you [REG 1622.30 (c)]. There are only two exceptions:

1. If you are or become a doctor, dentist, or veterinarian, you are not eligible for the fatherhood III-A [REG 1622.30(c)].
2. If you requested and received a II-S student deferment after June 30, 1967, you are not eligible for the fatherhood III-A. At least one court ruled that this applied only to men who received *undergraduate* II-S deferments after that date (*Gregory v. Hershey*, 2 SSLR 3524, E.D. Mich., 1969); the government is appealing this decision.

Even if the child was born after April 23, 1970, you are eligible for continued III-A deferment if the local board was notified of the pregnancy before that date and before it issued you an induction order. This is so even if the doctor's letter was sent after April 23,

1970, provided some evidence or a written request was sent before that date [Operations Bulletin No. 338, May 20, 1970]. You will be eligible for continued III-A if you sent evidence of the child's birth, preferably a copy of the birth certificate.

You may lose your III-A deferment if you are divorced or separated from your wife and the child is in her custody. However, if the child spends part of the time with you, and if you regularly provide for the child in your home, it is possible that you may still qualify. Even if you no longer qualify for the fatherhood III-A, your responsibility for the child's welfare may make you eligible for the "hardship" III-A, discussed below.

If you didn't notify your board prior to April 23, 1970, that you qualified for deferment as a father, it cannot give you a fatherhood III-A, but it can consider you for the "hardship" III-A.

HARDSHIP III-A

A local board will give you a III-A deferment if it is convinced that there is no way to prevent "extreme hardship" to your dependents except by deferring you. You do not lose your right to a hardship III-A because you received a student deferment, the April 23, 1970, changes didn't affect this deferment, and it isn't necessary for the dependent to live with you, so some fathers who don't qualify for the fatherhood III-A can get a hardship III-A. Doctors are technically eligible for this classification but rarely receive it.

This deferment can be given to prevent hardship

> . . . (1) to [your] wife, divorced wife, child, parent, grandparent, brother, or sister . . . or (2) to a person under 18 years of age or a person of any age who is physically or mentally handicapped . . . .

However, the dependent must be a U.S. citizen or live in the U.S. or its possessions [REG 1622.30(b)].

The test is whether the dependent needs you. The need may be some form of the following:

1. Financial—you may be deferred if your contributions are essential to the dependent's income and won't be replaced by Army pay and allowances or relatives if you are drafted.

2. Psychological—whether or not you provide financial support, you may be deferred if the dependent would have an emotional breakdown or severe psychological troubles if you were drafted; you will need to send your draft board letters by a psychiatrist, psychologist, family doctor, or other expert saying so.

3. Personal services—whether or not you provide financial support, you may be deferred if the dependent needs your assistance in managing the day-to-day affairs of the home, providing nursing or therapy, or other services, and no one else can reasonably be expected to take your place.

If you claim that "extreme hardship" to your dependents would result from drafting you, your local board is likely to try to determine whether your support can be replaced. If your dependent is getting welfare payments in addition to your aid, the board may ask the welfare agency whether it would increase the welfare if you were drafted (the answer is likely to be yes). If your dependent is not a child, the board is likely to want to know whether he can support himself. If you are supporting a parent or some other person who is old or disabled, you should get doctors' letters and other evidence to show that he can't work or at least can't earn enough to support himself.

The board will usually send a Dependency Questionnaire (Form 118) if you claim a hardship III-A (see form on next page), and it will use your answers to Series III to try to decide whether another relative would (not just *could*, but *would*) take over the support. If there are relatives but they can't or won't contribute enough to replace your support, you should get letters from them or others who know your family situation (a clergyman's letter is often helpful) explaining why they can't help.

In Series I, Question 3, of the Dependency Questionnaire, enter the total income of each dependent from all sources in the box marked "Approximate Annual Income." Include not only cash income but the value of anything he receives, including bills others pay for him (if he lives with you, include a share of the rent or mortgage payment you pay; if five people live in the home, his share is one-fifth). In the last column, marked "Amount Contributed by

SELECTIVE SERVICE SYSTEM

DEPENDENCY QUESTIONNAIRE

Form approved
Budget Bureau No. 33-R0158

DATE QUESTIONNAIRE RETURNED _____

Date of Mailing _____

COMPLETE AND RETURN BEFORE _____

(Local Board Stamp)

1. Name of Registrant

(Last) (First) (Middle)

2. Selective Service No.

3. Date of Birth (Month) (Day)

4. Class

5. Mailing address

(Number and street or R.F.D. route) (City, town, or village) (County) (State) (Zip code)

(The above items, except the date questionnaire returned, are to be filled in by the local board before questionnaire is mailed)

INSTRUCTIONS (Read Carefully)

1. The law requires you to complete and return this questionnaire on or before the date shown to the right above in order that your local board will have information to make a determination on your request for deferment on grounds of dependency.
2. When a question in any series does not apply, enter "NONE" or "DOES NOT APPLY."
3. You and a claimed dependent(s) may enter on page 4, any statements you feel may be important.
4. The information you furnish should be accurate and will help the local board to properly classify you.
5. Your statements will remain confidential, as prescribed by Selective Service Regulations.
6. FILL OUT WITH TYPEWRITER, OR PRINT IN INK, EXCEPT FOR THE SIGNATURES.
7. Be sure you *sign and date* the form in the appropriate places.

_____
(Member, Executive Secretary or Clerk of Local Board)

STATEMENTS OF THE REGISTRANT

CONFIDENTIAL AS PRESCRIBED IN THE SELECTIVE SERVICE REGULATIONS

Series 1—MARITAL STATUS AND DEPENDENTS

1. (a) I (check one): ☐ have never been married ☐ am a widower
   ☐ am married ☐ am divorced

   (b) I (check one if applicable): ☐ DO ☐ DO NOT live with my wife; if not, her address is ....

   (c) We were married at .... , on ....
   (Place) (Date)

2. (a) I have the following children under 18 years of age who live with me in my home:

   Name .... Age .... Name .... Age ....

   Name .... Age .... Name .... Age ....

   (b) If you have no children listed under 2(a) above, and your wife is pregnant, attach a physician's statement that the child has been conceived, the probable date of its delivery, and the evidence upon which his positive diagnosis of pregnancy is based.

3. (a) List below the persons, other than children listed in 2(a) above, who are wholly or partially dependent upon you for support and show appropriate information.
   (b) IF ANY DEPENDENT IS PHYSICALLY OR MENTALLY HANDICAPPED, ATTACH A PHYSICIAN'S STATEMENT AS TO THE PERSON'S CONDITION.

Dependent	Relationship	Age	Approximate Annual Income	Amount Contributed By Me Annually
Name Address			$	$
Name Address			$	$
Name Address			$	$
Name Address			$	$

SSS Form 118   (Revised 3-4-69) (Previous printings obsolete)

(1)

Series II—REGISTRANT'S FAMILY

List below all the living members of your immediate family who are 16 years of age or over, *other than those listed in Series I*, including your father, mother, brothers, sisters, father-in-law and mother-in-law. (Use page 4 if necessary)

	Relationship	Age	Approximate Annual Income	Amount This Relative can Contribute to Support
Name Address				
Name Address				
Name Address				
Name Address				
Name Address				

Series III—EMPLOYMENT STATUS OF REGISTRANT

1. My total income from all sources during the last 12 months was $ _____ Of this amount, $ _____ was in salary or wages, $ _____ was in other income _____

2. The job I am now working at is _____
   (Give full title of your job)

3. My average earnings from this employment are $ _____ per week, before taxes.

4. My employer is _____ (Name of company or proprietor. If working for yourself, enter "Self")
   _____
   (Address of place of employment, street or rural route, city, and State)

5. I have worked at this job since _____, 19____

6. I have been unemployed since _____, 19____

144

Series IV—FINANCIAL CONDITION

1. I (Check one): ☐ own my own home. ☐ am buying my own home (Complete 2 below).
   ☐ am renting my living accommodations (Complete 3 below).

2. Amount of original mortgage was $............ and the balance due is $............
   Monthly payments of $............ are made to ....
   _____
   (Name and address)

3. I pay rent in the amount of $............ per month to ....
   _____
   (Name and address)

4. I (Check one): ☐ DO ☐ DO NOT own an automobile used primarily for ....
   It was purchased ☐ New ☐ Used on .... and I still owe approximately $............ of the
   (Date)
   purchase price.

5. Itemize below all your monthly expenses. (Use additional sheet if necessary)

Item	Amount	Item	Amount

Series V—EMPLOYMENT STATUS OF REGISTRANT'S WIFE

1. My wife (Check one) ☐ IS ☐ IS NOT working at a job for pay.

2. She is employed by ....
   ....(Show employer and address)
   as ....
   (Position or kind of work)

3. Her earnings are $ .... per ☐ HOUR ☐ DAY ☐ MONTH ☐ YEAR

4. She was last employed on ....
   (Date employment ended—if never employed, so state)
   by ....
   (Name and address of wife's former employer)

REGISTRANT'S CERTIFICATE

I certify that I am the registrant named and described in the foregoing statements in this questionnaire; that I have read (or have had read to me) the statements made by and about me, and that each and every such statement is true and complete to the best of my knowledge, information, and belief.

Registrant sign here ☛ ....
(Signature or mark of registrant)

Date ....
....
(No. and Street or P.O. address)

....
(City)   (State)   (Zip Code)

Telephone No. ....

....
(Signature of witness to mark of registrant)

If another person has assisted you in completing this questionnaire, such person shall sign the following statement:

I have assisted the registrant herein named in preparation of this questionnaire because ....

....
(For example—registrant unable to read and write English, etc.)

....
(Signature of person who has assisted)

....
(No. and Street or P.O. address)

Date..

....
(City)   (State)   (Zip Code)

NOTICE TO REGISTRANT

YOU OR YOUR DEPENDENT MAY ENTER ON PAGE 4 OR ON ATTACHED SHEETS ANY ADDITIONAL STATEMENTS WHICH YOU BELIEVE SHOULD BE BROUGHT TO THE ATTENTION OF THE LOCAL BOARD FOR CONSIDERATION IN DETERMINING YOUR CLASSIFICATION. IF YOUR DEFERMENT REQUEST IS FOR HARDSHIP CONSIDERATIONS OTHER THAN FINANCIAL, SET FORTH SUCH CLAIM IN DETAIL IN THIS SECTION. YOU MAY ATTACH STATEMENTS OF PHYSICIANS, NEIGHBORS, FRIENDS, RELATIVES, ETC, WHO ARE FAMILIAR WITH THE FACTS UPON WHICH YOUR CLAIM IS BASED.

(3)

Series VI—STATEMENT OF REGISTRANT
(Use additional sheets if necessary)

....
(Signature of registrant)

....
(Date)

Series VII—STATEMENT OF DEPENDENT
(Use additional sheets if necessary)

....

....

....

....

....

....

....

....

....

....

....
(Signature of dependent)

....
(Date)

(4)

U. S. GOVERNMENT PRINTING OFFICE : 1969 OF—337—701

Me Annually," enter the contribution you make to this dependent's income, including not only cash but the value of anything else you provide—a share of the rent, food, clothing, medical and other bills you pay, health or other insurance you pay for. It is a good idea to write out a detailed monthly budget in the space on page 4 or an attached page. You aren't required to contribute any particular portion of the dependent's income. You must show that your support is necessary, that removing it would leave the dependent in "extreme hardship."

The board will also consider whether the Army will pay a dependency allowance. These allowances are paid to some dependents of servicemen. The armed forces will count your wife, unmarried legitimate children under 21, and unmarried stepchildren and adopted children under 21 who are dependent on you. In addition, if they were receiving more than half of their support from you, they will count parents, stepparents and adopted parents, people who have had a relationship to you like that of parents, and permanently disabled legitimate children over 21. No other relatives or other dependents can receive this allowance. If you have dependents who qualify, the armed forces will deduct $40 a month from your pay and add an additional amount depending on how many qualified dependents you have. The total amount payable to the dependent is $100 a month for one dependent, $130.60 for two, or $145 for three or more [LBM 17]. To qualify for the III-A hardship deferment on financial grounds, you would have to show that your dependents wouldn't qualify for the allowance or that it wouldn't be enough to replace your support and prevent "extreme hardship." In fact, it is extremely difficult to get a III-A on purely financial grounds.

Of course, no amount of money can replace you if the dependency is based on psychological problems or your personal services, and the law recognizes this [MSSA 6(h)(2), REG 1622.30(d)]. When these kinds of dependency exist in addition to or instead of the financial dependency, you should emphasize this in letters to your draft board and get others to write testifying that they know your dependents would have great difficulty in getting along without you.

Letters in support of an "extreme hardship" claim can best be written by your family friends, neighbors, family doctor, psychiatrist, minister, employer, social worker, and others who know the family situation.

A most useful letter will often be written by the dependent himself, if able to do so. In addition to your own letter and form, and the letters you get from other people, you should ask your dependent to write to your local board explaining the situation and asking that you be deferred. When this is done, the dependent must be notified of the draft board's decision when you are, and has the same right to appeal as you have.

However, only you have the right to ask for a personal appearance with your local board, and you should use this opportunity if you possibly can. When your personal appearance is scheduled, you should take your best witness with you. That will often be the dependent himself, even if a child, but sometimes you will be wiser to take your minister or doctor or some other person who can explain the situation to the board. You should also take copies of financial records to prove your support, including canceled checks or receipts for rent and medical or other bills, and income tax returns for you and your dependents.

The III-A deferment for extreme hardship to dependents is one of the toughest classifications to get. The Dependency Questionnaire may be confusing, it may be difficult to get enough evidence, and it will often be difficult to convince the board that the hardship is real.

This deferment should be available to men from really poor families who are trying to help out, but in practice they often are unable to get it because they don't have records or don't write or speak well enough to explain the situation to a draft board. As a result, this deferment is given mainly to middle-class men because they are more articulate and can convince the board. The help of a draft counselor is especially important when you are applying for this deferment. He may be able to explain the form, help you get evidence, and help you find people who can testify for you.

CHAPTER TWELVE

MINISTERS,
MEN PREPARING FOR THE MINISTRY: IV-D
ALIENS: IV-C
VETERANS, SOLE SURVIVING SONS: IV-A

This chapter discusses three unrelated classifications. If you are eligible for one of them you will probably receive it without difficulty when you send your draft board the necessary evidence. However, a relatively small number of men who claim one of these classifications run into difficulties, and these few have very complicated draft problems. If you are one, the brief discussion in this chapter will be inadequate. You will need the help of an expert counselor, one of the national draft counseling services listed in Chapter 21, or possibly an attorney experienced in dealing with these problems.

MINISTERS, SEMINARY STUDENTS, AND PRE-SEMINARY STUDENTS

By act of Congress, the IV-D classification must be given to you if you are in one of the three groups that qualify for this exemption [MSSA 6(g), REG 1622.43]:

1. "Regular or duly ordained ministers of religion"

2. Full-time seminary students sponsored by denominational bodies

3. Full-time students preparing to enter seminaries in which they are pre-enrolled, who are sponsored by denominational bodies

The law defines the two types of ministers who must be given the IV-D classification [MSSA 16(g)]. You are a "duly ordained" minister if you have received the ordination ritual of a church or sect, and preach and teach the principles of your religion as your "regular and customary vocation." You are a "regular" minister if you are not ordained but preach and teach the principles of your religion as your "customary vocation" and are recognized by your religion as a minister. In either case, you must be qualified to conduct the "public worship" of your faith and must serve a body of believers or potential believers. The definition in the law, as interpreted by the courts in many complicated cases, should be broad enough to include ministers of unconventional religions, including those who preach in public places and from door to door, provided they meet the "customary vocation" requirement.

You may fulfill the "customary vocation" part of the definition if your ministerial duties are your principal activity, receiving the greatest part of your working time and attention. The complications arise when you work part of the time as a minister and part of the time at an unrelated job, and many court decisions have tried to deal with this situation. Some courts have ruled that you can receive the IV-D classification if you give more hours per week to ministerial duties than to other work, and Selective Service traditionally considers 100 hours per month the minimum time you must spend on ministerial duties to qualify. But these are only general guidelines, and some exceptions have been made. The general principle seems to be that the IV-D registrant must give first place in his life to his duties as a minister and regard his other work merely as a means to continue his religious service.

You may be in the second group entitled to the IV-D classification if you are a full-time student in a "recognized" theological or divinity school under the direction of a "recognized" church or religious organization. To be "recognized," a theological school "should enjoy a good reputation and its graduates should be accepted, by the church sponsoring the registrant, for ministerial duties." A "recognized" church or religious organization "should be able to show that it was established on the basis of a community of faith and belief, doctrines and practices of a religious character, and that it engages primarily in religious activities" [LBM 56]. The local board is required to decide whether the school and church are "recognized," but may ask the advice of state and national directors of Selective Service. There are no official lists, nor could there be without a probable violation of the First Amendment to the Constitution.

If you are applying for a IV-D classification as a seminary student, you will need to send your local board a statement from your sponsoring church or organization saying that you are preparing for the ministry under its direction. You should also have your school send a statement showing that you are "satisfactorily pursuing a full-time course of instruction."

You may be in the third group of IV-D registrants if you are pre-enrolled in a "recognized" seminary under the direction of a "recognized" church or religious organization and you are a full-time, satisfactory student in a course of instruction which will prepare you for admission to the seminary. Thus if you are a college student preparing for a ministerial career, you do not need a II-S deferment. If you qualify as a pre-enrolled, sponsored preparatory student, you may be classified IV-D. You would need to submit the same kind of evidence as the seminary student.

ALIENS

Relatively few aliens are eligible for the IV-C classification. Many noncitizens are exempted from even registering for the American draft (see page 33). Most aliens admitted for permanent residence (immigrants) are subject to the draft just as citizens are, except when they are outside the United States. There are special provisions for those admitted as temporary residents (nonimmigrants).

If you are a permanent resident alien, you must register for the draft and are subject to the same rules as registrants who are U.S. citizens. There are two exceptions. By ruling of the U.S. Attorney General (42 Opinions of the Attorney General 28, April 1968; 1 SSLR 3073), if you are a citizen of one of the 15 countries (listed on page 33) which have treaties providing for exemption of their citizens while they are in the U.S., you may be exempt from the draft (though not necessarily classified IV-C) even though you are a permanent resident of the U.S. if you file an Application by Alien for Relief from Training and Service in the Armed Forces (Form 130), but filing this form will permanently bar you from U.S. citizenship. Selective Service has disagreed with the Attorney General about this right of "treaty aliens," and a lawyer's help may be needed if a draft board refuses to honor it.

In addition, if you are an alien with status as a permanent resident of the U.S., you are classified IV-C during any period when you are outside the United States and its territories. This reclassification would have the effect of canceling an induction order if one had been issued to you, but would not erase a violation of the Selective Service law committed before leaving the country [REG 1622.42(c)]. If you are an alien and plan to travel outside the United States but want to be able to return, you should notify your local board by letter before you leave, or within 10 days after you leave, of your address abroad, the intended date of return, and the reasons for your trip, enclosing evidence if possible of the reasons for traveling abroad. This can be important because you may be denied readmission to the U.S. or later deported if you have left to avoid military service, so evidence that your trip was necessary because of a family emergency, business, education, or other legitimate purpose may help insure that you can return. Before you leave, you should also apply for a Permit for Registrant to Depart from the United States (Form 300); even if it is denied, applying for it would show your intention to return (for details, see Chapter 7). When you return to the United States, you should write your local board within 10 days that you are back, and it must then reclassify you, giving you full appeal rights.

If you have a temporary visa but are required to register, you must be classified IV-C until your time in the U.S. totals more than one year, whether in one visit or several added together [REG 1622.42(a)].

After you have been in the country on a temporary visa for over a year, you are taken out of the IV-C classification, but you are eligible for any other classification a citizen could qualify for. However, even after a year's residence, you may receive the IV-C classification by filing an Application by Alien for Relief from Training and Service in the Armed Forces (Form 130) at any time

Form approved.
Budget Bureau No. 33-R0250

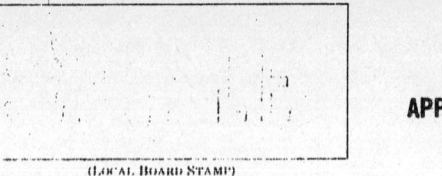

SELECTIVE SERVICE SYSTEM

APPLICATION BY ALIEN FOR RELIEF FROM TRAINING AND SERVICE IN THE ARMED FORCES

............................., 19......
(Date)

(LOCAL BOARD STAMP)

STATE OF .... } ss:
COUNTY OF ....

I, ..., ..., ...; I am a
   (Last name)   (First name)   (Middle name)

do solemnly swear (or affirm) that I am a citizen of ....;
   (Country)

registrant of Local Board ...., ..., ...;
   (Number)   (City)   (County)   (State)

my Selective Service number is [   ]; my alien registration number is ....;

I last entered the United States on .... at ....
   (Month, day, and year)   (Place of entry)

on .... as ....
   (Name of airline, vessel, etc.)   (Specify visitor, student, businessman, or other)

for the purpose of .... under a
   (Study, travel, business, research, etc.)

.... Visa numbered .... and that I have not been
(Type of visa)   (Number of visa)

admitted to the United States for permanent residence.

156

I hereby apply for relief from liability for training and service in the Armed Forces of the United States on the ground that I am an alien. I have read (or have had read to me) and understand the NOTICE given below, and I understand that if I am relieved from liability for such training and service on such ground, I shall be permanently ineligible to become a citizen of the United States. I further understand that I shall be ineligible to receive an immigrant visa and shall be excluded from entry into the United States for permanent residence.

Subscribed and sworn to before me this .... day of ...., 19.......

....
(Signature of person administering oath)

....
(Title of person administering oath)

....
(Signature of registrant)

NOTICE

Section 4 (a) of the Military Selective Service Act of 1967 provides in part that "Any male alien who is between the ages of 18 years and 6 months and 26 years, at the time fixed for registration, or who attains the age of 18 years and 6 months after having been required to register pursuant to section 3 of this title, or who is otherwise liable as provided in section 6(h) of this title, who has remained in the United States in a status other than that of a permanent resident for a period exceeding 1 year (other than an alien exempted from registration under this title and regulations prescribed thereunder) shall be liable for training and service in the Armed Forces of the United States, except that any such alien shall be relieved from liability for training and service under this title if, prior to his induction into the Armed Forces he has made application to be relieved from such liability in the manner prescribed by and in accordance with rules and regulations prescribed by the President; but any alien who makes such application *shall thereafter be debarred from becoming a citizen of the United States.* (Italics supplied.) Any alien who is so relieved also shall be permanently ineligible thereafter to become a citizen of the United States by reason of section 315 of the Immigration and Nationality Act (8 U.S.C. 1426), which provides that ". . . any alien who applies or has applied for exemption or discharge from training or service in the Armed Forces or in the National Security Training Corps on the ground that he is an alien, and is or was relieved or discharged from such training or service on such ground, shall be permanently ineligible to become a citizen of the United States." By reason of section 212(a)(22) of the Immigration and Nationality Act (8 U.S.C. 1182), a person who is ineligible to citizenship is hereby also ineligible to receive an immigrant visa and is excluded from admission into the United States, Puerto Rico, Guam and the Virgin Islands for permanent residence.

SSS Form 130 (Revised 1-8-69) (Previous printings are obsolete) (OVER)

FIRST PROOF

157

INSTRUCTIONS

This form shall be executed by the registrant in duplicate. The local board shall forward the original to the Director of Selective Service through the State Director of Selective Service and shall retain the duplicate in the registrant's Cover Sheet (SSS Form 101).

The oath may be administered by—
  (1) Any civil officer authorized to administer oaths generally.
  (2) Any commissioned officer of the land or naval forces assigned for duty with the Selective Service System.
  (3) Any member, executive secretary or clerk of a local board or board of appeal.
  (4) Any government appeal agent or associate government appeal agent.
  (5) Any duly authorized advisor to registrants.
  (6) Any postmaster, acting postmaster, or assistant postmaster.

U.S. GOVERNMENT PRINTING OFFICE : 1969OL-331-752

(Reverse of SSS Form 130)

---

before you are actually inducted into the armed forces [MSSA 4(a), REG 1622.42(b), LBM 23]. Filing this form with your local board will permanently bar you from U.S. citizenship. It may also make it difficult to get readmitted to the U.S. if you leave, so if you plan to travel outside the U.S. after filing the Form 130 but want to return, you should get the advice of an attorney experienced in immigration law before you leave.

If you registered at a time when you were required to, but have since become a member of one of the groups exempted from registration (discussed on page 33) you should be classified IV-C when you notify your local board of the changed circumstances [REG 1622.42(d)]. This may apply if you have a temporary visa and become an employee of the embassy or United Nations mission of your country, for example, or if you are a temporary or permanent resident and are living in the Canal Zone. It should also apply if you are a physician or other medical specialist in the United States for training or research, were admitted as an immigrant before July 1, 1967, after you were 26 years old, and leave the United States before you are ordered inducted into military service and are readmitted as a J-1 nonimmigrant [LBM 23]. It may also apply if you were a U.S. citizen but emigrated to another country and renounced your U.S. citizenship before the date you were scheduled for induction into the armed forces (see Chapter 17 for discussion of this complex subject).

If you entered the U.S. on a temporary visa, you are also eligible for the IV-C classification during any period when you are outside the country, but you may have even more difficulty being readmitted than a permanent resident would (see discussion above).

In addition, whether you are a temporary or permanent U.S. resident, if you have served at least 18 months in the armed forces of a country with which the U.S. has a mutual defense treaty, you may be eligible for the IV-A classification (see discussion below).

For a more detailed discussion, see the memo "Aliens and the Draft," available for 9¢ from any CCCO office (addresses on page 255—enclose a self-addressed long envelope with 6¢ postage).

VETERANS AND SOLE SURVIVING SONS

If you have completed military service in the U.S. armed forces, you may be classified IV-A, depending on how long you have served and the type of discharge you received. You must receive the IV-A classification:

1. If you were discharged or transferred to the reserves *for the convenience of the government* after serving honorably on active duty in any branch of the armed forces for at least six months [REG 1622.40(a)(1)]. This does not include active duty for training for reservists.

2. If you have served honorably on active duty in any branch of the armed forces for at least one year [REG 1622.40(a)(2)].

3. If you have served as a commissioned officer in the Public Health Service or the Environmental Science Services Administration for at least two years [REG 1622.40(a)(3)] (for information about this type of service, see Chapter 8).

4. If you have completed the full enlistment term as a member of the Ready Reserves of any branch of the armed forces, or as a member of a National Guard unit (usually six to eight years) [REG 1622.40(a)(5), (6), (7), (8), (9)].

Two other groups of registrants are eligible for the IV-A classification.

If you have performed at least 18 months of active duty in the armed forces of another country, you may receive the IV-A classification, provided that the other country has a mutual defense agreement with the United States and that it exempts from its armed forces American citizens who have served for 18 months in the U.S. armed forces [REG 1622.40(a)(4)]. There are 44 countries with such agreements [listed in LBM 76]. If you qualify for this exemption, you should ask the embassy or a consulate of the country in whose armed forces you have served to send your local board a certificate written in English verifying your service.

If you are the only living son in your family, and either your father or a brother or sister died as a result of service in the U.S. armed forces, whether on active duty or as a result of injury or disease received in military service, you must be classified IV-A as a sole surviving son [MSSA 6(o), REG 1622.40(a)(10)]. You may be eligible for this exemption even if your father is still living, for example if your only brother died as a result of military service. If you are entitled to this classification, you should send your local board a copy of a document showing that a member of your family died as a result of service in the armed forces; if you don't have evidence, the Veterans Administration may be able to help you get it. Draft boards can usually get this sort of information from the Veterans Administration, and it may be useful to ask your local board to write directly to the VA.

Under a Supreme Court decision, you must still receive the sole surviving son exemption though the "family unit" no longer exists —for example, if you are the only son of a father who died as a result of military service and your mother has also died. Since the purpose of this exemption is not only to provide "solace and consolation" to the remaining family, but also "to avoid extinguishing the male line of a family by facilitating the death in action of the only surviving son" and to allow "fairness to the registrant who has lost his father in the service of his country," the IV-A classification should also be given to the registrant whose father died as a result of military service and whose mother later remarried and had additional sons (*McKart v. U.S.*, 395 U.S. 185, 2 SSLR 3023, 1969).

CHAPTER THIRTEEN

REJECTION FOR PHYSICAL, MENTAL, OR ADMINISTRATIVE REASONS: I-Y, IV-F

You are found fit or unfit for military service according to standards set up by the Army, not by the Selective Service System. The same standards should apply whether you are being considered for regular military service, noncombatant military service, or civilian work as a conscientious objector. There are no differences between the physical standards for men who enlist and men who are drafted (with the exception of doctors and other medical specialists). The same physical standards apply to all branches of military service, but there are different mental (intelligence) standards. Different standards may also apply to those who want special assignments within a branch of the service, such as submarine duty in the Navy or pilot training in the Air Force.

The physical and psychological standards are in Chapter 2 (Medical Fitness Standards for Appointment, Enlistment, and Induction) of Army Regulation 40-501. This chapter (and additional sections in appendices) consists of a list of medical and other conditions which will disqualify you for military service. The list is too long to include in this book, but you can get a complete copy of the regulation for less than $2.00 from the Superintendent of Documents, Government Printing Office, Washington, D.C. 20402. Order catalog item D 101.9—AR 40-501 Reprint, *Medical Service: Standards of Medical Fitness* (including Changes 1–25 and any additional changes that have been issued). Chapter 2 is reprinted in the "I-Y and IV-F: Appendix" memo sold for 21¢ by all three offices of CCCO (addresses on page 255); enclose a self-addressed long envelope with 12¢ postage.

If you have a condition listed in Chapter 2 of this Regulation, you cannot serve in the armed forces except in case of war or national emergency, and you should be classified I-Y. If your condition is also listed in Chapter 6 (Medical Fitness Standards for Mobilization), you are not acceptable even in wartime and you should be classified IV-F.

If you have a disqualifying condition, you can be reclassified I-Y or IV-F on the basis of an evaluation by your local board, usually based on the recommendation of its medical advisor, or more often on the basis of a pre-induction physical examination or an examination when you are sent for induction. This chapter discusses these procedures and suggests ways to be sure any disqualifying condition you have is properly recognized.

INTERVIEW WITH LOCAL BOARD MEDICAL ADVISOR

You are required to notify your local board in writing within 10 days after you learn of any change in your circumstances which could affect your classification [REG 1625.1(b)]. This includes information about your physical and mental condition, and information about criminal convictions which could affect administrative (sometimes called "moral") acceptability.

If you are classified I-A, I-A-O, or I-O and you notify your local board that you have one of the medical conditions on the official list [AR 40-501, Chapter 2], the local board must order you to have an interview with its medical advisor (see page 28) to determine whether you should be reclassified [REG 1628.2(b)]. Many local boards seem not to know about this requirement in the Regulations, so you should specifically request an interview with the medical advisor; it may even be useful to call the board's attention to Regulation 1628.2(b) in your letter.

This interview can be transferred if you are so far from your local board that traveling to see its medical advisor would be a hardship. When you receive the Notice to Registrant to Appear for Medical Interview (Form 219), you should take it to a nearby local board and arrange for transfer in the same way as for an armed forces physical examination (see page 78).

The medical advisor, who serves without pay, can consider any evidence you have submitted to him or to the local board [REG 1628.3], so you should submit all the evidence you can get from your own doctors, hospitals, or other sources. There is little point in asking for a medical interview for a minor condition not on the list.

You should ask your own doctors to write (and preferably type) full reports of your disqualifying condition, including a complete description in medical terms, the medical history, the ways in which the condition may disable you under military conditions, any treatment you need or are receiving, and how long the condition is likely to last. The reports should include copies of X-rays, laboratory reports, special tests, or other evidence of the existence or seriousness of the condition. If medical consultants were involved in diagnosing it, their reports should also be included. If you had to be hospitalized or had an operation, including a copy of the hospital record may be useful.

All evidence given to you should be photocopied so you will have at least four extra copies made for your personal file. Send the originals to your local board when you request the interview with the medical advisor. Take another copy to the medical advisor when he interviews you. These items won't be returned to you; they will be kept by your local board and become a part of your official file.

At the interview, the medical advisor can perform whatever examination he considers necessary, but he cannot have X-rays or laboratory tests made. He then sends his report to the local board. If he considers you unsuitable for military service, the local board can reclassify you I-Y or IV-F, though it isn't required to. During the 1969 fiscal year, over 127,000 men were found disqualified by local boards without armed forces physical examinations.

If you are not deferred as a result of the interview with the medical advisor, you must still receive the armed forces physical examination before you can be inducted. Thus, the medical interview is an extra process which may be helpful in getting your disqualifying condition properly considered or may do you no good, but it can't take away any of your rights. Of course, the medical advisor's opinion may influence the doctors at the later examination.

Approval Not Required

SELECTIVE SERVICE SYSTEM

NOTICE TO REGISTRANT TO APPEAR FOR MEDICAL INTERVIEW

(Local Board Stamp)

Date of mailing

(Month) (Day) (Year)

Selective Service No.

You are hereby directed to report for a medical interview at the place and time designated below:

_____
(Place of reporting)

on _____ at _____
     (Date)   (Hour)

(Member, Executive Secretary, or clerk of Local Board)

IMPORTANT NOTICE

This medical interview will be of a preliminary nature, for the purpose of disclosing those obvious defects or manifest conditions which would disqualify you for service in the armed forces, and will not finally determine your acceptability for military service. Should you be found to have no obviously disqualifying defects you will be ordered to report for an Armed Forces Physical Examination.

If you are so far from the place designated above that reporting in compliance with this Notice will be a hardship, take this Notice immediately to the local board for the area in which you are now located and make written request for a transfer for medical interview.

Failure to comply with this Notice will result in your being declared a delinquent and subject to the penalties provided by the Military Selective Service Act of 1967.

SSS FORM 219 (Revised 2-6-64) (Previous printings may be used)   GPO 941-633

The interview with the medical advisor is intended as a way to screen men whose conditions can be recognized without the expense and paperwork involved in an armed forces physical examination [LBM 78]. It therefore is improper for a local board to send you for a regular pre-induction examination at the Armed Forces Examining and Entrance Station in place of the medical interview, although this is sometimes done.

The interview with the medical advisor can also be useful if you have already taken and passed a pre-induction physical examination and later discover that you have a disqualifying condition. Selective Service takes the view that re-evaluation should generally be done by the AFEES, not the medical advisor, but it leaves open the possibility of an interview with the medical advisor for a newly discovered medical condition which "has not been previously presented and evaluated" by either the medical advisor or the AFEES (Operations Bulletin No. 327, issued August 23, 1968).

PRE-INDUCTION PHYSICAL EXAMINATION

The pre-induction physical examination (also called armed forces physical examination) must be taken and passed before you can be ordered for induction into the armed forces, whether you requested an early examination or waited for the board to order you to take one (see Chapter 6 for detailed discussion). The exceptions are volunteers for induction and men ordered to pre-inductions who didn't take them, but even they receive full examinations on the day set for induction. Volunteers are sometimes sent for the examination before they are ordered to report for induction; the decision is up to each local board.

After it orders you to take a pre-induction physical examination, your local board should send all evidence in your file that relates to your medical condition to the Armed Forces Examining and Entrance Station (AFEES), including any evidence previously considered by the local board medical advisor. However, to guard against the possibility that some evidence may not reach the AFEES, you should take one of your own copies of the evidence of your disqualifying condition with you to the examination. If you didn't send evidence to your local board, or if the evidence in your file is more than a few months old, you should get new, up-to-date evidence from your doctors to take with you.

Before you receive the physical examination, you will be required to fill out a number of forms. One of these, Standard Form 89, Report of Medical History (reproduced on the following pages), calls for information about illnesses and other medical conditions you have had in the past or now have, both physical and psychological. You should complete this form very carefully. Since the conditions you list on it are more likely to receive attention during the examination, you should go over the form ahead of time so you can give complete answers. If you are claiming a disqualifying medical condition, beware Question 17 asking you to describe your general health. Your health may be "poor" although your spirits are high.

Since the examination may be hasty, you should point out to the doctors that you have evidence of a disqualifying condition, and if necessary be insistent that it be considered carefully.

During the examination you will also be required to fill out a form listing arrests and convictions. The AFEES can't find you acceptable for military service if you have been convicted of a felony (defined as a crime with a maximum penalty of more than a year in prison, regardless of how long you actually served), but the records of all men with serious criminal records are reviewed by a Moral Waiver Determination Board. This board evaluates the seriousness of the crime and the likelihood of rehabilitation to decide whether to consider you suitable for military service. In the fiscal year ended June 30, 1969, it gave "moral waivers" to 87% of those whose files it reviewed. If you were convicted of a felony and don't receive a moral waiver, you will be considered administratively (or "morally") unfit for the armed forces [AR 601-270, 3-9a]. If you have not been convicted of a felony but have less serious criminal convictions or a long police record, you may sometimes be considered administratively unfit [AR 601-270, 3-9b] or medically unfit because of "personality disorders" [AR 40-501, 2-34a(1)].

If you are in the custody of a court (on bail while awaiting trial

Standard Form 89
(Rev. March 1965)
Bureau of the Budget
Circular A-32

REPORT OF MEDICAL HISTORY

THIS INFORMATION IS FOR OFFICIAL USE ONLY AND WILL NOT BE RELEASED TO UNAUTHORIZED PERSONS

89-106-01

1. LAST NAME—FIRST NAME—MIDDLE NAME	2. GRADE AND COMPONENT OR POSITION	3. IDENTIFICATION NO.
4. HOME ADDRESS (Number, street or RFD, city or town, State and ZIP Code)	5. PURPOSE OF EXAMINATION	6. DATE OF EXAMINATION

7. SEX	8. RACE	9. TOTAL YEARS GOVERNMENT SERVICE	10. AGENCY	11. ORGANIZATION UNIT
		MILITARY / CIVILIAN		

12. DATE OF BIRTH	13. PLACE OF BIRTH	14. NAME, RELATIONSHIP, AND ADDRESS OF NEXT OF KIN

15. EXAMINING FACILITY OR EXAMINER, AND ADDRESS

16. OTHER INFORMATION

17. STATEMENT OF EXAMINEE'S PRESENT HEALTH IN OWN WORDS *(Follow by description of past history, if complaint exists)*

18. FAMILY HISTORY

RELATION	AGE	STATE OF HEALTH	IF DEAD, CAUSE OF DEATH	AGE AT DEATH
FATHER				
MOTHER				
SPOUSE				
BROTHERS AND SISTERS				
CHILDREN				

19. HAS ANY BLOOD RELATION *(Parent, brother, sister, other)* OR HUSBAND OR WIFE

YES	NO	*(Check each item)*	RELATION(S)
		HAD TUBERCULOSIS	
		HAD SYPHILIS	
		HAD DIABETES	
		HAD CANCER	
		HAD KIDNEY TROUBLE	
		HAD HEART TROUBLE	
		HAD STOMACH TROUBLE	
		HAD RHEUMATISM *(Arthritis)*	
		HAD ASTHMA, HAY FEVER, HIVES	
		HAD EPILEPSY *(Fits)*	

20. HAVE YOU EVER HAD OR HAVE YOU NOW (Place check at left of each item)

YES	NO	(Check each item)	YES	NO	(Check each item)	YES	NO	(Check each item)
		SCARLET FEVER, ERYSIPELAS			GOITER			"TRICK" OR LOCKED KNEE
		DIPHTHERIA			TUBERCULOSIS			FOOT TROUBLE
		RHEUMATIC FEVER			SOAKING SWEATS (Night sweats)			NEURITIS
		SWOLLEN OR PAINFUL JOINTS			ASTHMA			PARALYSIS (Inc. infantile)
		MUMPS			SHORTNESS OF BREATH			EPILEPSY OR FITS
		COLOR BLINDNESS			PAIN OR PRESSURE IN CHEST			CAR, TRAIN, SEA, OR AIR SICKNESS
		FREQUENT OR SEVERE HEADACHE			CHRONIC COUGH			FREQUENT TROUBLE SLEEPING
		DIZZINESS OR FAINTING SPELLS			PALPITATION OR POUNDING HEART			FREQUENT OR TERRIFYING NIGHTMARES
		EYE TROUBLE			HIGH OR LOW BLOOD PRESSURE			DEPRESSION OR EXCESSIVE WORRY
		EAR, NOSE OR THROAT TROUBLE			CRAMPS IN YOUR LEGS			LOSS OF MEMORY OR AMNESIA
		RUNNING EARS			FREQUENT INDIGESTION			BED WETTING
		HEARING LOSS			STOMACH, LIVER OR INTESTINAL TROUBLE			NERVOUS TROUBLE OF ANY SORT
		CHRONIC OR FREQUENT COLDS			GALL BLADDER TROUBLE OR GALL STONES			ANY DRUG OR NARCOTIC HABIT
		SEVERE TOOTH OR GUM TROUBLE			LAMENESS			EXCESSIVE DRINKING HABIT
		SINUSITIS			ANY REACTION TO SERUM, DRUG OR MEDICINE			HOMOSEXUAL TENDENCIES
		HAY FEVER			LOSS OF ARM, LEG, FINGER, OR TOE			PERIODS OF UNCONSCIOUSNESS
		HISTORY OF HEAD INJURY			PAINFUL OR "TRICK" SHOULDER OR ELBOW			
		SKIN DISEASES			BACK TROUBLE OF ANY KIND			

21. HAVE YOU EVER (Check each item)

YES	NO	(Check each item)	YES	NO	
		WORN GLASSES—CONTACT LENS			ATTEMPTED SUICIDE
		WORN AN ARTIFICIAL EYE			BEEN A SLEEP WALKER
		WORN HEARING AIDS			LIVED WITH ANYONE WHO HAD TUBERCULOSIS
		STUTTERED OR STAMMERED			COUGHED UP BLOOD
		WORN A BRACE OR BACK SUPPORT			BLED EXCESSIVELY AFTER INJURY OR TOOTH EXTRACTION

COMMITTED SUICIDE ☐
BEEN INSANE ☐

22. FEMALES ONLY: A. HAVE YOU EVER —

YES	NO	
		BEEN PREGNANT
		HAD A VAGINAL DISCHARGE
		BEEN TREATED FOR A FEMALE DISORDER
		HAD PAINFUL MENSTRUATION
		HAD IRREGULAR MENSTRUATION

B. COMPLETE THE FOLLOWING:

AGE AT ONSET OF MENSTRUATION _____
INTERVAL BETWEEN PERIODS _____
DURATION OF PERIODS _____
DATE OF LAST PERIOD _____
QUANTITY: ☐ NORMAL ☐ EXCESSIVE ☐ SCANTY

23. HOW MANY JOBS HAVE YOU HAD IN THE PAST THREE YEARS?

24. WHAT IS THE LONGEST PERIOD YOU HELD ANY OF THESE JOBS? MONTHS

25. WHAT IS YOUR USUAL OCCUPATION?

26. ARE YOU (Check one)
☐ RIGHT HANDED ☐ LEFT HANDED

YES	NO	CHECK EACH ITEM YES OR NO. EVERY ITEM CHECKED "YES" MUST BE FULLY EXPLAINED IN BLANK SPACE ON RIGHT	
		27. HAVE YOU BEEN REFUSED EMPLOYMENT OR BEEN UNABLE TO HOLD A JOB BECAUSE OF:	
		A. SENSITIVITY TO CHEMICALS, DUST, SUNLIGHT, ETC.	
		B. INABILITY TO PERFORM CERTAIN MOTIONS	
		C. INABILITY TO ASSUME CERTAIN POSITIONS	
		D. OTHER MEDICAL REASONS (*if yes, give reasons*)	
		28. HAVE YOU EVER WORKED WITH RADIOACTIVE SUBSTANCE?	
		29. DID YOU HAVE DIFFICULTY WITH SCHOOL STUDIES OR TEACHERS? (*If yes, give details*)	
		30. HAVE YOU EVER BEEN DENIED LIFE INSURANCE? (*If yes, state reason and give details*)	
		31. HAVE YOU HAD, OR HAVE YOU BEEN ADVISED TO HAVE, ANY OPERATIONS? (*If yes, describe and give age at which occurred*)	
		32. HAVE YOU EVER BEEN A PATIENT (*Committed or voluntary*) IN A MENTAL HOSPITAL OR SANITORIUM? (*If yes, specify when, where, why, and name of doctor, and complete address of hospital or clinic*)	
		33. HAVE YOU EVER HAD ANY ILLNESS OR INJURY OTHER THAN THOSE ALREADY NOTED? (*If yes, specify when, where, and give details*)	
		34. HAVE YOU CONSULTED OR BEEN TREATED BY CLINICS, PHYSICIANS, HEALERS, OR OTHER PRACTITIONERS WITHIN THE PAST 5 YEARS? (*If yes, give complete address of doctor, hospital, clinic, and details*)	
		35. HAVE YOU TREATED YOURSELF FOR ILLNESSES OTHER THAN MINOR COLDS? (*If yes, which illnesses*)	
		36. HAVE YOU EVER BEEN REJECTED FOR MILITARY SERVICE BECAUSE OF PHYSICAL, MENTAL, OR OTHER REASONS? (*If yes, give date and reason for rejection*)	

37. HAVE YOU EVER BEEN DISCHARGED FROM MILITARY SERVICE BECAUSE OF PHYSICAL, MENTAL, OR OTHER REASONS? *(If yes, give date, reason, and type of discharge; whether honorable, other than honorable, for unfitness or unsuitability)*

38. HAVE YOU EVER RECEIVED, IS THERE PENDING, OR HAVE YOU APPLIED FOR PENSION OR COMPENSATION FOR EXISTING DISABILITY? *(If yes, specify what kind, granted by whom, and what amount, when, why)*

WARNING: A FALSE OR DISHONEST ANSWER TO ANY OF THE QUESTIONS ON THIS FORM MAY BE PUNISHED BY FINE OR IMPRISONMENT (18 U.S.C. 1001).

I CERTIFY THAT I HAVE REVIEWED THE FOREGOING INFORMATION SUPPLIED BY ME AND THAT IT IS TRUE AND COMPLETE TO THE BEST OF MY KNOWLEDGE. I AUTHORIZE ANY OF THE DOCTORS, HOSPITALS, OR CLINICS MENTIONED ABOVE TO FURNISH THE GOVERNMENT A COMPLETE TRANSCRIPT OF MY MEDICAL RECORD FOR PURPOSES OF PROCESSING MY APPLICATION FOR THIS EMPLOYMENT OR SERVICE.

TYPED OR PRINTED NAME OF EXAMINEE | SIGNATURE

39. PHYSICIAN'S SUMMARY AND ELABORATION OF ALL PERTINENT DATA *(Physician shall comment on all positive answers in items 20 thru 38)*

TYPED OR PRINTED NAME OF PHYSICIAN OR EXAMINER | DATE | SIGNATURE

NUMBER OF ATTACHED SHEETS

☆ U.S. GOVERNMENT PRINTING OFFICE : 1967 OF—267-459

or on parole, for example), you cannot be found acceptable until you have an unconditional release from custody [AR 601-270, 3-9c and d].

During the examination you will also be asked to fill out and sign an Armed Forces Security Questionnaire (DD Form 98). This form consists of a list of nearly 300 organizations which have been declared subversive by the Attorney General, only a handful of which still exist, followed by a series of questions asking whether you have ever had any relationship to any of them. If you claim membership in a listed organization or claim to be a Communist, you will not be considered acceptable for military service until a security investigation has been completed, a process which may take a few weeks, several months, or even longer. If you refuse to answer the questions, or qualify your answers without claiming to be a Communist or a member of one of the listed organizations, you may still be found acceptable without delay or investigation [AR 601-270, 5-6].

The form indicates that you have a right to refuse to answer on Fifth Amendment grounds (possible self-incrimination), but most lawyers believe you have a right to refuse to answer questions about political affiliations even if you don't fear self-incrimination. Many people object to loyalty questionnaires because they see them as infringements of the Constitutional rights to freedom of association and belief guaranteed by the First Amendment. Refusal to answer the Armed Forces Security Questionnaire is not a violation of any law.

Another part of the pre-induction examination is the Armed Forces Qualification Test, an aptitude and general information test to determine your mental acceptability. If you fail this test, you are given further mental tests, and your educational background is considered to determine whether you have failed deliberately. High school graduates are usually considered acceptable even if they fail the mental tests [AR 601-270, 4-10 and 4-11].

During fiscal year 1969, over 470,000 men, or 46% of those sent for pre-induction physical examinations, were found unacceptable, about three-fourths of them for medical reasons and the rest for mental or administrative reasons.

At the conclusion of the examination, your local board will be notified of the results and will receive copies of all the forms containing the details of the examination. Since these are in your file, you are able to examine and copy them if you wish (see pages 21 and 51 for details of your right to examine your file). The local board must notify you officially of the results by sending you a Statement of Acceptability (DD Form 62), illustrated on page 80, which must indicate whether you were found acceptable or unacceptable. If you receive a I-Y with no expiration date from your local board and want to learn whether you are likely to be called back for a re-examination, visit your local board and look at the original copy of the Statement of Acceptability in your file to see whether a recommendation was made in the space which is blacked out on your copy.

However, even before this official notification, you should know whether you passed the pre-induction physical examination because the regulations require that the AFEES officials tell you before you leave [AR 601-270, 4-20h(12)]. Therefore, if you are told that you have been found acceptable but believe you should have been disqualified, you should take action immediately as suggested below.

AFTER THE PRE-INDUCTION EXAMINATION

First, write a summary of the examination to send to your local board for your file. Try to recall the names of any doctors (most wear name tags) who didn't take time to carefully read your medical evidence, who inspected your condition carelessly, or who made discourteous remarks. Include everything which indicates you didn't receive a fair evaluation.

Selective Service Regulations do not permit you to appeal the results of a pre-induction physical examination unless it results in a change in your classification, and even then the usual personal appearance and appeal rights are unlikely to gain recognition of a medical condition, though they may be useful as a way to protect you from induction while you try other means to have the evaluation changed. Most men are already classified I-A before they take the examination, so no Selective Service appeal is possible.

However, it is possible to use unofficial but sometimes effective appeal procedures to get further consideration of medical claims, not through Selective Service but by writing to the Army.

If you and your doctor disagree with the results of your pre-induction physical examination, you should write immediately to The Surgeon, U.S. Army Recruiting Command, Hampton, Virginia 23369. You should explain in your letter why you believe the decision at the AFEES was in error and enclose copies of your medical evidence and your description of the examination. If your claim is convincing, you will be given a more thorough examination.

If you are not satisfied with the results of your appeal to The Surgeon, you can write to Chief, Physical Standards Division, Office of the Surgeon General, Department of the Army, Washington, D.C. 20315. Again, explain why your condition needs further evaluation and enclose copies of the medical evidence and your description of the examination.

Needless to say, letters should be sent to these officials only if your condition is genuine and you have good evidence, for they will be less inclined to intervene in cases of genuine need if they receive many false or unconvincing requests.

EXAMINATION AT INDUCTION

A complete armed forces physical examination is valid for one year. Your local board can issue an induction order even if you passed the examination more than a year ago, or if you failed to take a scheduled pre-induction examination or volunteered for induction and have never had a pre-induction examination, but on the day of induction you must be given a complete examination.

If your pre-induction physical examination was taken less than a year ago, you do not receive the complete examination but are given a "physical inspection" on the day of induction. This is a much less complete check, but if you have submitted new evidence of a disqualifying condition it should be carefully considered [AR 601-270, 4-21].

The Armed Forces Security Questionnaire (DD Form 98) is valid for only 120 days, and you will be asked to sign that it is still accurate if your pre-induction examination was taken longer than four months before your induction date. You will also be asked to fill out a more detailed security questionnaire, the Statement of Personal History (DD Form 398), which is usually sent to you by your local board with the induction order. Refusal to complete these won't delay induction, unless you claim to be a Communist or a member of an organization on the Attorney General's list, in which case induction is postponed and a security investigation is made [AR 601-270, 5-6 and 5-31].

During fiscal year 1969, over 57,000 men, or 18% of those who reported for induction, were found unacceptable at the point of induction.

IF YOU ARE FOUND UNACCEPTABLE

Occasionally a man who wants to get into the armed forces is rejected at the physical examination and wants to appeal the decision. If this is your desire, you should use the unofficial appeal procedures described above, enclosing doctors' letters showing that you do not have the condition for which you were rejected or that it is not serious enough to interfere with military duty.

Many, perhaps most, men who are rejected are pleased to be excused from military duty. When the local board receives the notice from the AFEES that you were found unacceptable, it should reclassify you I-Y or IV-F at its next meeting unless you have become eligible for a lower classification. Sometimes the AFEES suggests that you should be returned in a few months for another examination, but you should still be reclassified so that you will have full appeal rights if you are later re-examined and found acceptable.

No Selective Service classification is necessarily permanent. New evidence or a change of circumstances can always result in reclassification. Men classified I-Y or IV-F can be sent for another examination at any time, though repeat examinations are much more common in I-Y than IV-F.

If you are found unacceptable at an armed forces physical examination but the doctors believe your disqualification is temporary, they must still reject you [AR 601-270, 4-22c] but will usually tell your local board to send you for another examination at a specified time, often after three or six months. You cannot receive an induction order during this time and your board should classify you I-Y or IV-F. You must first take and pass another pre-induction examination, and receive a new Statement of Acceptability, before an induction order can be issued. Before sending you for a new examination, your local board may send you for an interview with its medical advisor to decide whether you are likely to pass the new examination [LBM 78]. Of course, you cannot be found acceptable merely on the advice of the medical advisor. If he considers you acceptable, you are sent for another examination at the AFEES. You will receive a complete physical examination if your previous examination was more than a year earlier, or a "physical inspection" if it was less than a year earlier. If you are found acceptable, your local board is notified and will usually reclassify you from I-Y or IV-F at its next meeting. You have full Selective Service appeal rights as well as the chance to use the unofficial appeal processes described above.

PART IV

CONSCIENTIOUS OBJECTION

"Nothing contained in this title shall be construed to require any person to be subject to combatant training and service in the armed forces of the United States who, by reason of religious training and belief, is conscientiously opposed to participation in war in any form. As used in this subsection, the term 'religious training and belief' does not include essentially political, sociological, or philosophical views, or a merely personal moral code. Any person claiming exemption from combatant training and service because of such conscientious objections whose claim is sustained by the local board shall, if he is inducted into the armed forces under this title, be assigned to noncombatant service as defined by the President, or shall, if he is found to be conscientiously opposed to participation in such noncombatant service, in lieu of such induction, be ordered by his local board, subject to such regulations as the President may prescribe, to perform for a period equal to the period prescribed in section 4(b) such civilian work contributing to the maintenance of the national health, safety, or interest as the local board pursuant to Presidential regulations may deem appropriate and any such person who knowingly fails or neglects to obey any such order from his local board shall be deemed, for the purposes of section 12 of this title, to have knowingly failed or neglected to perform a duty required of him under this title."

[MSSA 6(j)]

CHAPTER FOURTEEN

APPLYING AS A CONSCIENTIOUS OBJECTOR

In simplest terms, you are a conscientious objector (CO) if you are strongly opposed to participating in war. If you apply for a CO classification and your local board accepts your claim, you will be drafted at the usual time if you don't qualify for a deferment but must be assigned to a special form of service.

For a much more detailed discussion, see the *Handbook for Conscientious Objectors* (Philadelphia: CCCO, 11th edition, 1970, $1.00).

There are two classifications for conscientious objectors. If you have strong moral objections to killing in war and to carrying arms, you should apply for the I-A-O classification; as a I-A-O you may be drafted into the Army but must be assigned to noncombatant duty—usually the Army Medical Corps. If you are morally opposed to any form of military service, for example because you view even Army medics as contributing to the war-making job of the Army, you should apply for the I-O classification; as a I-O you may be ordered to spend two years in civilian alternative service approved by your local board—work "contributing to the maintenance of the national health, safety, or interest." (These two types of service are discussed in Chapter 15.) It is improper for a draft board to "compromise" with a I-O applicant by giving him a I-A-O [LBM 107].

Whether you apply for a I-A-O or a I-O classification, you must meet three requirements to be recognized as a CO. First, your objection must be based on "religious training and belief." Second, you must be "opposed to participation in war in any form." Third, your claim must be sincere. The remainder of this chapter discusses these three qualifications and the procedure for applying as a CO.

RELIGIOUS TRAINING AND BELIEF

"Religious training and belief" isn't defined in the law except in a negative way: the term "does not include essentially political, sociological, or philosophical views, or a merely personal moral code."

Until 1967, the law defined the term as "an individual's belief in a relation to a Supreme Being involving duties superior to those arising from any human relation." This language was removed from the 1967 law, and the 1968 revision of the Special Form for Conscientious Objector (Form 150) removed the questions about belief in a Supreme Being (see form, page 186). Therefore, it is necessary to turn to court decisions to learn the meaning of "religious training and belief."

In 1965, the Supreme Court, in *U.S. v. Seeger* (380 U.S. 163), discussed the meaning of "religious training and belief" and offered a very broad definition:

> Within that phrase would come all sincere religious beliefs which are based upon a power or being, or upon a faith, to which all else is subordinate or upon which all else is ultimately dependent. The test might be stated in these words: A sincere and meaningful belief which occupies in the life of its possessor a place parallel to that filled by the God of those admittedly qualifying for the exemption comes within the statutory definition.

Even before the *Seeger* decision you didn't have to base your claim on membership in a church or on a conventional belief in God. But since Seeger was an agnostic, the decision made it clear that any belief or value which you live by, which is so basic to your own thinking that it is your personal religion, can lead you to be a CO and will meet the legal requirement.

In June 1970, the Supreme Court reaffirmed this definition of religion in *Welsh v. U.S.* (. . . U.S. . . ., 3 SSLR 3001), concluding that the law "exempts from military service all those whose consciences, spurred by deeply held moral, ethical, or religious beliefs, would give them no rest or peace if they allowed themselves to become a part of an instrument of war."

This definition of "religious training and belief" is so broad that it would be hard to think of any sincere CO who doesn't qualify. Every person lives by some beliefs, some set of basic values, though it may be hard to put them into words. "The belief upon which conscientious objection is based must be the primary controlling force in the man's life" [LBM 107].

In response to *Welsh,* the Selective Service System notified local boards that registrants may qualify on the basis of "solely moral or ethical beliefs, even though the registrant himself may not characterize these beliefs as 'religious' in the traditional sense, or may expressly characterize them as not 'religious.' " [LBM 107]. The *Welsh* decision held:

> If an individual deeply and sincerely holds beliefs which are purely ethical or moral in source and content but which nevertheless impose upon him a duty of conscience to refrain from participating in any war at any time, those beliefs certainly occupy in the life of that individual "a place parallel to that filled by . . . God" in traditionally religious persons. Because his beliefs function as a religion in his life, such an individual is as much entitled to a "religious" conscientious objector exemption under Section 6(j) as is someone who derives his conscientious opposition to war from traditional religious convictions.

Seeger called himself religious and Welsh did not. The court ruled that the principal difference was words rather than beliefs. In *Seeger* the Court said that if a registrant considered himself religious this should be given "great weight" by Selective Service. That still stands, and if you can accept the Court's broad definition of "religious" you'll have an easier time getting CO status. But in *Welsh* the Court ruled that if one says he isn't religious, that statement should be examined in the light of *Seeger* and *Welsh* since "very few registrants are fully aware of the broad scope of the word 'religious' as used in Section 6(j). . . ." If your beliefs fit within the Court's definition, Selective Service must recognize that you meet the requirement.

What about the exclusion of "essentially political, sociological, or philosophical views, or a merely personal moral code"? You certainly have political, sociological, or philosophical views; you just can't base your CO claim on them. Nor can your claim be denied because of them, unless they contradict your CO claim. If you live by certain values, these are basic, and your political, sociological, or philosophical views reflect these more basic beliefs. You should be turned down only if your objection to war "does not rest at all upon moral, ethical, or religious principle but instead rests solely upon considerations of policy, pragmatism, or expediency" (*Welsh v. U.S.*).

PARTICIPATION IN WAR IN ANY FORM

The Selective Service System generally interprets the "participation in war in any form" requirement to mean that a CO must be opposed to all war. Therefore, it would not give you a CO classification if you expressed a willingness to fight in some wars but not in others.

Supreme Court decisions have indicated that a CO doesn't have to be opposed to all violence, however. If you believe in self-defense, or the defense of your family, or would use violence if necessary to protect a friend from attack, you can still be recognized as a CO if you are opposed to war (*Sicurella v. U.S.*, 348 U.S. 385, 1955). In other words, you don't have to be a pacifist, as that word is ordinarily used.

Although Selective Service interprets the law to require that you be opposed to all war, it should be pointed out that the law is phrased in the present tense: "any person . . . who . . . *is* conscientiously opposed. . . ." And the statement you sign on the Special Form for Conscientious Objector (Form 150) starts, "I *am,* by reason of my religious training and belief, conscientiously opposed. . . ." Therefore, it seems to many lawyers, it is not necessary to decide whether you might have fought in a past war or whether you may feel differently about a future or hypothetical war. If you had been alive and old enough for military service at the time of World War II, the Civil War, or the American Revolution, you would have been a different person, formed by different experiences. Similarly, to make up your mind whether you would fight in some future war, you would need to know today how you will feel at a future date. How can you know what information, experiences, and convictions would influence you then? All that seems necessary under the present law is to decide whether you, the actual you, can participate in the real wars of today. Many a "selective objector" has obtained a CO classification on the grounds that he is *now* an objector to "participation in war in any form."

However, if you are sure that you can fight in war under some foreseeable circumstances but not others, you are not likely to receive a CO classification.

Many Western religions teach a "just war" concept, requiring a moral judgment about the particular war you are faced with, and usually setting up a basis for making the judgment. If this is your position, and you believe you should go to war under some real circumstances but you have examined the wars in which the United States is currently engaged and concluded that these are unjust, and therefore that you can't participate without violating your beliefs, you may well not be considered eligible for a CO classification by Selective Service. The law, as now interpreted, does not make provision for the "unjust war" or "selective" objector. The Supreme Court did not reach this question in *U.S. v. Sisson* (. . . U.S. . . ., 3 SSLR . . ., 1970), but agreed to decide other cases that raise it in its 1970–71 term. Meanwhile it is impossible to say whether the selective objector position will ultimately be upheld or turned down. It is safe to say, however, that the Selective Service System rejects this interpretation and will turn down your application if you indicate that you are opposed to some wars but not all [LBM 107].

SINCERITY

If you claim to be opposed to war by reason of your religious beliefs, your draft board will decide whether in its opinion you are sincere—that is, whether you are telling the truth. "The board should be convinced by information presented to it that the registrant's personal history reveals views and actions strong enough to demonstrate that expediency is not the basis of his claim" [LBM 107]. Your claim can't legally be turned down merely because the board doesn't believe you, though in practice this often seems to happen. It is hard to explain religious convictions and harder still to "prove" you hold them. Therefore, courts have ruled that a CO claim can't arbitrarily be turned down by a skeptical draft board. Only on the basis of facts in the individual's file which indicate that his claim might be insincere will a federal court uphold the rejection of a CO claim (*Dickinson v. U.S.,* 346 U.S. 389, 1953; *Witmer v. U.S.,* 348 U.S. 375, 1955).

The board will use your answers to Form 150, discussed below, to try to decide whether your claim is sincere. It should also consider the letters of support you have submitted, anything said by you and your witnesses at a personal appearance, and all other evidence offered by you or others. Before 1967, there was provision in the law for a hearing and an FBI investigation as part of the appeal procedure to collect information about your sincerity, but this is no longer done. The local board has the power to contact your references, call witnesses, and ask welfare or governmental agencies to supply information, but these powers are very rarely used in CO claims outside the state of Washington. As a result, nearly all of the information the board will have comes from you and those you ask to give information about you.

WHEN TO APPLY

The local board must send you a copy of the Special Form for Conscientious Objector (Form 150) whenever you request it [REG 1621.11]. It is certainly best, however, to apply as soon as you realize that you are a CO. In fact, the requirement that you notify your board within 10 days of new information that could affect your classification may make it a legal obligation to apply as a CO as soon as you are sure of your beliefs.

Even if it were not required, it would be sensible to apply as early as possible, to reduce the board's suspicion that your claim was made just because you expected to be drafted into the Army. There is little danger in applying early. Even if you still need to refine your thinking, the CO claim should be made; you can add more complete answers or better evidence at any time.

Filing a CO claim doesn't keep you from receiving or keeping any deferments you are entitled to. The board is required to put you into the lowest classification for which you are eligible, and all deferments are lower than the two CO classifications. Your local board shouldn't even consider the CO application as long as you are deferred. Some men suspect that the board may be unwilling to give a hardship-to-dependents deferment, or some other deferment granted at the discretion of the board, if they have filed CO claims, and this does occasionally happen. But more often boards seem to prefer to give deferments to COs, perhaps to put off the necessity of deciding about the CO claim.

The first chance to make a CO claim is when you file the Classification Questionnaire (Form 100), normally at age 18 (see Chapter 4). If you sign Series VIII, the Form 150 should be mailed to you promptly, though sometimes a letter must be sent to remind the board to mail it.

If you don't claim to be a CO when you answer the Classification Questionnaire, any CO claim made after that is considered a "late claim." It must still be considered, but you will need to explain how your beliefs have developed or matured since you filed the Classification Questionnaire. From the board's point of view, not signing Series VIII on that form indicates you were not a CO at that time.

Even a CO claim made after the board has sent you an induction order must be given some consideration, but this is the hardest claim to get recognized. To get a reopening of your classification at this point, you will probably have to convince the board that your beliefs crystallized or matured only *after* your board issued the induction order, and therefore that your late claim represents "a change in the registrant's status resulting from circumstances over which the registrant had no control" [REG 1625.2]. The lower courts cannot agree whether a local board is obligated to reopen in this situation, but the Supreme Court has agreed to decide this question during its 1970–71 term (*Ehlert v. U.S.*). Anyone who decides to make a CO claim after he has received an induction order needs the help of a very experienced counselor or attorney.

Form approved.
Budget Bureau No. 83-RO115

SELECTIVE SERVICE SYSTEM
SPECIAL FORM FOR CONSCIENTIOUS OBJECTOR

┌─ DATE QUESTIONNAIRE RECEIVED ─┐
            AT LOCAL BOARD

Date of Mailing _____

Complete and return within 30 days.

2. Selective Service No.

(Local Board Stamp)

1. Name of Registrant (First)   (Middle)   (Last)

3. Mailing address (Number and street, city, county and State, and ZIP Code)

(The above items, except the date received back at local board, are to be filled in by the local board before the questionnaire is mailed.)

INSTRUCTIONS

A registrant who claims to be a conscientious objector shall offer information in substantiation of his claim on this special form which, when filed, shall become a part of his Classification Questionnaire (SSS Form 100).

Section 6(j) of the Military Selective Service Act of 1967 provides:

"Nothing contained in this title shall be construed to require any person to be subject to combatant training and service in the Armed Forces of the United States who, by reason of religious training and belief, is conscientiously opposed to participation in war in any form. As used in this subsection, the term 'religious training and belief' does not include essentially political, sociological, or philosophical views, or a merely personal moral code. Any person claiming exemption from combatant training and service because of such conscientious objections whose claim is sustained by the local board shall, if he is inducted into the Armed Forces under this title, be assigned to noncombatant service as defined by the President, or shall, if he is found to be conscientiously opposed to participation in such noncombatant service, in lieu of such induction, be ordered by his local board, subject to such regulations as the President may prescribe, to perform for a period equal to the period prescribed in section 4(b) such civilian work contributing to the maintenance of the national health, safety, or interest as the local board pursuant to Presidential regulations may deem appropriate and any such person who knowingly fails or neglects to obey any such order from his local board shall be deemed, for the purposes of section 12 of this title, to have knowingly failed or neglected to perform a duty required of him under this title."

Series I.—CLAIM FOR EXEMPTION

INSTRUCTIONS.—The registrant should sign his name to either statement A or B in this series. If he cannot sign either one, he must indicate why.

A I am, by reason of my religious training and belief, conscientiously opposed to participation in war in any form. I, therefore, claim exemption from combatant training and service in the Armed Forces, but am prepared to serve in a noncombatant capacity if called. (Registrants granted this status are classified I-A-O.)

(Signature of registrant)

B I am, by reason of my religious training and belief, conscientiously opposed to participation in war in any form and I am further conscientiously opposed to participation in noncombatant training and service in the Armed Forces. I, therefore, claim exemption from both combatant and noncombatant training and service in the Armed Forces, but am prepared to perform civilian alternative service if called. (Registrants granted this status are classified I-O.)

(Signature of registrant)

Series II.—RELIGIOUS TRAINING AND BELIEF

INSTRUCTIONS.—If more space is needed use extra sheets of paper.

1. Describe the nature of your belief which is the basis of your claim and state why you consider it to be based on religious training and belief.

2. Explain how, when and from whom or from what source you received the religious training and acquired the religious belief which is the basis of your claim. (Include here, where applicable, such information as religion of parents and other members of family; childhood religious training; religious and general education; experiences at school and college; organizational memberships and affiliations; books and other readings which influenced you; association with clergymen, teachers, advisers or other individuals which affected you; and any other material which will help give the local board the fullest possible picture of how your beliefs developed.)

3. To what extent does your religious training and belief restrict you from ministering to the sick and injured, either civilian or military, or from serving in the Armed Forces as a noncombatant without weapons?

....
....
....
....
....
....
....

4. Have you ever given expression publicly or privately, written or oral, to the views herein expressed as the basis for your claim? Give examples.

....
....
....
....
....
....
....

Series III.—REFERENCES

You may provide your local board with any additional evidence from any source that would support your claim of conscientious objection. You may, if you choose, provide in the space below the names of references who could provide the local board with information regarding your religious training and belief. You may wish to suggest that these references, if given, write directly to the local board in support of your claim.

Name	Full Address	Occupation or Position	Relationship to You

(3)

REGISTRANT'S CERTIFICATE

INSTRUCTIONS.—Every registrant claiming to be a conscientious objector shall make this certificate.

NOTICE.—Imprisonment for not more than 5 years or a fine of not more than $10,000, or both such fine and imprisonment, is provided by law as a penalty for knowingly making or being a party to the making of any false statement or certificate regarding or bearing upon a classification. (Military Selective Service Act of 1967.)

I, _____, certify that I am the registrant named and described in the foregoing statements in this form; that I have read (or have had read to me) the statements made by and about me, and that each and every such statement is true and complete to the best of my knowledge, information, and belief. The statements made by me in the foregoing _____ in my own handwriting. *(are, are not)*

Registrant sign here ☞ _____
(Signature or mark of registrant)

_____
(Date)

_____
(Signature of witness to mark of registrant)

_____
(Date)

If another person has assisted the registrant in completing this form, such person shall sign the following statement:

I have assisted the registrant herein named in completing this form.

....
(Signature of person who has assisted)

....
(Occupation of person who has assisted)

....
(Address of person who has assisted)

....
(Date)

FILLING OUT FORM 150

Answering the questions on Form 150 is difficult. It involves trying to put into words the values by which you live—never an easy task. It is made harder in this case because you are explaining your beliefs to the members of your draft board, who are fairly certain not only to have entirely different beliefs but to be unhappy about those who disagree with them. Therefore, it is important that you try to write clearly, simply, and carefully.

Once you send for the Form 150, you are given 30 days to fill it out and return it. Although that's better than the 10 days allowed before the fall of 1968, it still isn't usually long enough to think out your beliefs, write your answers, discuss them with a counselor, and revise them, and at the same time to collect supporting letters from references. Therefore, it's a good idea to start your thinking, writing, and discussing before you actually receive the form, and if possible even before you send for it. A copy of the Form 150 begins on page 186.

The form consists of three important parts.

In Series I, you are asked to sign one of two statements to indicate whether you are claiming a I-A-O or a I-O classification. If you can't sign either statement for some reason, you are asked to explain why. Whatever the explanation, it is not likely to cause your draft board to classify you either I-A-O or I-O.

Series II asks four questions about your beliefs.

Question 1 should be answered with a concise essay on the basic beliefs you live by, why you think they are religious (in the broad sense of the *Seeger* and *Welsh* decisions), and why they lead you to be a CO. You are not expected to confine your answers to the few lines on the form; most applicants type their essays on separate sheets and write "see attached pages" on the form. Don't be long-winded, but give a full description of your beliefs as they relate to participation in war.

It is neither necessary nor helpful to discuss side issues. If you are opposed to war because you oppose all violence, it is useful to say so. If you believe in violence in defense of yourself and your family, but oppose the organized, massive violence of war, concentrate on your reasons for opposing war. The 1968 form, unlike the earlier one, doesn't ask for a complete discussion of your attitude toward the use of force, and there is usually no need to offer one. If you aren't sure what you would have done during past wars, you don't need to discuss them. You should, however, be prepared for such hypothetical questions at your personal appearance later.

Question 2 asks how your beliefs developed. The best answer is usually a chronological description of the development of your thinking on the subject, mentioning the influences and experiences along the way that brought you to your present position. This may be fairly short if you are 18 years old and base your claim on family or church background. If you are older, or if your beliefs are less conventional, this personal history should be more detailed, especially if you gave no hint of being a CO on your Classification Questionnaire. If you are applying at age 24 or 25, or after receiving an induction order, you will need a very complete history to show why your beliefs reached maturity at this time. If an organized religion influenced your beliefs, it may be helpful to include a copy of its official policy on conscientious objection; the statements of more than 60 religious organizations are reprinted in *Religious Statements on Conscientious Objection* (Washington: NISBCO, 7th edition, 1970, 75¢).

Question 3 asks whether, and if so why, you are unable to be a soldier in the Army Medical Corps or to serve as a civilian in a hospital. I-A-Os usually serve in the Medical Corps. I-Os often serve in civilian hospitals. If you believe in giving medical aid but object to doing so as a member of the armed forces, you would apply for I-O. In explaining why noncombatant military service would conflict with your beliefs, it may be helpful to think about the purpose of the service as well as the specific duties. Reading the discussion in Chapter 15 may be useful. Of course, you should show how this thinking relates to your religious beliefs as described in Question 1.

Question 4 gives you a chance to show that you sincerely try to live according to your beliefs—not just anti-war beliefs, but your basic underlying life values. Have your values caused you to enter into social service, religious work, anti-war or civil rights activity? Have your beliefs influenced your choice of work or study? How have you dealt with situations that might have involved violence?

Have you expressed your developing beliefs in term papers, letters, discussions, meetings, or even more public ways? A picture of a man struggling to live according to his beliefs should emerge.

Series III gives you a chance to add more evidence of sincerity. You may be able to attach school papers, newspaper clippings, speeches, or other items by or about you which illustrate that you sincerely try to express and live your beliefs. You certainly should send letters written by people who know you well—friends, clergyman, teachers, family friends, neighbors, employers, and even members of your family. Their letters should attest to the fact that you are sincerely opposed to all war for religious reasons; if they disagree with your position, it is helpful for them to say so. The instructions on the form suggest that the letters should be sent directly to the draft board, and some local boards may therefore expect this to be done. However, many men will prefer to have the letters returned to them for screening and copying, and to send them with the Form 150, and this is not forbidden. Not all well-motivated references write helpful letters, so it may be wise to examine the letters before they are sent in and to use only those that will help your claim. Draft boards rarely write to your references, so it will be up to you to get letters. Although only five spaces are given, you will probably want to get more letters than that. Some counselors suggest about six good letters; if you submit more, they are less likely to be read carefully by the members of your draft board. Quality is more important than quantity.

You must sign and date the certificate section at the end. A witness is required only if you are illiterate and must sign with a cross. A draft counselor must sign that he assisted you only if he worded your answers.

AFTER FORM 150 IS SUBMITTED

After you have returned your Form 150, your work is not done. A memorandum from the national director of Selective Service [LBM 41] suggests that your board ask you to attend a meeting before it decides whether to approve your claim, and at least one court has indicated that your claim cannot legally be turned down unless you have been offered this right (*U.S. v. Stout,* 415 F.2d

1190, 2 SSLR 3280, 4th Circuit, 1969). You should follow the suggestions in Chapter 5, on preparing for a personal appearance, with great care, and try to take at least one witness. This preclassification interview doesn't count as a personal appearance, so if the board gives you an unacceptable classification you can still have a personal appearance and try again to convince the board that your claim is sincere. More evidence can be submitted at any time, and you may well learn from the preclassification interview what it should be.

For a detailed discussion of the Form 150 and the meaning of the CO provisions in the Selective Service law, read the *Handbook for Conscientious Objectors* published by CCCO (see Chapter 21). It is especially important that you have the help of a draft counselor if you are making a CO claim.

It is also important that you think carefully about what you believe and how strongly you believe it, for you may have to show great persistence to be recognized as a CO. Local boards, and even appeal boards, often ignore court decisions and reject CO claims for improper reasons, and some COs have had to write to Selective Service state directors and other officials, or even to refuse induction and face the risks of trial, before their claims were recognized. Despite this apparent arbitrariness and unpredictability, there are only a handful of men now in prison who sought recognition as COs before receiving induction orders and used all appeals open to them.

CHAPTER FIFTEEN

NONCOMBATANT SERVICE AND CIVILIAN ALTERNATIVE SERVICE: I-A-O AND I-C, I-O AND I-W

Just as conscientious objectors have the same rights of deferment as other men, they have the same obligation to serve if called. If you get one of the two CO classifications, you will be drafted by the same lottery system and have to serve for the same two years as a man classified I-A. The difference is that you will be ordered to do a different type of service, intended to be consistent with your beliefs as a CO.

NONCOMBATANT MILITARY SERVICE: I-A-O, I-C

If you apply for a I-A-O classification, you are saying in effect, "I object to killing or carrying arms but am willing to serve in the armed forces, wear the uniform, and obey all orders which don't involve my using weapons." If you receive this classification and are inducted into the Army, you will receive your basic training at the Medical Training Center, Fort Sam Houston, San Antonio, Texas. You will receive roughly the same basic training as other soldiers, but without any weapons training. After basic training, you will receive individual training—probably as a "medical aidman." About 99% of all I-A-Os are assigned as medics, and the remainder serve as cooks, clerks, truck drivers, chaplains' assistants, and in other noncombatant assignments.

As a medic, you may perform acts of mercy, saving life, easing suffering, and preventing sickness, and you may sometimes be able to serve civilians in war zones as well as soldiers. You may find this period of service valuable and satisfying, and you are likely to be respected and depended upon by the combat soldiers you serve with. Men classified I-A-O provide about 6% to 8% of the Army's medical aidmen. You are just as likely to be sent into a combat area and to be placed on the front lines as a medic who isn't a CO, and you are actually more likely to be sent into combat than a I-A.

However, do not enter military service as a I-A-O imagining that the medics are somehow separate from the Army and its basic purpose. This view is contradicted by the Army:

> The Army Medical Service is a supporting service of the combat elements of the Army primarily concerned with the maintenance of the health and fighting efficiency of the troops. The mission of the medical service in a theater of operations is to conserve manpower by recommending, and providing technical supervision of the implementation of, measures for safeguarding the health of the troops, effective medical care, and early return to duty; and to contribute directly to the military effort by providing adequate medical treatment and rapid orderly evacuation of the sick and wounded. [Army Field Manual 8-10, *Medical Service, Theater of Operations,* November 1959, page 17.]

In trying to decide whether to apply for a I-A-O or I-O classification, therefore, you should consider what degree of cooperation with the military your beliefs will permit. Few COs are unwilling to give medical assistance and other aid to injured and sick persons. But in deciding whether you can serve as an Army medic, you must consider not only the kind of service you will perform but the context and overall purpose as well. If your beliefs as a CO allow you to perform life-saving duties without regard to the fact that your services are regarded by the Army as a necessary part of its war-making function, you may find yourself satisfied with the I-A-O classification. If not, you will need to consider the I-O classification.

While you are performing military service as a I-A-O, you are classified I-C. After your service is completed, you are classified IV-A. You are not eligible to re-enlist in the armed forces, but you receive the same veterans' benefits as other ex-soldiers.

CIVILIAN ALTERNATIVE SERVICE: I-O, I-W

If your convictions do not allow you to serve in any military capacity, even as a noncombatant, you may be classified I-O by your draft board. This classification allows the board to assign you to a civilian alternative service job at the time other men your age are drafted into the Army. Perhaps because I-O registrants do not serve in the armed forces (and therefore do not help fill the local board's monthly quota), this classification is usually much harder to get than I-A-O. Even so, there are more I-Os than I-A-Os. About 2,000 I-A-Os per year complete the Army's noncombatant training program, while at the end of April 1970, nearly 38,000 men were classified as I-O type conscientious objectors, including over 9,000 then performing civilian alternative service, and the number has been steadily increasing (*Selective Service News,* April–May 1970).

If you receive the I-O classification, you will be processed in the usual way. You are still eligible for any deferments (except I-S(C), discussed in Chapter 9), and can appeal a I-O classification like any other. You will be ordered to take an armed forces physical examination when you are close to being called for service, if you haven't already passed one. Unlike men in other classifications, as a I-O you may refuse to take the examination without violating the Regulations, but you will then be considered acceptable for civilian work [LBM 64]. If you believe you should be rejected for medical reasons, you will probably take the examination and follow the steps outlined in Chapter 13.

If you are classified I-O, the Regulations require that you submit to your local board a list of up to three types of work which you are able and willing to do. This is to be done "within ten days after a Statement of Acceptability (DD Form 62) has been mailed to [you] by the local board or within ten days after [you have] failed to report for or submit to armed forces physical examination" [REG 1660.20(a)]. In practice, the local board takes the initiative by sending you a Special Report for Class I-O Registrants (Form 152) [LBM 64].

However, it is not necessary to wait until you receive this form. If you wish to speed up the process, you can volunteer by letter or

Form 151 at any time, before or after you have received a I-O classification. If you volunteer before you are classified I-O, the board must immediately consider your CO application [REG 1660.10]. Unfortunately, some boards, particularly in Minnesota, send Form 151 to all registrants who request Form 150, seeming to imply that a CO should be willing to give up any deferments he qualifies for and perform civilian work immediately, and giving the impression that those who don't volunteer may be assumed to be insincere. This sort of pressure is inconsistent with the idea of "volunteering," and the practice seems improper and perhaps illegal.

You will be required to spend two years in "civilian work contributing to the maintenance of the national health, safety, or interest" [MSSA 6(j)]. You can work for a government agency, federal, state, or local. You can also work for a nonprofit private organization, provided your work serves the public, not just the members of the organization [REG 1660.1]. You usually cannot work in your home community, though this is subject to definition in a highly mobile society and in any case can be permitted at the local board's discretion [REG 1660.21(a)]. The national director advises that "the position should be one that cannot readily be filled from the available competitive labor force" and "should constitute a disruption of the registrant's normal way of life somewhat comparable to the disruption of a registrant who is inducted into the Armed Forces" [LBM 64], which often means only low-paying or unattractive jobs are approved. The instructions on Form 152 formerly provided that "it will be the policy of the Selective Service System whenever possible to order you to civilian work which will most fully utilize your experience, education and training," but the revised form dated September 15, 1969, left off this sentence, suggesting a change of policy. It should be noted that the director's memorandum is only advisory, while Selective Service forms are part of the Regulations [REG 1606.51(a)].

Many boards insist that your civilian work assignment be chosen from the lists at local boards (the instructions to Series I of Form 152 reflect this illegal practice). These lists include organizations which often employ COs and have general approval from the state or national director of Selective Service, but have no official stand-

Form approved.
Budget Bureau No. 38-R127.

SELECTIVE SERVICE SYSTEM

APPLICATION OF VOLUNTEER FOR CIVILIAN WORK

(Stamp of the local board of jurisdiction as determined by item 2 of the Registration Card (SSS Form 1))

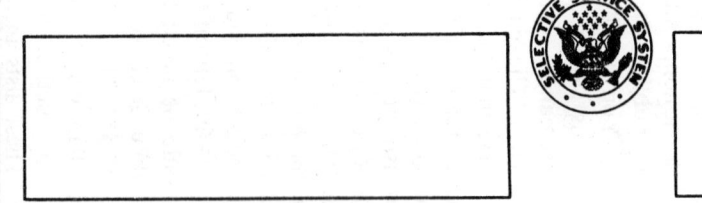

(Stamp of local board at which application is filed if other than local board of jurisdiction)

I hereby volunteer for civilian work contributing to the maintenance of the national health, safety, or interest and request that I be ordered to perform this work under the provisions of the Military Selective Service Act of 1967, and the rules and regulations prescribed thereunder. For this purpose, I waive all rights of personal appearance and appeal if I am classified as available for such civilian work, and I consent to my being ordered to perform this work at any time convenient to the Government.

My Selective Service number is

My Local Board is No. _____ at _____
(City, town or county, State, and ZIP Code)

I was born _____ _____ _____
(Month) (Day) (Year)

My mailing address is _____
(Number and street or R.F.D. route)

_____ _____ _____ _____
(City, town, or village) (County) (State) (ZIP Code)

_____
(Signature of registrant)

_____
(Date of application)

Instructions: Prepare in duplicate, the original for filing in the Cover Sheet (SSS Form 101), the duplicate for delivery to the registrant.

SSS Form 151

Form approved.
Budget Bureau No. 83-R128.

SELECTIVE SERVICE SYSTEM
SPECIAL REPORT FOR CLASS I-O REGISTRANTS

(Local Board Stamp)

DATE REPORT RECEIVED AT LOCAL BOARD _____

Date of mailing _____

Complete and return before _____ (Selective Service Number)

To _____
　　(Last name)　　(First name)　　(Middle name)

Mailing address _____
　　(Street and number)　(City, town, or village)　(State)　(ZIP Code)

TO CLASS I-O REGISTRANTS:

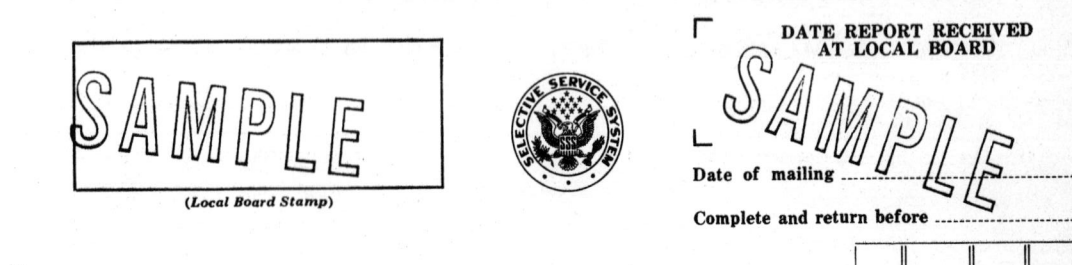

A registrant placed in Class I-O who has received his Certificate of Acceptability (DD Form 62) or who failed to report for or submit to Armed Forces physical examination shall, in accordance with Selective Service Regulations prescribed by the President, be ordered by his local board to perform for a period of twenty-four (24) consecutive months such civilian work contributing to the maintenance of the national health, safety, or interest as the local board may deem appropriate.

The Selective Service Regulations require you to submit to your local board, within ten (10) days after a Certificate of Acceptability (DD Form 62) is mailed to you or within ten (10) days after you have failed to report for or submit to an Armed Forces physical examination, three (3) types of approved civilian work which you are qualified to perform and which you offer to perform in lieu of induction into the Armed Forces. A list of the types of approved civilian work is on file in local board offices. The types of work you offer to perform, your prior work experience, and your other pertinent qualifications should be set forth under the appropriate items of this form.

204

By submitting a choice of employment you have an opportunity to select the type of work you will be more interested in and perhaps best qualified to do. There may be opportunities for performing approved types of work with nonprofit organizations, associations, or corporations or with local, State, or Federal governmental agencies. If you are qualified for positions that require special skills, training, technical knowledge, or professional education and experience, you should list any additional information that will be of assistance to the employer in assigning you to work that can utilize your highest level of aptitude and skill.

If you fail to submit to the local board the types of work which you offer to perform, or if the local board finds that none of the types of work submitted by you has been approved, or is appropriate, it will submit to you by letter three (3) types of approved work which it deems appropriate for you to perform. Within ten (10) days after such letter has been mailed to you by the local board, you shall file with the local board a written statement signifying acceptance or rejection of any or all of the types of work submitted. If any types are acceptable to you the local board will order you to perform one of the types of work which you have offered to perform. If you do not offer to perform any of the types of work submitted by the local board, a meeting will be held at a time and place of which you will be mailed notice and at which you will have an opportunity to reach an agreement with the local board as to the type of work which you will perform. If no agreement can be reached at such meeting the local board, after approval by the Director of Selective Service, will order you to perform such work as is deemed appropriate by the local board.

In no case will you be required to perform work until you have been mailed an Order to Report for Civilian Work and Statement of Employer (SSS Form 153). This order will allow you a minimum of ten (10) days after the date on which it is mailed to you to report for work. However, your local board will not order you to work prior to the time you would have been ordered to report for induction if you had not been classified in Class I-O unless you file with the local board an Application of Volunteer for Civilian Work (SSS Form 151) which establishes that you desire to be ordered to work as soon as possible without regard to your normal order of selection.

In the event you have applied to one of the approved employers for work and have a definite answer to your application, you should show this in Series II on the form. The local board cannot secure special skilled positions for you.

The Military Selective Service Act of 1967, provides that any person who knowingly fails or neglects to obey an order from his local board to perform civilian work, as required by section 6 (j) thereof, shall be deemed to have violated the provisions of the Military Selective Service Act of 1967, and shall be subject to the punishment provided by that act.

....
(Clerk, Executive Secretary, or member of the local board)

SSS Form 152 (Rev. 9-15-69)
(Previous printings may be used.)

1

SERIES I—WORK QUALIFICATIONS

In accordance with Selective Service Regulations I am submitting in order of preference, three (3) types of approved civilian work, selected from a list on file at a selective service local board, which I am qualified to do and which I offer to perform in lieu of induction into the Armed Forces as follows:

1. **First Type:**

   ....

2. **Second Type:**

   ....

3. **Third Type:**

   ....

SERIES II—APPLICATION FOR APPROVED EMPLOYMENT

If you have applied to an approved employer for civilian work contributing to the national health, safety, or interest, and he has accepted your application, indicate:

Name of employer ....

Address of employer ....
                       (Number and street)   (City)   (State)   (ZIP Code)

Type of employment ....

Remarks ....

....
(Signature of registrant)

2

Fill out work experience record on opposite side.

SERIES III—IMPORTANT CIVILIAN WORK EXPERIENCE

Describe your longest and most important jobs— Begin with your most recent job

1.
A. Name of Employer: | Name job and describe exactly what you did and how you did it:

Address

Employer's business

| Date Job Started | Date Job Ended | Final Pay Per Wk. |

B. Name of Employer: | Name job and describe exactly what you did and how you did it:

Address

Employer's business

| Date Job Started | Date Job Ended | Final Pay Per Wk. |

C. Name of Employer: | Name job and describe exactly what you did and how you did it:

Address

Employer's business

| Date Job Started | Date Job Ended | Final Pay Per Wk. |

D. Name of Employer: | Name job and describe exactly what you did and how you did it:

Address

Employer's business

| Date Job Started | Date Job Ended | Final Pay Per Wk. |

2. ABILITIES AND INTERESTS

SPECIAL SKILLS (Check those in which you have experience)

......Accounting	......Child Welfare	......Electricity	......Animal Husbandry
......Bookkeeping	......Handicrafts	......Mechanics	......Fruit Growing
......Filing	......Playground Supervision	......Plumbing	......Gardening
......Shorthand	......Group Singing	......Licensed Car Driver	......Cooking
......Typing	......Painting	......Licensed Truck Driver	......Sewing
......Nursing	......Masonry	......Dairying	......Laundry
......Teaching	......Carpentry	......Poultry Farming	......Other (Describe below)

Other _____

Describe training, experience, and degree of proficiency in the skills in which you are most interested.

_____
_____
_____

List any special hobbies or interests you may have _____

3. LANGUAGES, other than English (check appropriate space) S-speak; R-read; W-write:

	Spanish			French			German			Low German			Other ( )		
	S	R	W	S	R	W	S	R	W	S	R	W	S	R	W
Fairly well															
Fluently															

3

4. EDUCATION:

A. I have completed .... years of elementary school, ... years of junior high school, and .... years of high school.
(Number) (Number) (Number)

B. I .... graduated from high school.
(was, was not)

C. I have had the following schooling other than elementary and high school (if none, write "None"):

Name of College, University, Preparatory, Trade, or Business School	Course of Study	Length of Time Attended, Degrees or Certificates Granted

REGISTRANT'S CERTIFICATE

I, ..., certify that I am the registrant named and described in the foregoing statements in this report; that I have read (or have had read to me) the statements made by and about me, and that each and every such statement is true and complete to the best of my knowledge, information, and belief. The statements made by me in the foregoing .... in my own handwriting.
(are, are not)

Registrant sign here ☞ ....
(Signature or mark of registrant)

Date ....

....
(Signature of witness to mark of registrant)

THE REGISTRANT WILL MAKE NO ENTRIES IN THIS SPACE

The registrant identified above is found qualified for the following types of civilian work contributing to the national health, safety, or interest in the order shown:

1. _____

2. _____

3. _____

_____
(Signature of local board member or employer)

_____
(Title)

_____
(Date)

ing [LBM 64]. Your local board can allow you to perform suitable work not on these lists if you find a job and submit a letter from the employer offering to hire you for two years and explaining that the work and the organization meet the requirements for civilian alternative service. Since most of the jobs on the local board lists are in general hospitals, mental institutions, and old people's or children's homes, you may prefer to find your own job if your interests and abilities equip you for a different sort of work. In recent years, local boards have sometimes approved work in medical research, forestry, settlement houses, agricultural research, and work for state highway and sanitation departments, and occasionally even in VISTA, United Nations agencies, organizing and service in poverty programs, teaching, legal aid, and draft counseling. The Peace Corps cannot be approved, but similar programs of work overseas, sponsored by private and religious organizations, employ COs. It must be emphasized, however, that while a local board has almost absolute power to decide whether a particular job is "appropriate" [REG 1660.20], the national and state directors really make most of the decisions.

Some draft counseling services have lists of job openings suitable for alternative service. A list of many employing agencies is published by the National Interreligious Service Board for Conscientious Objectors (address on page 255), entitled *Guide to Alternative Service* ($1.00). Interesting jobs are often included in *Invest Yourself* (50¢; goes to $1.00 for the expanded 1971 edition issued December 1970), published annually by the Commission on Voluntary Service & Action, 475 Riverside Drive, Room 830, New York, New York 10027. Work toward "basic change in American institutions in the directions of world peace, social and economic justice, individual freedom, and democracy" is listed bimonthly in the newsletter published by Vocations for Social Change, Canyon, California 94516 (free; contributions requested), which also lists other work directories. Not all of the jobs in these latter two sources can be used as alternative service, however.

If the jobs you submit are rejected, the board must submit three choices it has made, and you will be assigned to one of these if you accept it. If you reject all three, you will be asked to attend a meeting of the local board with a representative of the state director, who will "offer his assistance in reaching an agreement." If no agreement is reached, the local board will select a job, with the approval of the national director, and order you to perform it [REG 1660.20, LBM 14]. Although these four steps have time limits specified in the Regulations, in practice you will usually be given extra time to find a job or make arrangements with a prospective employer, if you are willing to cooperate by finding work which your local board is willing to approve.

When a job is selected, the local board will issue an Order to Report for Civilian Work and Statement of Employer (Form 153). If you report, you will be classified I-W while you are doing civilian work.

You should receive the normal pay, vacation, and other benefits of your job while you are in civilian alternative service, and be treated just as other employees are, and you are as free as other employees to devote your spare time to education, political activity, or whatever you prefer. The employer may fire you, in which case the state director of Selective Service for the state where you are working must assign you to similar work elsewhere. However, you are not free to leave your job without the permission of the state or national director until your two years are over.

Under some circumstances, you may be allowed to transfer to a different employer, be given retroactive credit for work done before you were officially ordered to begin, or be released early from civilian work [REG 1660.21(c) and (d), LBM 64]. After you have completed the required time, you will be classified in I-W(Rel.).

Work in civilian service as a I-W can be for some a way of demonstrating peaceful alternatives to war through social service. However, if you have difficulty in imagining any form of alternative service acceptable to a draft board which could satisfy your sense of religious or humanitarian vocation, or if you are conscientiously opposed to the draft law itself, you may find yourself troubled by the idea of conscripted service in the context of a military manpower system. Some men who could qualify as conscientious objectors, but who were opposed on principle not only to military service but to any forced service, have rejected I-O status and refused to cooperate with the draft.

SELECTIVE SERVICE SYSTEM

Form approved.
Budget Bureau No. 33-R0129

ORDER TO REPORT FOR CIVILIAN WORK AND STATEMENT OF EMPLOYER

(Date of mailing)

(LOCAL BOARD STAMP)

(Selective Service Number)

To _____
    (First name)   (Middle name)   (Last name)

Mailing address _____
    (Street and number)   (City)   (State)   (ZIP Code)

Having been found to be acceptable for civilian work contributing to the maintenance of the national health, safety, or interest you have been assigned to _____
(Type of work)

located at _____
(Name and address of employer)

You are ordered to report to the local board named above at _____ (Hour) m. on the _____ day of _____, 19__, where you will be given instructions to proceed to the place of employment.

You are ordered to report for employment pursuant to the instructions of the local board, to remain in employment for twenty-four (24) consecutive months or until such time as you are released or transferred by proper authority.

You will be instructed as to your duties at the place of employment.

Failure to report at the hour and on the day named in this order, or to proceed to the place of employment pursuant to instructions, or to remain in this employment the specified time will constitute a violation of the Military Selective Service Act of 1967, which is punishable by fine or imprisonment or both.

_____
(Member, Executive Secretary, or Clerk of Local Board)

Employer: The registrant to whom the above order was issued has been directed to report to your institution or place of business by _____. Please complete the following statement as soon as possible after this reporting date and return 3 copies to his local board, whose address is shown in the upper left-hand corner.

STATEMENT OF EMPLOYER

The registrant *(check one)* ☐ Reported for work on _____
                                                            (Date)
                              ☐ Reported but refused to accept the work offered to him.
                              ☐ Failed to report and had not reported as of the date of this statement.

Name of Employer _____

Address of Employer _____
                        (Street address)   (City)   (State)   (ZIP Code)

_____
(Signature of employer or agent)   (Title)   (Date)

SSS Form 153 (Revised 5-14-69) (Previous printings are obsolete) (See Instructions on reverse side)

INSTRUCTIONS

An original and five copies of this form shall be prepared by the local board for each registrant ordered to report for civilian work contributing to the national health, safety or interest. The original shall be mailed to the registrant at least ten (10) days before the day set for him to report to the local board and a copy filed in his Cover Sheet (SSS Form 101). Four copies shall be mailed to the employer, one completed copy to be retained by the employer, three completed copies to be returned to the local board. The local board shall file one completed copy in the registrant's Cover Sheet (SSS Form 101), and forward two completed copies to the State Director of Selective Service, one to be retained for his use, the other to be forwarded to the Director of Selective Service.

(Reverse of SSS Form 153)

PART V

EMIGRATION

"Many of our forefathers came to this country to get out from under the burden of conscription in Europe. I have yet to hear these ancestors referred to as 'draft dodgers,' or the men now going to Canada referred to as 'Pilgrims.' "

ANONYMOUS

"Canada should be a 'refuge from militarism' . . . Prime Minister Trudeau said here. . . . We are opposed to militarism."

TORONTO DAILY STAR
MARCH 20, 1970

CHAPTER SIXTEEN

LEAVING TO AVOID THE DRAFT

What kinds of men emigrate because of the draft? The only safe generalization is that, more than most men, they do not want to be drafted, but have chosen not to confront it and accept the risk of prison. They have a variety of reasons. Many are nonpolitical; although they may despise the draft, they are not prepared to commit civil disobedience aimed at influencing others, as are the resisters discussed in Chapter 18. Others are political but don't think going to prison will have an effect on public opinion worth their sacrifice. Still others have come to feel that America is not worth trying to change, or is so far gone as to be hopeless. Many fear the effect of prison on career, marriage, family relationships, or psychological condition. They are often attracted to a country like Canada because it seems a new, open frontier.

A large number of draft emigrants are motivated at least partly by opposition to the war in Indo-China. Some are opposed to that war but would participate in other wars, and therefore don't expect to be recognized as conscientious objectors (see Chapter 14). Perhaps a majority of those who have emigrated had other draft alternatives but either didn't know of them, rejected them on principle, or objected to more basic aspects of American life than the draft.

Those who emigrate are often well educated, usually with some college, often with one or more degrees. This is partly because it's easier to be admitted to most countries as a permanent resident if you have education and skills, and partly because fewer uneducated men think of opposing military service by leaving their native country.

If you are going to leave because of the draft, it may be important to get answers to a number of questions. The most important of these is "Why?" The answer may seem obvious, but many of those who go find that it isn't. Some discover that their reasons for going weren't as strong as the attachments to home, family, and familiar way of life. Some feel they have deserted their friends at a time when they were needed, when it was essential to change America into a more just and peaceful country, and that they can have little influence on America's future from abroad. A number have decided to return and face trial.

But they are in the minority. Most emigrants have not returned. Some are entirely happy in their new lives. Others aren't satisfied but would rather have their dissatisfaction than a prison term.

WHEN TO LEAVE

As long as you are going to a country that isn't interested in your draft status and won't deport or extradite you because of it (discussed below), it makes little difference legally when you leave. There are possible advantages (also discussed below) to going before the date you are supposed to report for induction, but in most cases these aren't important. You are still able to leave after refusing induction or failing to report. It is also possible to leave after you are arrested for a draft offense, but leaving while you are on bail awaiting trial may present special problems, probably including loss of the bail and a more severe punishment if you ever return, and may make it harder for other men to get out on bail.

WHERE TO GO

You should, theoretically at least, be able to go to any country that meets three tests:

1. You find it an attractive place to live, and can earn a living there.
2. It won't extradite you for your draft violation.
3. You can get the right to live there permanently.

You will have to judge the first element for yourself on the basis of as much information as you can get, and preferably advance visits to see how well you will like the new country as a permanent home. You may want to consider whether you will be eligible for that country's draft, if it has one.

You must also consider the possibility of extradition, the legal process by which you may be turned over to American authorities to be tried for a crime of which the United States had accused you. Extradition is possible only for a crime listed in the treaties between the United States and the country you are in. There seem to be only a few countries whose extradition treaties with the United States include draft offenses, and all of these are in Latin America: Argentina, Chile, Colombia, the Dominican Republic, Ecuador, El Salvador, Guatemala, Honduras, Mexico, Nicaragua, and Panama. Despite the treaties, with the exception of Mexico, where there are reports of men being returned to the United States by Mexican officials without any formal legal action, we have never heard of extradition from these countries actually taking place in draft cases.

Getting a visa as an immigrant or permanent resident may be a problem in some countries. Many Americans find England attractive because it is English speaking, temperate in climate, culturally rich, and without a draft. But it is almost impossible to be admitted to England as an immigrant, so it is rarely an option.

Because of these three considerations, most draft emigrants choose Canada. Its extradition treaty does not include draft offenses. It is English speaking, economically and culturally similar to the United States in many areas, and an attractive land with attractive people and a liberal government. It has no draft. And it is in need of more people with education and job skills, so it readily grants "landed immigrant" status to those who meet its standards. Chapter 17 is devoted to the details of emigration to Canada.

CAN YOU EVER RETURN?

It must be emphasized that the draft emigrant must choose a *permanent* home. If you leave the United States to avoid the draft, there is no certainty that you can ever return, even for a visit. There are two possible reasons for this, depending on whether you remain a U.S. citizen or renounce your citizenship.

If You Remain a U.S. Citizen

It is not illegal to move to another country, but you remain legally subject to the draft as long as you remain a U.S. citizen, regardless of where you live or whether you have legal status as a visitor, student, or immigrant there.

Therefore, your draft board will continue processing your file after you leave. If you fail to perform any duty—to notify it of your mailing address, to return questionnaires it sends to you, to take a pre-induction physical examination—you have broken the Selective Service law. Even if you perform these duties, you are likely, at the normal time, to be sent an induction order. If you don't submit to induction into the Army, or report for civilian work if you are classified as a I-O conscientious objector, you are almost certain to be reported for prosecution to the U.S. Attorney. A warrant for your arrest will in time be issued, and it will be waiting for you if you ever return to American territory. There is no time limit; it will be outstanding indefinitely. (There is a five-year statute of limitations for draft offenses, after which you can't be prosecuted, but it apparently applies only if you remain in the United States.)

Some emigrants hope that a general amnesty will eventually be declared for men who have left the United States because of the draft, perhaps after the Vietnam war is over. This would have the effect of canceling arrest warrants and leaving draft emigrants free to return without fear of arrest and prosecution. But the United States has no history of such amnesties, and this is at best a distant hope, dependent on future changes in U.S. policies and public opinion.

Without an amnesty, you can expect that a warrant will eventually be issued for your arrest and that you can thereafter return only if you decide to accept arrest and trial for your draft offense.

If You Give Up Your U.S. Citizenship

There are two ways to lose U.S. citizenship. The first is by becoming a citizen of another country, since the United States no longer recognizes dual citizenship. However, this may take a long time—five years from the time you are admitted to Canada as a landed immigrant, for example. Violations of American laws committed while you were still a U.S. citizen will not be canceled by giving up that citizenship, and you will still be subject to arrest if you return to the United States even though you have become a citizen of another country.

However, it is possible to give up your U.S. citizenship even before you become a citizen of another country. You must go to a U.S. embassy or consulate in another country and go through the brief formality of "renouncing" your U.S. citizenship. The papers are filed with the U.S. State Department and you cease to be a U.S. citizen and are not subject to American laws.

If you move to another country and renounce your American citizenship before you have violated the draft law, you are not subject to arrest if you return. This means you should be sure that you have fulfilled all draft obligations—such as notifying your local board of your new address—up to the time you renounce your citizenship. Probably the last possible time to renounce citizenship to avoid prosecution would be just before the date you were supposed to report for induction or civilian work. When you notify your draft board that you are living abroad and have renounced your U.S. citizenship, it should probably reclassify you IV-C as an alien living outside the U.S. (see page 158).

There are at least two serious disadvantages to renouncing citizenship.

First, there is no certainty that you could ever re-enter the United States. The U.S. must admit its citizens, but you would no longer be a U.S. citizen. If the U.S. government denied permission to visit, you might have no legal remedy. Whether officials at border crossing points will have lists of "unwelcome visitors" in the future, and whether they would include men who emigrated and renounced citizenship because of the draft, cannot now be determined. Even if you are able to visit, there is little prospect that you could ever return to live in the United States. Since the only practical advantage of renouncing citizenship is keeping open the possibility of returning to the U.S. without being arrested, these possibilities must be given serious thought.

Second, until you are admitted to citizenship in your new country, you are not a citizen of any country. You have no passport for travel outside your host country. And if you violate the conditions of your admission—in some cases this could be done by being arrested on a narcotics charge, by applying for public welfare, or by needing to be placed in a mental or tuberculosis institution—you would be entirely without a country; you would have no right to remain in the new country or return to the United States, and would have to go wherever you could be admitted. Being "stateless" may be the worst of all conditions.

Furthermore, renunciation of your original citizenship may create problems when you apply for citizenship in the new country. It may even make you ineligible to stay as a visitor in some countries. For all of these reasons, very few draft-age Americans who emigrate to other countries renounce their U.S. citizenship, and most of the organizations in Canada and other countries that assist and advise draft emigrants recommend against it.

CURRENT INFORMATION

If you are planning to emigrate, it is advisable to visit the country in which you would live—and if possible the city—before making a final decision. You should look into living conditions, employment opportunities, and attitudes toward American draft emigrants. You should also talk with one of the organizations there that aid and advise draft emigrants; such committees exist in Canada and a number of European countries. Foreign embassies and consulates in the United States may have some information. It is important to have up-to-date information on immigration rules and practices, and advice on the best ways to proceed. The organizations that aid draft emigrants may also provide help in getting settled, finding work, and meeting new friends. Chapter 21 lists some sources of information about emigration.

CHAPTER SEVENTEEN

EMIGRATION TO CANADA

Since most Americans who leave the United States to avoid being drafted go to Canada, this chapter supplies information about the Canadian immigration laws which may effect you if you decide to go there.

It is not possible in this short chapter to provide full details. For fuller details, read the *Manual for Draft-Age Immigrants to Canada,* 5th edition, edited by Byron Wall (Toronto: House of Anansi, 1970, $2.00), and consult the Canadian organizations listed in Chapter 21. In addition, these practices, like all others discussed in this book, are always subject to change, so it is especially important that you be in touch with an organization in Canada which aids American draft emigrants before you make final plans. All we have tried to give in this chapter is a general picture to help you decide whether you are interested in emigrating to Canada and whether you are likely to be admitted.

Many Americans find Canada an attractive country. In most areas it is very like the United States in way of life, economy, culture, and speech, with an element of England added. In Quebec province and the other French-speaking areas, it resembles provincial France with American and English elements. There is conflict between the English- and French-speaking sections, resulting in movements toward separatism for the French-speaking areas. Canada's politics are generally liberal by American standards, with a government more like that of England than that of the U.S. Its climate and geography are varied. It is much more rural than the United States and has far more unsettled frontier, though its cities are as cosmopolitan, as interesting, and sometimes as beset with problems as ours, including unemployment for the less skilled. It is geographically slightly larger than the United States, but has a population of only 20 million, so it is far less involved in the international conflicts that preoccupy most larger countries. Its economy is dominated by American-owned corporations, and its government generally cooperates with that of the United States, but it has an independence of spirit that makes it quite different from the client states of Latin America.

The government of Canada does not offer formal asylum to Americans escaping from the draft, but Canadian immigration laws do not exclude you because of your draft status. Since Canada has no draft, and seems unlikely to start one after its unhappy experience with the World War II draft, the extradition treaties between Canada and the United States do not include any crimes related to the draft and you would be considered for admission without regard to your draft status.

To be admitted to Canada, you must have two kinds of qualifications. First, you must not fall into a "prohibited class." Second, you must meet the requirements for one of three kinds of admission: visitor, student, or landed immigrant.

PROHIBITED CLASSES

If you fall into one of the "prohibited classes," you are not eligible for admission to Canada. In addition, if you enter legally but fall into a prohibited class during your first five years in Canada, you can be deported. After five years, even if you don't become a Canadian citizen, you can be deported only for offenses in the first two groups listed below, or for falsifying on your admission form. If you become a citizen, you can't be deported for any reason. These are the prohibited classes:

1. Subversives. This might include people who have ever been members or associates of organizations subversive to democratic government, or those believed on reasonable grounds to be likely "to engage in or advocate subversion" or likely "to engage in espionage, sabotage, or any other subversive activity directed against Canada or detrimental to the security of Canada." Clearly this is subject to interpretation

and in practice tends to be limited. For example, the Communist Party is legal in Canada.

2. Narcotics users. Use, or even a reasonable suspicion of use, of any narcotic, unless more than five years earlier, is grounds for exclusion. Marijuana is regarded as a narcotic.

3. Criminals. Conviction or confession of a crime involving "moral turpitude" makes one ineligible for admission. "Moral turpitude," though not defined in the law, probably includes only serious crimes. This might not be enforced if the sentence was completed more than five years earlier, or two years earlier if the immigrant was convicted before he was 21.

4. Other excluded persons. Also excluded are prostitutes, homosexuals, mentally or physically defective or seriously diseased persons, chronic alcoholics, and "persons who are . . . or are likely to become public charges."

Of course, if you fall into one of the categories that exclude you from Canada, it is quite likely that you would also be found unsuitable for military service in the United States. The main exceptions are criminal convictions (discussed in Chapter 13), involvement with marijuana, and receipt of public welfare.

REQUIREMENTS FOR ADMISSION

Visitors

Millions of Americans visit Canada every year. Admission is normally a quick, easy process—a few questions about where you were born, where you are going in Canada, and how long you plan to stay, and a customs inspection of your baggage. If your appearance is unconventional, if you don't have enough money for a visit ($10 a day is assumed necessary), or if you have much more baggage than a visit requires, you are likely to be questioned more closely.

You can stay in Canada as a visitor for a maximum of six months. You can't go to school unless you change to student admission status (which can be done from within Canada). You also can't work unless you get a special permit or change to landed immigrant status (which also can be done from within Canada).

Students

If you have a letter of admission to a Canadian school and evidence that you have enough money to live in Canada (cash, bankbooks, evidence of a scholarship, or a letter from your parents saying they will support you), you generally will have no difficulty being admitted. Student admission is for a year at a time and may be renewed as long as you continue your studies. Your wife can be admitted with you, but neither of you can work without special permission. If you decide to stay in Canada after graduation, you can apply for landed immigrant status from within Canada. You will be just as eligible for a student deferment from your American draft board while you are a full-time student at a Canadian college as you would be at an American college (see Chapter 9).

Landed Immigrants

Only in this category are you admitted permanently to Canada. You are eligible to work, travel, or study. (You will be given student status if you indicate your intention to study when you apply for admission, but if you enter as a landed immigrant and later decide to become a student, your status will not be affected.) You will have the same rights as Canadian citizens except the right to vote, to hold certain government jobs, and to receive a Canadian passport (but you can still travel on your American passport, and even get it renewed, as long as you remain a U.S. citizen). After five years, you can apply for Canadian citizenship, or can remain in Canada without becoming a citizen.

Under the Immigration Regulations which went into effect on October 1, 1967, you can apply for landed immigrant status in any of five ways:

1. At the border. This is the fastest way. Generally it is recommended if your qualifications are uncertain, because rejection is usually informal; you will usually be able to withdraw your application if you are told that it will not be approved,

and you can apply again elsewhere without having your previous rejection on the record.
2. From within Canada. You can enter as a visitor or student, and once in Canada apply for permanent status (in the case of the student, after you have finished your studies). This way is recommended only if your qualifications are good and you don't mind being unable to work until your application is approved—unless you get a special permit, which may not be easy to get. Approval may take a few weeks or a few months. If you are rejected, however, it may be difficult or impossible to try again, and you will have to leave Canada. The advantage of applying from within Canada is that you are safe from arrest for a draft violation while you are in Canada and have some time to collect the documents for your application for landed immigrant status, or to reconsider your decision.
3. By nomination or sponsorship. If you have a close relative in Canada who will take financial responsibility for you, admission will usually be very easy. The application is then filed by your relative, who might be a husband or wife, fiancé or fiancée, parent, grandparent, child, brother or sister, aunt or uncle, nephew or niece. You may be in Canada (as a visitor or student) or outside Canada when the application is filed.
4. By mail from outside Canada. This may take a number of months, but if your qualifications are very good it is a relatively easy way to complete all your arrangements before you actually leave the U.S. It avoids the interview involved in most other forms of application, which may be a disadvantage if you can make a good impression, or an advantage if you are likely to become nervous and make a poor impression. Since you are expected to wait for a reply after you have mailed your application, you should not apply by mail if your draft status may force you to leave the U.S. quickly.
5. At a Canadian consulate. You can file your application and receive your interview at the Canadian consulates in many major U.S. cities. You may have to wait as long as if you

applied by mail, but will have the advantage of the interview to impress the official with your personal qualities.

However you apply, you will be evaluated on the same basis. You must score 50 out of a possible 100 "assessment units" unless you are sponsored or nominated (in which case there are different and easier requirements). The units are given for the following qualifications:

1. Education and vocational training—up to 20 units—one for each year of school, apprenticeship, or other training.

2. Personal assessment—up to 15 units—given by the immigration officer on the basis of his evaluation of your adaptability, motivation, initiative, and general suitability for successfully settling in Canada.

3. Occupational demand—up to 15 units—based on estimates by the Immigration Department of the need for workers in Canada in your occupational field.

4. Occupational skill—up to 10 units—based on your highest skill, regardless of what work you actually intend to do, from 10 units for professionals to one for unskilled workers.

5. Age—up to 10 units—all 10 if your age is between 18 and 35, minus one unit for every year over 35.

6. Arranged employment—10 units—given if you have a definite job offer in Canada with prospects of continuity—given only if you apply from outside Canada or at the border, not if you apply from within Canada.

7. Knowledge of English and French—up to 10 units—five each for fluent knowledge of English and French, fewer units if you are less fluent.

8. Relative—up to 5 units—five for a relative in the city where you will live who will help you, three if the relative lives elsewhere in Canada.

9. Employment opportunities in the area of destination—up to 5 units—based on the need for workers in the part of Canada where you will live.

There are special rules if you are planning to start a business in Canada and show you have the money and ability to succeed, or if you plan to retire there.

The application form for landed immigrants asks about these and other qualifications, including the places where you have lived and worked, the amount of money you are taking in or will later transfer to Canada, any debts you have, your marital status and children, organizations you belong to, criminal convictions, and health. You will need a number of documents or notarized letters to prove your identity, citizenship, marriage, education and training, ownership of the assets you claim to have, and other facts depending on individual circumstances. If your application is approved, you will be required to submit a report of a thorough medical examination.

The unit system makes admission as a landed immigrant a fairly objective process, though the judgment of the immigration officer is involved in some items. If you earn at least 50 units, don't fall into a prohibited class, and demonstrate that you have enough money to support yourself until you have a job (at least several hundred dollars), you are almost certain to be admitted. Even with 50 units, if the immigration officer believes that your scores "do not reflect the particular applicant's chances of establishing himself in Canada," he may reject you, but he then must explain the reasons in writing and receive the approval of a superior officer. Such rejections are unusual.

Most draft emigrants should meet these standards with little difficulty. Even if the immigration officer isn't impressed with you, you would receive 12 units for high school graduation and one for every year of college and graduate study, 10 for being under 35 years old, 5 for speaking English, and more depending on your occupational skills and plans. Even if you feel confident you will qualify, you would be wise to visit the city where you will live and try to get a firm job offer there (conditional, of course, on your being admitted); this will give you 10 extra units. Most major cities in Canada have committees to aid draft immigrants, and they can sometimes help find jobs. Their information on immigration is likely to be much more current than that in this or any other book, especially in the cases of the major groups listed in Chapter 21.

There are often rumors that Canada is about to "close the border." These have always proved untrue. Even if the border is "closed," it will merely mean that you can't apply for landed immigrant status at the border. The other four ways, including entering as a visitor and applying from within Canada, would remain available.

PART VI

TRIAL AND PRISON

"Unjust laws exist: shall we be content to obey them, or shall we endeavor to amend them, and obey them until we have succeeded, or shall we transgress them at once? Men generally, under such a government as this, think that they ought to wait until they have persuaded the majority to alter them. They think that, if they should resist, the remedy would be worse than the evil . . . .

"If the injustice is part of the necessary friction of the machine of government, let it go, let it go: perchance it will wear smooth,— certainly the machine will wear out. If the injustice has a spring, or a pulley, or a rope, or a crank, exclusively for itself, then perhaps you may consider whether the remedy will not be worse than the evil; but if it is of such a nature that it requires you to be the agent of injustice to another, then, I say, break the law. Let your life be a counter friction to stop the machine. What I have to do is to see, at any rate, that I do not lend myself to the wrong which I condemn."

HENRY DAVID THOREAU, "CIVIL DISOBEDIENCE" (1849)

CHAPTER EIGHTEEN

TWO KINDS OF PRISONER—THE NONCOOPERATOR AND THE UNSUCCESSFUL COOPERATOR

The "Penalties" section of the Selective Service law provides that ". . . any person who . . . evades or refuses registration or service in the armed forces . . . or who in any manner shall knowingly fail or refuse to perform any duty required of him under or in the execution of this title, or rules, regulations, or directions made pursuant to this title . . . shall, upon conviction in any district court of the United States of competent jurisdiction, be punished by imprisonment for not more than five years or a fine of not more than $10,000 or by both such fine and imprisonment . . ." [MSSA 12(a)].

Despite this severe penalty, thousands of men have refused to be inducted into the armed forces or refused other duties provided in the law. Nearly all have done so with full knowledge of the possible penalty. Many men have been convicted and sentenced to prison or placed on probation.

Nearly all of those who are actually sent to prison for violations of the Selective Service law are acting out of a firm belief that they are doing the right thing. Their beliefs are so strong that they would rather risk prison than violate them. If you feel this way, this chapter and the two that follow may give you some idea of why a minority of draft-age men openly violate the Selective Service law. Chapter 19 describes what is likely to happen to you in court and what chance you have to win there. And, in case you lose or plead guilty, Chapter 20 tells a little about life in a federal prison and the after-effects.

Most men who are tried for Selective Service violations can be divided into two groups. Those who are opposed to the draft law or the policies it supports, and on principle refuse to obey its requirements, may be called "noncooperators." Others obey the Selective Service law so long as they are put into the classifications they feel they can accept. They refuse to obey the law when they are denied those classifications and are ordered to report for induction or civilian alternative service, and may therefore be called "unsuccessful cooperators." This distinction is convenient for discussion, but in fact many men fall somewhere between cooperators and noncooperators.

NONCOOPERATORS

There have always been a small number of men with strong objections to the draft. The number has increased greatly during the past few years as draft calls have risen because of the unpopular war in Indo-China. Those who refuse to cooperate express a wide variety of reasons for their actions.

Over the 20 years that America has had a "peacetime" draft, most noncooperators have acted out a feeling that they are opposed to more than their own participation in war or military service. Therefore, they are unwilling to enter either civilian or noncombatant service when ordered by their draft boards.

Some act from strong opposition to the military. Although Selective Service is technically a civilian agency, its principal function is of course to provide men for the armed forces. Accepting its legitimacy, even by asking for a CO classification and doing work approved by the draft board, seems to some men an acceptance of the right of draft boards to order other men into the Army. Those who take this position feel that no man should be required to serve in the armed forces. To them, cooperating with draft boards is no different from cooperating with the armed forces.

In other cases, noncooperators believe that the draft itself is unacceptable. They consider it an effort by the government to control and regiment the individual citizen. They resent having to register and keep their boards informed of their addresses and of any actions that could affect their classifications. They reject the idea that a group of people in the community—usually much older but not necessarily wiser than they—have a right to decide on behalf of the government whether they should be allowed to go to school, to work, or to live with their families. They will not willingly give up the right to control their own lives, even to an official government agency, and see this attempt to limit their freedom as illegitimate and dictatorial. Although the courts disagree, they sometimes argue that the Thirteenth Amendment to the Constitution, which forbids "involuntary servitude," should make the draft illegal.

Many of today's noncooperators are responding particularly to the Indo-China war. They believe that men are being drafted to fight in a war which is immoral or illegal. They often point out that the Nuremberg trials of Nazi leaders after World War II were based on the principle that men are responsible for war crimes even if they were simply obeying the laws of their country or the orders given by their superiors. To them, the United States is involved in a war of aggression and is violating treaty obligations as well as international law.

As defined here, noncooperation is essentially an individual act, whether phrased in terms of conscience, religious belief, or political or social philosophy.

However, today at least several thousand noncooperators feel that this is not enough. They wish not only to act justly themselves (as they view it) but also to influence others. They feel an obligation to make their acts politically and socially relevant, to attempt to bring their views to the attention not only of the government but of the people. Those who take this view usually call themselves draft resisters.

The resister is likely to try to make his position as public as possible. By making public statements, holding meetings and demonstrations, being interviewed by newspaper and television reporters, distributing leaflets, and talking with as many others as possible, the draft resister tries to organize a strong enough movement to influence public opinion, stall the machinery of war, and in time affect the course of history. Conceivably he has already done so.

Probably most of those who join the resistance groups which have sprung up since 1967 in nearly every large city and on many college campuses are primarily opposed to the war in Indo-China. But many are opposed to all war, to the draft, and to the conditions and social institutions which produce war and injustice.

There are almost as many resistance philosophies as there are resistance groups, but they seem to be variations of two essential attitudes. Probably best known to newspaper readers is the view that resisters should use their own public acts of civil disobedience, often including destroying draft cards or returning them to the government, as an organizing instrument to make their views known to others who feel the same way, and at the same time to challenge government policy. Less known, but perhaps more widely held, is the view that resisters should avoid breaking the law as long as possible to work toward organizing for basic social change, but refuse to be drafted if they finally receive induction orders.

Viewed as a form of protest, draft resistance clearly has been effective in calling attention to the resisters' position. The price of this attention, of course, has been the alienation of many people who might agree with, or at least respect, the anti-war position but are repelled by the illegal and spectacular acts, and as a result regard even the most principled and disciplined resisters as anti-social and irresponsibly rebellious. However, their views would be much easier to ignore if they stayed strictly within the law. Press attention to the resistance movement has resulted from the dramatic and illegal nature of some of its actions—especially the burning and returning of draft cards and the destruction of Selective Service files.

A collection of statements by noncooperators and other war objectors, explaining why they took their various stands, appears in *We Won't Go,* edited by Alice Lynd (Boston: Beacon Press, 1968, $1.95). For a more intimate view of resisters, see Dr. Willard Gaylin's *In the Service of Their Country: War Resisters in Prison* (New York: Viking Press, 1970, $6.95).

UNSUCCESSFUL COOPERATORS

By far the largest number of those who violate the Selective Service law don't define themselves as noncooperators. However they may feel about war, the draft, or Vietnam, they are willing to obey the law if they are given the status they think they are entitled to. If they violate the law, it is because they don't believe they have been properly classified by Selective Service.

A great many of those who refuse to accept military service or civilian alternative service are members of the Watchtower Bible and Tract Society, usually called Jehovah's Witnesses, who ask to be classified IV-D as ministers but are turned down. This group regards all of its members as ministers, responsible for teaching, speaking, and distributing literature, but on principle none of them are paid for their work as ministers and missionaries. As a result, most of them work to support their families and use their free time for ministerial duties. Their claims for IV-D classification are therefore usually rejected (see page 153), and they are generally given the I-O classification as conscientious objectors. Some accept and perform civilian alternative service, but many refuse to accept any classification except IV-D because they believe their responsibilities to serve as ministers spreading God's word in the world must come before any service demanded by the government. More Jehovah's Witnesses go to prison for draft refusal than members of any other group, but increasing numbers are offered probation and accept it despite the usual condition that they work at a service job like that required of conscientious objectors.

Another large group in prison consists of members of the Religion of Islam (often called Black Muslims), who are conscientious objectors to the war in Indo-China and perhaps all war. Since most make no effort to obtain CO status from Selective Service, when they refuse induction there is virtually no legal defense available.

A small number of unsuccessful cooperators are men who filed claims as conscientious objectors but were turned down and refused to be inducted into military service. Before 1965 a number of CO applicants were rejected by draft boards that said their claims weren't based on "religious training and belief," but the broad definition of the *Seeger* decision (see Chapter 14) has virtually eliminated court convictions in these cases. Today most convictions of unsuccessful CO claimants occur because the applicant doesn't provide evidence to support his claims, doesn't use his appeal rights, or waits until a crisis develops (often the loss of a deferment or receipt of an induction order) before making his claim, thus calling his sincerity into question. Since the courts have very limited power to review the decisions made by draft boards (see Chapter 19), rejection for "insincerity" may be hard to challenge in court. Even so, most of those who go to prison lose at their trials by failing to use all possible Selective Service appeal rights before refusing induction. Nearly all of those who are persistent and careful in trying to gain recognition within the Selective Service System are eventually successful in either being recognized as COs or receiving some other status acceptable to them. Nonetheless, every year a small number of unsuccessful CO applicants, despite careful efforts to have their claims recognized, end up in court. It is men in this group who have a reasonable chance of being acquitted.

CHAPTER NINETEEN

LEGAL DEFENSE AND SENTENCES

If you provide as much evidence as possible for the classification for which you feel you qualify, use all your procedural rights, and persist in your claim, the chances are very good that Selective Service will recognize it. If not, your final chance may be the courts. A successful effort to make Selective Service obey the law may not only help you but establish principles that will protect the rights of others.

Your day in court requires a good attorney, one who knows not only the general principles of law but also the special and rapidly changing problems involved in draft cases. If you expect to carry your case to the courts, you should choose an attorney and get his advice early in the process—if possible, as soon as it appears you will end up in court. If you are unable to pay for legal help, you are entitled to a court-appointed attorney. In some places the courts appoint attorneys who are especially interested in and informed about Selective Service law, but otherwise court-appointed attorneys are often unfamiliar with Selective Service law and should be encouraged to contact CCCO or another counseling service. The organizations listed in Chapter 21 can help you find an attorney.

There are three ways you may obtain judicial review of the decisions of Selective Service. By far the most common is a criminal defense—defending yourself in court from a charge of breaking the law, often by refusing induction. The second is a "petition for a writ of habeas corpus"—allowing yourself to be inducted but immediately asking the court to release you from the armed forces on the grounds that your induction order was illegal. The third is an injunction—a court order stopping the induction order before you have obeyed or disobeyed it.

If you refuse induction—or refuse an order to perform civilian work as a conscientious objector, or some other requirement of the draft law—you can expect to be arrested, usually within a few months, and tried in the Federal District Court where you refused induction or where you were ordered to work. If you plead "not guilty," you are not necessarily denying that you refused induction. More often, you are saying that your induction order was illegally issued by your draft board, and therefore that no crime was committed when you disobeyed it. If the court accepts your argument, you will be found not guilty and the indictment will be dismissed. Your file will be sent back to Selective Service to reconsider. If, however, the court disagrees and rules that you disobeyed a legal order, you will be found guilty of violating the Selective Service Act. A prison sentence is then a real possibility, though not the only possibility.

If you are more willing to risk two years in the military than a term of imprisonment, you can accept induction into the Army, but make arrangements in advance with an attorney to file papers immediately requesting a court order—called a "writ of habeas corpus"—releasing you from military custody. You would use the same legal arguments in this case as you would use to defend yourself if you refused induction. You can file a habeas corpus action at any time, but its chances of success are greater if filed as quickly as possible. If the court agrees with your arguments, you will be ordered released from the armed forces. If your argument fails, you will remain a soldier. Therefore, if you believe your conscience will not allow you to obey military orders, you may find this a less satisfactory way to get a court review. If you remain in the armed forces but refuse to obey orders, you are likely to face court-martial, with fewer rights than civilian courts allow and punishment under often worse conditions.

Injunctive action is an effort to convince a court in advance that any induction order that might be issued to you under the circumstances would be unlawful, and that induction would result in substantial damage to you. The 1967 Selective Service Act attempts to prevent injunctive action, but Supreme Court rulings allow injunctions in some cases: if you are being denied a legal right which does not depend on Selective Service's judgment of the facts, provided you have used all available appeals (*Oestereich v. Selective Service Board,* 393 U.S. 233, 1968; *Breen v. Selective Service Local Board No. 16,* 396 U.S. 460, 2 SSLR 3373, 1970). If you get an injunction, it will stop the draft board from inducting you without the risks involved in refusing or accepting induction, but today this is possible only in a minority of cases.

Of course, the law is always subject to reinterpretation by the courts. Federal courts have traditionally been greatly influenced by past decisions, called precedents, especially those of the U.S. Courts of Appeal and the Supreme Court. Today, however, this is less true than at any time in the past. Federal judges feel less bound by decisions made during World War II and before. This may be partially because the courts seem to be getting more sophisticated, more aware of the realities of modern life; partially because today there isn't the spirit of national unity which in all-out war causes courts to overlook all but the most glaring violations of individual rights by the government; and partially because strained relations between Congress and the courts, and between the Justice Department and Selective Service, have encouraged the courts to give closer attention to legal errors by Selective Service. As a result, new principles are being developed by courts, and some of the information in this and other chapters may be outdated by the latest court decisions before you read this book.

Under present court decisions, whether you go to court for a criminal defense, habeas corpus, or injunction, there are basically five kinds of arguments you can use to try to show that it is illegal to induct you: (1) that the Selective Service Act, or part of it, is unconstitutional, (2) that some provision of the Regulations issued by the President is illegal because it is in conflict with the Act passed by Congress, (3) that your classification was denied because Selective Service misunderstood the law or misinterpreted it as applied to you, (4) that you have been harmed because the draft board didn't follow the correct procedures, and (5) that your draft board was arbitrary and had no factual basis for denying the classification you requested.

Before you can offer the last four of these arguments, however, the courts usually require that you make every possible effort to get satisfaction within the Selective Service System. You must use all appeals that you are entitled to, must take any pre-induction physical examinations, and (except when injunction is permitted) must report for induction and take the physical examination—and then either accept induction and ask for habeas corpus, or refuse induction and face trial. If you simply don't report for induction, or fail to use any other opportunity that might result in your being excused from military service, the courts may rule that you have failed to "exhaust your administrative remedies" and they may then refuse to listen to your arguments, though this may not happen in cases where a draft board's "expertise" or "discretion" is not involved (*McKart v. U.S.*, 395 U.S. 185, 2 SSLR 3023, 1969). There are important exceptions to these rules, and you will need a lawyer's advice before making your decisions.

Although your own lawyer will need to work out the specifics as they apply to you, we will give a brief description of these basic arguments that can be offered in court.

The first argument is that the draft law, or some parts of the law or Regulations—at least as applied to a given case—is unconstitutional. Failures so far are: (1) Conscription without a declaration of war is unconstitutional. (2) The war in Indo-China is illegal, and therefore drafting men to fight in it is unconstitutional. (3) Any draft is a violation of the Thirteenth Amendment to the Constitution forbidding involuntary servitude. (4) It is unconstitutional for a man to be drafted by a board which excludes members of his race from membership. Although the Constitutional arguments are rarely successful, they have been used effectively to broaden the definition of conscientious objection (discussed in Chapter 14) and to limit somewhat the arbitrary powers of draft boards.

The second argument, based on conflict between the Act and the Regulations, succeeds on rare occasions. It was the basis for several court decisions to extend the I-S(C) classification (see page 125) and III-A fatherhood deferment (see page 139) to some graduate students and was successful in ending draft board use of the Regulations to take deferments away from men declared delinquent (discussed in Chapter 7).

The third argument, based on "error in law," has been used successfully in a number of CO cases. It has produced broad interpretations of sections of the law which Selective Service had tried to limit, including the Supreme Court's definition of "religious training and belief" in the *Seeger* and *Welsh* decisions (see Chapter 14) and of the sole surviving son classification in the *McKart* decision (see Chapter 12).

The fourth argument, based on the Constitutional protection of due process, is more often successful than any other. If a procedural error was made by Selective Service (or sometimes by the Army officials at the Armed Forces Examining and Entrance Station), and it is shown that it took away a right of value to you, the judge is very likely to rule in your favor, provided you used available means to try to get the error corrected. If you were improperly denied a reopening of your classification when you submitted new information, were not given personal appearances and appeals you were entitled to, were not given the required time or forms to submit information, or if classifications or orders were issued by the wrong officials, you may often use these as grounds for court action. A close review of your Selective Service file by a very experienced counselor, an attorney, or one of the offices of CCCO will sometimes reveal unsuspected procedural errors.

The fifth argument, also based on the due process guarantee in the Fifth Amendment to the Constitution, is that the action of Selective Service has been arbitrary and capricious because there was no factual basis for your classification. The courts have ruled that a draft board must have some reason, or rational "basis in fact," for the classification it gave and for the denial of the classification requested (*Estep v. U.S.,* 327 U.S. 114, 1946; *Dickinson v. U.S.,* 346 U.S. 389, 1953). In other words, your draft board can't legally refuse to give you a CO classification or a deferment if you submit information which establishes that you apparently meet the qualifications for that classification, unless there is information in your file that indicates you may not qualify for it. However, this allows a very limited review by the courts. The judge will not determine whether the draft board made a good decision; if he finds *any* facts in your file which support the board's action, he may refuse to overturn it, though some courts have required that draft boards put written explanations of their decisions into the file (*U.S. v. Haughton,* 413 F.2d 736, 2 SSLR 3173, 9th Circuit, 1969;

U.S. v. Broyles, 2 SSLR 3562, 4th Circuit, 1970). If the file has *no* evidence supporting the board's action, that action will be ruled arbitrary and therefore illegal.

In the last reported fiscal year, 1969, out of 1,746 men charged in court with Selective Service violations, 97 were found not guilty and 748 had their charges dismissed, in many cases to allow them to enter the armed forces. Of the remaining 901 men, 511 entered guilty pleas and 390 were found guilty after trial.

SENTENCES

What are the consequences if you are convicted in court of violating the Selective Service Act?

Perhaps the best that can happen is probation or a suspended sentence, which in practice are much the same thing. You would be under the supervision of a probation officer for a period set by the judge, up to five years, and might need the probation officer's permission to change jobs or leave the federal court district where you live and work; and you are obliged to report to him regularly. Their strictness varies greatly. If you broke the law for conscientious reasons, the judge will probably insist that your work be "in the national interest," similar to civilian alternative service (discussed in Chapter 15). If you violate the conditions, you can be sent to prison for the length of time of your initial suspended sentence or the length of your probation, or you can be resentenced by the same judge who gave you the first sentence. In the 1969 fiscal year, 350 of the 901 convicted men were given probation by judges in 34 states.

If you are sentenced under the Youth Corrections Act, the maximum sentence is four years' imprisonment and two years' parole, which is like probation. After its completion, your conviction usually is "erased" and you have no criminal record.

The maximum sentence is five years' imprisonment and a $10,000 fine. Fines are seldom imposed. In fiscal year 1969, of the 545 men given prison sentences, five-year sentences were given to 88 men, three- to five-year sentences were given to 262 men, one- to three-year sentences were given to 155 men, and 40 men were given sentences of one year or less. The average sentence was 36 months, lower than the 1968 average of 37 months, but up from an average of 32 months in 1967 and 26 months in 1966.

Some lawyers are convinced that, in practice, the likelihood of a successful defense or favorable sentence in Federal District Court depends more on the attitudes of the judge than the legal merits of your position, but this is less true if you elect to carry your case onward to the Courts of Appeal.

CHAPTER TWENTY

PRISON AND AFTER

The growth in the number of conscientious objectors and draft resisters inevitably means many young men are spending up to five years in one of the 32 institutions run by the Federal Bureau of Prisons.

After a six-year period during which the total number of federal prisoners steadily declined, the total rose in 1968 to 20,250 prisoners, and the average age dropped one year. The director of the Bureau of Prisons does not offer an explanation, but the cause was probably the draft. In the 1968 fiscal year, 580 Selective Service violators received prison sentences, compared with 666 in 1967, 301 in 1966, and 189 in 1965. The increased use of probation caused the number to drop to 545 in fiscal 1969.

Jehovah's Witnesses (see Chapter 18) make up the largest single group of draft violators in prison at any given time; currently there are several hundred. Draft resisters, Muslims, and unsuccessful CO claimants make up most of the remainder.

Those who are merely trying to avoid military service, but are not motivated by any strong principle, seldom go to prison. They usually accept an opportunity to "volunteer" for the Army when they are caught. Only if the Army doesn't want them—for example, because of a criminal record—do they sometimes end up in prison.

Selective Service violators can be found in about 18 of the 32 federal institutions. The most used of these are the Federal Prison Camp, Allenwood, Pennsylvania (minimum security); the Federal Correctional Institution, Sandstone, Minnesota (medium security); the Medical Center for Federal Prisoners, Springfield, Missouri (in medium-security dormitories for able-bodied men, to help run the institution); the Federal Reformatory, Lompoc, California (for young adults); and the Federal Prison Camp, Safford, Arizona (minimum security). With rare exceptions, draft violators are not put in penitentiaries, which are maximum-security prisons, but they sometimes serve their sentences on medium-security prison farms attached to penitentiaries.

Each institution is different, in part because the wardens have leeway in deciding the visiting hours, the educational and recreational programs, censorship, and other administrative matters.

Obviously, healthy-minded young men intensely dislike being prisoners, ordered about from dawn to dusk by men who seem much like the more disagreeable inmates but wear the symbols of power. The frustration over endless rules and regulations, the monotony of unchanging routine, the lack of privacy, the meaninglessness of work assignments, and the realization that one has after all ended up just a number in a wrinkled uniform, all take their toll. But a few months or years in prison is not a fate worse than death, if only because it has a court-determined time limit.

The first hint, therefore, if prison is in your future, is to think in terms of going *through* prison, rather than *to* prison. It is not an end to your dreams but, at very worst, a nightmare from which you will eventually awaken.

It need not be that bad. To a substantial degree, it will be up to you. Your fellow prisoners will not be successful criminals or they would not be in prison. Most will not be professionals, which in part explains their getting caught. Often the same inadequacies which drive one man to drink cause another to commit an occasional crime. If you have a concern for others and orient yourself to their problems, you may have an exhausting but rewarding time in prison.

Men in prison are often considered social discards, and draft violators must accept the same label. Often, however, they have inner resources not available to the average inmate, and these will intrigue other inmates and ought to be shared. Perhaps nothing is more rewarding than sharing resources which will be increased, rather than diminished, in the process.

The second hint on "doing time" in a manner that will add to your wisdom is to use your initiative. Don't do only what you are told to do, or your decision-making powers may be impaired for weeks or months after release, or even permanently. Concentrate on areas where there are choices, and create choices.

Offer to teach a class in something you know a good bit about, whether it has wide appeal or not. See if you can set up a drama, poetry, or music group. Organize sports competitions or a prison newspaper. Involve as many other inmates as possible. Not only does success benefit many others, but even an unsuccessful attempt can create a sense of shared purpose and common effort. And time will slip by. Seek undeveloped talents in those around you. Take correspondence courses, which can be arranged, and encourage others to do so. See if the chaplain would sponsor discussion groups.

A prison experience is always difficult, but it can be a source of growth and even satisfaction if it comes about as a result of doing what to you is the right thing. Even in a totalitarian society, as each prison is, interesting and worthwhile things can be done.

The last hint is of a different nature. Many of the stories one hears about homosexual activity in jails and prisons are true. But forced sexual activity is less common in federal prisons than in city and county jails and state prisons. It is true that virtually any draft-age prisoner will be "propositioned" repeatedly, but physical assaults are rare. The vast majority of men, in prison or out, have a strong preference for willing sex partners, even though they may use aggressive methods to determine whether someone who appeals to them might be willing if they "play their cards right." If you are able to convey an active dislike for the prospect of a sexual relationship with another prisoner, you can be reasonably certain his threats of attack will remain verbal. Perhaps that is the most one can ask of sexually starved members of an artificial community. Certainly the armed forces have similar problems.

In any event, virtually no one serves the entire sentence given him by the judge. You become eligible for parole after serving one-third of your sentence, though it isn't usually granted the first time you are eligible. If sentenced under the Youth Corrections Act, you can be given parole at any time, and thus may experience a longer period of uncertainty. Unless you get into serious trouble in prison, you can count on being released after serving about two-thirds of your sentence, because of what is called "good time."

Thus, if you receive a five-year sentence—which would be unusually long, since the national average is now about three years—you would ordinarily spend three years in prison even if you didn't make parole. In general, the longer your sentence, the more likely you are to make parole. As a result, sentences tend to be somewhat equalized, and most men are released after no more than one and a half to two years in prison.

AFTER PRISON

Just as veterans enjoy special status in our society, with permanent advantages over nonveterans, so the man who goes to prison for a felony suffers permanent disadvantages. Ex-felons cannot vote or hold elective office in many states, nor work for the state government. Only California seems to distinguish between conventional ex-felons and those whose crimes were caused by their beliefs. In that state the latter can now vote, after many years of being disfranchised. Some state laws go farther and make it difficult or even impossible to obtain the licenses necessary for certain kinds of work. Doctors and lawyers will have an unusually difficult time pursuing their professions. Practices vary depending on state laws, so it is impossible to generalize adequately.

Jobs requiring security clearance, with the federal government directly or with firms holding certain defense contracts, are likely to be closed to convicted draft violators, and even recognized COs for that matter. Ordinarily, however, these men are not interested in jobs requiring security clearance.

We know of no case where a draft violator was denied a Presidential pardon on request, when the applicant was no longer of draft age. Such a pardon, requested on special forms addressed to the United States Pardon Attorney, removes all the restrictions discussed above.

As indicated in the previous chapter, if you are sentenced under the Youth Corrections Act you do not face the employment problems of convicted felons.

Who can predict whether the next generation will ask, "Dad, what did you do to stop the spread of communism in Southeast

Asia?" or "Dad, what did you do to stop the war in Indo-China?" Prison, and its aftermath, is bearable if it comes as a result of following your conscience. If you are in doubt, it may not be. Whether in doubt or not, try to be mature enough to accept the consequences.

PART VII

OTHER SOURCES OF AID

"Every person shall be deemed to have notice of the requirements of the Military Selective Service Act of 1967, upon publication by the President of a proclamation or other public notice fixing a time for any registration. This provision shall apply not only to registrants but to all other persons."

[REG 1641.1]

CHAPTER TWENTY-ONE

DRAFT COUNSELING AND LEGAL AID

NATIONAL COUNSELING ORGANIZATIONS

1. CCCO/An Agency for Military and Draft Counseling
   National office: 2016 Walnut Street, Philadelphia, Pennsylvania 19103; 215/568-7971
   Western Region office: 437 Market Street, San Francisco, California 94105; 415/397-6917
   Midwest office: Midwest Committee for Draft Counseling (MCDC), 711 S. Dearborn Street, Chicago, Illinois 60605; 312/427-3350

Refers to local draft counselors and to attorneys; or if none is near enough, provides counseling in person and by mail on all draft matters. Trains draft counselors; publishes *Handbook for Conscientious Objectors* ($1.00), *Draft Counselor's Manual* ($2.50 including *Handbook*), and memorandums on deferments and legal problems; publishes *News Notes* (free) five times a year.

2. National Interreligious Service Board for Conscientious Objectors (NISBCO)
   550 Washington Building, 15th Street and New York Avenue, N.W., Washington, D.C. 20005; 202/393-4868

Counsels in person and by mail, specializing in church-oriented COs; assists COs in communicating with Selective Service National Headquarters; publishes *Religious Statements on Conscientious Objection* (75¢), *Guide to Alternative Service* ($1.00), various memorandums, and the monthly *Reporter for Conscience Sake* ($2.00/year).

In addition to these, many religious organizations provide aid with draft matters, primarily to men applying as COs, and most peace and pacifist organizations offer counseling.

There are attorneys' panels formed or in formation in a number of cities to give legal assistance in draft cases, often with provision for fees based on ability to pay. Draft counselors and counseling services can often suggest experienced lawyers in their areas.

CANADIAN COUNSELING ORGANIZATIONS

1. Toronto Anti-Draft Programme
   2347 Yonge Street (P.O. Box 41, Station K), Toronto 315, Ontario, Canada; 416/481-0241
2. Committee to Aid American War Objectors
   628 E. Georgia Street (P.O. Box 4231), Vancouver 9, British Columbia, Canada; 604/255-1918

These two organizations are the largest, and generally the best informed, of more than 20 groups in Canadian cities which aid American draft emigrants. They can refer to the others, which provide more limited legal advice, information about local conditions, and aid in settling and finding work.

LOCAL COUNSELORS AND COUNSELING SERVICES

Because our space and information are limited, we have not tried to list all draft counseling services. Some areas have many, and the nearest listed group may be able to refer you to one nearer you or offering the particular help you need; if one organization serves as a coordinator or referral service for an area, we have tried to list it. Other areas have no counseling services of which we are aware. We do not endorse the quality of the listed counseling services, since we are unable to stay currently informed about them all. You will have to make your own evaluation, as suggested in Chapter 1.

If a telephone number is listed, it is usually a good idea to phone to learn counseling hours or make an appointment. Mailing addresses, if different, are given in parentheses. The list is arranged by Zip Codes.

Massachusetts

Amherst, MA 01002: Valley Peace Center, 1 Cook Place; 413/253-3683

Worcester, MA 01602: Draft Information Service, 134 Chandler Street; 617/755-8170

Worcester, MA 01609: Interfaith Center for Draft Information, Worcester Area Council of Churches, 63 Wachusett Street; 617/757-8385

Cambridge, MA 02138: Harvard Draft Counseling Center, Phillips Brooks House, Harvard University; 617/495-5529

Newton, MA 02158: Newton Community Peace Center, 474 Centre Street; 617/969-7900

Boston, MA 02215: Boston University Draft Counseling Service, 185 Bay State Road; 617/353-3638

New Hampshire

Concord, NH 03301: New Hampshire Civil Liberties Union Selective Service Committee, 3 Pleasant Street; 603/485-7185

Maine

Biddeford, ME 04005: York County Draft Counseling and Educational Center, Saint Francis College, Decary Hall Room 121; 207/282-1515

Vermont

Putney, VT 05346: Windham Draft Counseling Service, Student Union Room 206, Box 477; 802/387-5511, ext. 204

Burlington, VT 05401: Burlington Draft Counselor's Community, c/o Meacham, 434 S. Winooski Avenue; 802/864-4607

Connecticut

West Hartford, CT 06119: American Friends Service Committee, 144 S. Quaker Lane; 203/232-9521

Storrs, CT 06268: Storrs Draft Information Committee, Community House, North Eagleville Road; 203/429-5900

Voluntown, CT 06384: New England Committee for Nonviolent Action, R.F.D. 1, Box 197b; 203/376-9970

New Haven, CT 06520: New Haven Draft Information Center, 425 College Street; 203/624-6657

Stamford, CT 06905: Draft Counseling and Information Service of So. Fairfield County, 1101 Bedford Street; 203/323-9129

New Jersey

Montclair, NJ 07042: Draft Information and Counseling Service of New Jersey, 2 Erie Street; 201/744-3263

Princeton, NJ 08540: Draft Information Center, 173 Nassau Street; 609/924-5487

New York

New York, NY 10003: American Friends Service Committee, 15 Rutherford Place; 212/777-4600

New York, NY 10012: War Resisters League, 339 Lafayette Street; 212/228-0450

Brooklyn, NY 11215: Brooklyn Draft Information and Counseling Service, 53 Prospect Park West (Ethical Culture); 212/SO 8-3701

Garden City, NY 11530: Long Island Draft Information and Counseling Service, 38 Old Country Road (1363 Pine Court, East Meadow, NY 11554); 516/WE 1-5765

Melville, L.I., NY 11746: Suffolk Draft Information Service, 19 W. Lyons Street; 516/ AR 1-4672

Albany, NY 12208: Capital Area Peace Center, 727 Madison Avenue; 518/463-8297

Poughkeepsie, NY 12603: Draft Counselling and Information Service of Dutchess County, 249 Hooker Avenue; 914/471-9616

Oswego, NY 13126: Oswego County Draft Information Center, Wesley House, 4 West End Avenue; 315/343-1797

Syracuse, NY 13210: American Friends Service Committee, 821 Euclid Avenue; 315/475-9469

Binghamton, NY 13901: Harpur College Draft Counselling Service, Harpur College, SUNY at Binghamton; 607/798-9018

Buffalo, NY 14211: Draft Counseling Center of Greater Buffalo, 72 N. Parade Avenue; 716/897-2871

Ithaca, NY 14850: Cornell Draft Information Service, 316 Anabel Taylor Hall, Cornell University; 607/256-4229

Pennsylvania

Pittsburgh, PA 15213: Pittsburgh Draft Information Center, 4401 Fifth Avenue; 412/682-2751
Erie, PA 16501: Gannon College Draft Information Service, Gannon College, Perry Square; 814/456-7523, ext. 326
Philadelphia, PA 19102: Philadelphia Draft Information Center, 153 N. 16th Street; 215/LO 3-4431, LO 3-6474

Delaware

Wilmington, DE 19801: Delaware Draft Counseling & Educational Service, 1106 N. Adams Street; 302/658-7602

District of Columbia

Washington, DC 20008: Washington Area Peace Action, 2111 Florida Avenue, N.W.; 202/234-2000

Maryland

Baltimore, MD 21218: American Friends Service Committee, 319 E. 25th Street; 301/366-7200

Virginia

Hampton, VA 23368: Peninsula Draft Counseling Service, c/o Howard Schonberger, Box 6043, Hampton Institute; 703/722-6581, ext. 402

North Carolina

High Point, NC 27261: American Friends Service Committee, 1818 S. Main Street (P.O. Box 1791); 919/882-0109
Chapel Hill, NC 27514: Chapel Hill Draft Counseling Service, c/o Student Government Office, Carolina Union, University of North Carolina; 919/933-3903
Charlotte, NC 28207: Charlotte Draft Counseling Service, 2039 Vail Avenue; 704/333-3979

South Carolina

Columbia, SC 29211: St. Mark's Universal Life Church, 2319 Park Street (P.O. Box 1197); 803/254-8878

Georgia

Atlanta, GA 30309: Atlanta Workshop in Nonviolence, 253 North Avenue N.E. (P.O. Box 7477); 404/875-0646

Augusta, GA 30904: Augusta Draft Information Service, c/o Marguerite Rece, 3021 Fox Spring Road; 404/738-5262

Florida

Tallahassee, FL 32301: Tallahassee Draft Counseling Center, 548 W. Park Street; 904/224-4915, 222-3704

Coconut Grove (Miami), FL 33133: AFSC Peace Center of Miami, 3356 Virginia Street, Room 202; 305/443-9836

St. Petersburg, FL 33705: American Friends Service Committee, 130 19th Avenue S.E.; 813/894-0708

Alabama

Mobile, AL 36601: Deep South Draft Counseling Service, 105 S. Ann Street (P.O. Box 2612); 205/471-4642

Tennessee

Nashville, TN 37208: Nashville Draft Counselling Service, 911 18th Avenue, N.; 615/256-2544

Knoxville, TN 37916: Knoxville Draft Counselling Service, Tyson House, 824 Melrose Place; 615/523-5373

Mississippi

Greenville, MS 38701: Rims Barber, The Delta Ministry, 723 Nelson Street (Box 457); 601/334-4587

Jackson, MS 39202: Roger Mills, National Office of Rights of the Indigent, 538½ N. Farish; 601/948-7301

Kentucky

Louisville, KY 40202: Kentuckiana Military and Draft Counseling Project, 422 W. Liberty Street; 502/584-4417

Ohio

Columbus, OH 43210: Columbus Draft Project, 30 W. Woodruff; 614/291-5983

Bowling Green, OH 43402: Northwest Ohio Draft Counseling Service, 313 Thurstin; 419/353-8912
Toledo, OH 43604: Draft Information & Counseling Service, 401 Board of Trade Building; 419/242-7405
Oberlin, OH 44074: Oberlin Draft Information Center, Wilder Hall, Oberlin College; 216/774-1363
Cleveland, OH 44106: Draft Counseling Association, 11291 Euclid Avenue; 216/791-8294
Youngstown, OH 44504: Youngstown Community Draft Information, 838 Ohio Avenue; 216/746-8747
Cincinnati, OH 45220: Cincinnati Draft Information Service, 2699 Clifton Avenue; 513/861-5660
Dayton, OH 45406: American Friends Service Committee, 915 Salem Avenue; 513/278-4225
Athens, OH 45701: Draft Counseling Center, 18 N. College Street; 614/592-3913
Lima, OH 45805: Lima Draft Information Center, 875 W. Market Street; 419/228-4639

Indiana

Indianapolis, IN 46202: Indianapolis Draft Project, 222 E. 16th Street; 317/923-9563
Valparaiso, IN 46383: Porter County Draft Counseling Center, Student Union, E. Union Street; 219/462-3610
Gary, IN 46408: Lake County Draft Information Center, 3525 Jefferson Street; 219/887-5497
South Bend, IN 46625: South Bend Draft Union, 526 N. Hill Street; 219/232-3275
Ft. Wayne, IN 46805: Ft. Wayne Selective Service Information Center, 1127 (down) S. Clinton Street (P.O. Box 5144); 219/743-4692
Muncie, IN 47306: Ball State Draft Information Service, 300 N. College Avenue; 317/285-7091
Richmond, IN 47374: Eastern Indiana Draft Counseling Center, Box 7, Earlham College; 317/962-6561, ext. 279
Bloomington, IN 47401: I. U. Draft Information and Counseling Service, Indiana Memorial Union, Room 48-J, Indiana University; 812/337-1785

West Lafayette, IN 47906: Purdue Draft Counseling Service, Wesley Foundation, 435 State Street; 317/743-3861

Michigan

Ann Arbor, MI 48108: Draft Counseling Center, 502 E. Huron Street; 313/769-4414
Detroit, MI 48226: Detroit Draft Counseling Center, Central Methodist Church, 23 E. Adams Street; 313/965-5422
Flint, MI 48507: Selective Service Information Center, Unitarian Church, G-2474 S. Ballenger Highway; 313/232-4023
Saginaw, MI 48602: Saginaw Draft Counseling Center, Saginaw Valley Peace Watch, 1505 S. Michigan; 517/793-7721
Midland, MI 48640: Selective Service Information Center, 6220 N. Jefferson (P.O. Box 1101); 517/631-1162
East Lansing, MI 48823: Draft Information Center, 507 E. Grand River, Suite 205; 517/351-5283
Kalamazoo, MI 49007: Kalamazoo Draft Counseling Committee, 2210 Wilbur Street; 616/343-1969, 349-1754
Benton Harbor, MI 49022: Berrien County Draft Information Service, P.O. Box 991; 616/925-2629
Grand Rapids, MI 49502: Grand Rapids Draft Information Center, 129 E. Fulton Street; 616/454-8427
Traverse City, MI 49684: Grand Traverse Area Draft Information Center, College Council Room, Northwestern Michigan College; 616/946-5650, ext. 301
Marquette, MI 49855: Pastor D. Lothar Pietz, Lutheran Campus Ministry, Presbyterian Campus Ministry, 307 W. Fair Avenue; 906/225-1945

Iowa

Ames, IA 50010: Iowa State University Draft Center, Room 54, Memorial Union, Iowa State University; 515/294-1587
Grinnell, IA 50112: Grinnell Draft Information Center, 1205 Park Street; 515/236-6181, ext. 355
Des Moines, IA 50312: American Friends Service Committee, 4211 Grand Avenue; 515/274-0453
Waverly, IA 50677: Wartburg-Waverly Draft Counseling, Box 346, Wartburg College; 319/352-1200, ext. 305

Iowa City, IA 52240: Hawkeye Area Draft Information Center, 212 Dey Building, Iowa Avenue & Clinton Street; 319/337-9327
Cedar Rapids, IA 52401: Linn County Draft Information Center, 600 Third Avenue S.E.; 319/366-3622

Wisconsin

Whitewater, WI 53190: Draft Information Club, c/o Elsie Adams, Department of English, Wisconsin State University; 414/472-1045, 472-1046
Milwaukee, WI 53205: Milwaukee Area Draft Information Center, 1618 W. Wells Street (P.O. Box 3903); 414/342-0191
Milwaukee, WI 53211: Ecumenical Center for Draft Counseling, 2211 E. Kenwood Boulevard; 414/962-5855
Madison, WI 53715: Draft Counseling and Information Center, Friends of AFSC, 1001 University Avenue; 608/257-7979
Stevens Point, WI 54481: Stevens Point Draft Information Service, 1125 Fremont Street; 715/344-0034
La Crosse, WI 54601: Selective Service Information Center, 1732 State Street; 608/785-0666
Eau Claire, WI 54701: Eau Claire Draft Information Center, Ecumenical Religious Center, 110 Garfield Avenue; 715/834-7781
Appleton, WI 54911: Appleton Area Draft Counseling Service, 410 E. Washington Street; 414/733-7533

Minnesota

Minneapolis, MN 55404: Minnesota Draft Help, 529 Cedar Avenue, S. (P.O. Box 6041); 612/333-8471, 333-3717
Duluth, MN 55802: Draft Information Service—Duluth-Superior, 24 E. First Street; 218/727-5510
Mankato, MN 56001: Associated Campus Ministries, 331 Dillon Avenue; 507/387-3419
St. Cloud, MN 56301: St. Cloud Draft Information Center, 418 W. St. Germain (P.O. Box 432); 612/252-7226

South Dakota

Brookings, SD 57006: Campus Ministry Draft Information Service, 802 11th Avenue; 605/692-6332

Sioux Falls, SD 57105: Sioux Falls Draft Information Service, 1101 W. 28th Street, Room 16; 605/336-4323

Montana

Missoula, MT 59801: A.S.U.M. Selective Service Information Center, Associated Students Office, University of Montana; 406/243-5643

Illinois

Techny, IL 60082: North Shore Draft Information Group, Divine Word Seminary, 1835 Waukegan Road; 312/272-2700
DeKalb, IL 60115: DeKalb Association for Draft Counseling, 633 W. Locust Street; 815/758-0005
Evanston, IL 60202: Evanston Peace Center—Draft Counseling Service, 926 Chicago Avenue; 312/475-2260
Aurora, IL 60504: Aurora Draft Counseling Center, 33 S. Stolp Avenue; 312/896-9232
Chicago, IL 60605: American Friends Service Committee, 407 S. Dearborn Street; 312/427-2533
Rockford, IL 61103: Rockford Area Selective Service Information and Counseling Service, 412 Park Avenue; 815/962-7193
Rock Island, IL 61201: Quad-Citians for Peace Draft Information Center, 2808 5½ Avenue; 309/788-0781
Galesburg, IL 61401: Galesburg Selective Service Information Center, c/o First Baptist Church, Cherry and Tompkins Streets; 309/342-0149
Peoria, IL 61606: Peoria Draft Information Center, Room 204, 1005 N. University; 309/674-9453
Normal, IL 61761: Bloomington-Normal Selective Service Information Center, 210 W. Mulberry Street; 309/452-3733
Champaign, IL 61820: Champaign-Urbana Selective Service Information and Counselling Service, YMCA, 1001 S. Wright Street; 217/344-1351
Quincy, IL 62301: Quincy Selective Service and Military Careers Information Center, Quincy College; 217/224-0591
Springfield, IL 62701: Springfield Selective Service Information Center, Springfield Area Council of Churches, 322½ S. Sixth Street; 217/528-8449

Carbondale, IL 62901: Southern Illinois Draft Information and Counseling Center, Student Christian Foundation, 913 S. Illinois; 618/549-7387

Missouri

St. Louis, MO 63112: American Friends Service Committee, 447 DeBaliviere Avenue; 314/862-8070
St. Louis, MO 63130: Peace Information Center, 6244 Delmar Boulevard; 314/VO 2-5735
Kansas City, MO 64110: Vietnam Information Center, 4723½ Troost; 816/753-1619
Columbia, MO 65201: Columbia Friends Meeting, 813 Maryland Avenue; 314/445-7569

Kansas

Lawrence, KS 66044: Lawrence Peace Center, AFSC, 107 W. 7th Street; 913/842-7932
Manhattan, KS 66502: Service Careers Information Center, 1021 Denison Center; 913/JE 9-4281
Emporia, KS 66801: Kansas State Teachers College Counseling Services, 1200 Commercial Street; 316/343-1200, ext. 221 or 229
Winfield, KS 67156: Draft Counseling and Information Service, News Bureau, Southwestern College; 316/221-4150, ext. 54
Wichita, KS 67214: Wichita Draft Counseling Service, 607 N. Broadway; 316/264-9303

Nebraska

Omaha, NB 68104: Draft Information Service, 1616 N. 51st Street; 402/553-5316

Louisiana

New Orleans, LA 70125: New Orleans Peace Action Center, 8017 Palm Street; 504/482-2172
Lake Charles, LA 70601: Rev. Homer C. Singleton, Jr., 501 E. Sale Road; 318/477-2191, 477-3432

Oklahoma

Norman, OK 73069: University of Oklahoma Draft Counseling Center, 1508 Asp; 405/325-5471

Tulsa, OK 74104: Draft Information Centers, Canterbury Center for United Ministry, 2839 E. 5th Street; 918/939-5431

Texas

Denton, TX 76203: Denton Draft Counseling Service, United Ministry Center, 1501 Maple (Box 13765, North Texas State University); 817/382-6035

Waco, TX 76706: Waco Draft Information, P.O. Box 6395; 817/752-4886

Houston, TX 77004: Center for Selective Service Information, c/o MCMA, 208 Bruce Religion Center, University of Houston; 713/748-6600, ext. 1238, or 526-0030

San Antonio, TX 78206: American Friends Service Committee, 109 W. Durango Street (P.O. Box 1398); 512/223-3371

Edinburg, TX 78539: Valley Draft Counseling Service, 1605 W. Kuhn, Apt. 3; 512/383-6151

Austin, TX 78705: Austin Draft Information Center, 2330 Guadalupe; 512/477-3480

Colorado

Denver, CO 80203: American Friends Service Committee, 1460 Pennsylvania Street; 303/534-6285

Wyoming

Laramie, WY 82070: Laramie Draft Information Center, 11th and Grand Avenue (1215 Grand Avenue); 307/742-3791

Idaho

Pocatello, ID 83201: Rev. Willis Ludlow, Idaho State University Ecumenical Ministry, 836 S. 9th Street; 208/233-0247

Moscow, ID 83843: Campus Christian Center, 822 Elm; 208/882-2536

Utah

Salt Lake City, UT 84102: Utah Draft Information and Counseling Service, 232 University Street; 801/364-4357

Logan, UT 84321: Logan Draft Information and Counseling Service, 1315 E. 7th N.; 801/753-0002, 752-4668

Arizona

Tempe, AZ 85281: Phoenix Area Draft Counseling, 1414 S. McAllister; 602/966-9371

Tucson, AZ 85701: Tucson Draft Counseling Service, 45 W. Pennington, Suite 407; 602/623-7951

Flagstaff, AZ 86001: Flagstaff Draft Counseling Center, 408 S. Humphreys; 602/774-1572

Nevada

Las Vegas, NV 89109: Draft Counseling Center, P.O. Box 1913; 702/737-7040

Reno, NV 89507: Draft Information Center, Jot Travis Student Union, University of Nevada (P.O. Box 8057, University Station); 702/784-6505

California

Los Angeles, CA 90007: Selective Service Counseling Center, The Law Center, University Park, University of Southern California; 213/746-6092

Los Angeles, CA 90024: UCLA Draft Counseling Center, UCLA Law School, 405 Hilgard Avenue; 213/825-1707

Pasadena, CA 91102: American Friends Service Committee, 980 N. Fair Oaks (P.O. Box 991); 213/791-1978

San Diego, CA 92102: San Diego Draft Coffees, 1511 29th Street; 714/232-3671

Santa Ana, CA 92701: Orange County Peace Center, 204½ W. Third Street (P.O. Box 116); 714/836-8669

Ventura, CA 93001: Concerned Citizens for Peace, 4949 Foothill Road; 805/643-8749

Santa Barbara, CA 93105: Santa Barbara Draft Counseling Service (mailing address: 830 Calle Cortita); 805/962-4482

Bakersfield, CA 93301: Kern County Draft Information Service, 1527 19th Street, Room 209; 805/325-9937, 832-9171
Fresno, CA 93702: Fresno Draft Information Center, 1621 S. Cedar Avenue; 209/268-3864
San Francisco, CA 94110: Draft Help, 3684 18th Street; 415/863-0775
Palo Alto, CA 94301: Resistance Draft Counseling, 424 Lytton Avenue; 415/327-3108
Oakland, CA 94612: Oakland Draft Help, 597 15th Street; 415/451-1672
Berkeley, CA 94704: East Bay Draft Information and Counseling Center, 2320 Dana Street, Room 5; 415/841-7400
Sacramento, CA 95814: Sacramento Draft Help Center, 1715 15th Street; 916/447-9726

Hawaii

Honolulu, HI 96814: Draft and Military Information Center, 1212 University Avenue; 808/946-1113

Oregon

Portland, OR 97214: Portland Draft Counseling & Education Center, 215 S.E. Ninth Avenue; 503/236-1568
Eugene, OR 97403: Draft and Military Information Center, Room 2-B, Erb Memorial Union, University of Oregon; 503/342-1411, ext. 321 or 1907

Washington

Seattle, WA 98103: Seattle Draft Counseling Center, 6817 Greenwood Avenue N.; 206/SU 9-0252
Tacoma, WA 98406: Tacoma Draft and Military Services, 3019 N. 21st Street; 206/SK 9-2153
Chaney, WA 99004: Eastern Washington State College Draft Counseling, 208 Martin Hall, E.W.S.C.; 509/359-2366

Alaska

Fairbanks, AK 99701: Fairbanks Draft Counseling Service, 851 University Avenue; 907/479-6317

APPENDIX A

ADDRESSES OF SELECTIVE SERVICE DIRECTORS

Letters to the national director should be addressed to: Director, Selective Service National Headquarters, 1724 F Street, N.W., Washington, D.C. 20435

Letters to the state director should be addressed to: State Director, Selective Service State Headquarters, (followed by the address as given in the list below)

State or Territory	Address
Alabama	474 S. Court Street, Montgomery, 36104
Alaska	619 Fourth Avenue, Anchorage, 99501
Arizona	522 N. Central Avenue, Phoenix, 85004
Arkansas	700 W. Capitol, Little Rock, 72201
California	805 I Street, Sacramento, 95814
Canal Zone	P.O. Box 2014, Balboa Heights
Colorado	New Customhouse, 19th & California Streets, Denver, 80202
Connecticut	P.O. Box 1558, Hartford, 06101
Delaware	3202 Kirkwood Highway, Wilmington, 19808
District of Columbia	440 G Street, N.W., Washington, 20001
Florida	19 McMillan Street, P.O. Box 1988, St. Augustine, 32084
Georgia	901 W. Peachtree Street N.E., Atlanta, 30309
Guam	P.O. Box 3036, Agana, 96910
Hawaii	P.O. Box 4006, Honolulu, 96812
Idaho	550 W. Fort Street, Boise, 83702
Illinois	405 E. Washington Street, Springfield, 62701

Indiana	36 S. Pennsylvania Street, Indianapolis, 46204
Iowa	Building 68, Fort Des Moines, Des Moines, 50315
Kansas	10th and Van Buren Streets, Topeka, 66612
Kentucky	220 Steele Street, Frankfort, 40601
Louisiana	Building 601-5-A, 4400 Dauphine Street, New Orleans, 70140
Maine	Federal Building, 40 Western Avenue, Augusta, 04330
Maryland	31 Hopkins Plaza, Baltimore, 21201
Massachusetts	John F. Kennedy Federal Building, Boston, 02203
Michigan	P.O. Box 626, Lansing, 48903
Minnesota	180 E. Kellogg Boulevard, St. Paul, 55101
Mississippi	4785 Interstate 55 North, Jackson, 39206
Missouri	411 Madison Street, Jefferson City, 65101
Montana	P.O. Box 1183, Helena, 59601
Nebraska	941 O Street, Lincoln, 68508
Nevada	P.O. Box 644, Carson City, 89701
New Hampshire	P.O. Box 427, Concord, 03301
New Jersey	402 E. State Street, Trenton, 08608
New Mexico	P.O. Box 5175, Santa Fe, 87501
New York City	26 Federal Plaza, New York, 10007
New York State	441 Broadway, Albany, 12207
North Carolina	P.O. Box 9513, Morgan Street Station, Raleigh, 27603
North Dakota	P.O. Box 1417, Bismarck, 58501
Ohio	85 Marconi Boulevard, Columbus, 43215
Oklahoma	417 Post Office–Courthouse Building, Oklahoma City, 73102
Oregon	P.O. Box 4288, Portland, 97208
Pennsylvania	P.O. Box 1266, Harrisburg, 17108
Puerto Rico	P.O. Box 4031, San Juan, 00905
Rhode Island	1 Washington Avenue, Providence, 02905
South Carolina	1801 Assembly Street, Columbia, 29201
South Dakota	P.O. Box 1872, Rapid City, 57701

Tennessee	1717 West End Building, Nashville, 37203
Texas	209 W. 9th Street, Austin, 78701
Utah	102 Soldiers Circle, Fort Douglas, 84113
Vermont	P.O. Box 308, Montpelier, 05602
Virginia	400 N. 8th Street, Richmond, 23240
Virgin Islands	P.O. Box 360, Charlotte Amalie, St. Thomas, 00801
Washington	Washington National Guard Armory, S. 10th & Yakima, Tacoma, 98405
West Virginia	Federal Office Building, Charleston, 25301
Wisconsin	P.O. Box 2157, Madison, 53701
Wyoming	P.O. Box 2186, Cheyenne, 82001

APPENDIX B

BIRTHDAYS AND LOTTERY NUMBERS

Day	January 1944-1950	January 1951	February 1944-1950	February 1951	March 1944-1950	March 1951	April 1944-1950	April 1951	May 1944-1950	May 1951	June 1944-1950	June 1951
1	305	133	86	335	108	14	32	224	330	179	249	65
2	159	195	144	354	29	77	271	216	298	96	228	304
3	251	336	297	186	267	207	83	297	40	171	301	135
4	215	99	210	94	275	117	81	37	276	240	20	42
5	101	33	214	97	293	299	269	124	364	301	28	233
6	224	285	347	16	139	296	253	312	155	268	110	153
7	306	159	91	25	122	141	147	142	35	29	85	169
8	199	116	181	127	213	79	312	267	321	105	366	7
9	194	53	338	187	317	278	219	223	197	357	335	352
10	325	101	216	46	323	150	218	165	65	146	206	76
11	329	144	150	227	136	317	14	178	37	293	134	355
12	221	152	68	262	300	24	346	89	133	210	272	51
13	318	330	152	13	259	241	124	143	295	353	69	342
14	238	71	4	260	354	12	231	202	178	40	356	363
15	17	75	89	201	169	157	273	182	130	344	180	276
16	121	136	212	334	166	258	148	31	55	175	274	229
17	235	54	189	345	33	220	260	264	112	212	73	289
18	140	185	292	337	332	319	90	138	278	180	341	214
19	58	188	25	331	200	189	336	62	75	155	104	163
20	280	211	302	20	239	170	345	118	183	242	360	43
21	186	129	363	213	334	246	62	8	250	225	60	113
22	337	132	290	271	265	269	316	256	326	199	247	307
23	118	48	57	351	256	281	252	292	319	222	109	44
24	59	177	236	226	258	203	2	244	31	22	358	236
25	52	57	179	325	343	298	351	328	361	26	137	327
26	92	140	365	86	170	121	340	137	357	148	22	308
27	355	173	205	66	268	254	74	235	296	122	64	55
28	77	346	299	234	223	95	262	82	308	9	222	215
29	349	277	285	...	362	147	191	111	226	61	353	154
30	164	112	...	...	217	56	208	358	103	209	209	217
31	211	60	...	...	30	38	...	...	313	350	...	...

The initial of the last name, and if necessary the first table to decide which of two men with the same lottery

| 1-J | 2-G | 3-D | 4-X | 5-N | 6-O |
| 14-C | 15-F | 16-I | 17-K | 18-H | 19-S |

272

To learn your draft lottery number from this table, find the column for your month and year of birth and go down that column to the number opposite the day you were born.

July 1944-1950	1951	August 1944-1950	1951	September 1944-1950	1951	October 1944-1950	1951	November 1944-1950	1951	December 1944-1950	1951	Day
93	104	111	326	225	283	359	306	19	243	129	347	1
350	322	45	102	161	161	125	191	34	205	328	321	2
115	30	261	279	49	183	244	134	348	294	157	110	3
279	59	145	300	232	231	202	266	266	39	165	305	4
188	287	54	64	82	295	24	166	310	286	56	27	5
327	164	114	251	6	21	87	78	76	245	10	198	6
50	365	168	263	8	265	234	131	51	72	12	162	7
13	106	48	49	184	108	283	45	97	119	105	323	8
277	1	106	125	263	313	342	302	80	176	43	114	9
284	158	21	359	71	130	220	160	282	63	41	204	10
248	174	324	230	158	288	237	84	46	123	39	73	11
15	257	142	320	242	314	72	70	66	255	314	19	12
42	349	307	58	175	238	138	92	126	272	163	151	13
331	156	198	103	1	247	294	115	127	11	26	348	14
322	273	102	270	113	291	171	310	131	362	320	87	15
120	284	44	329	207	139	254	34	107	197	96	41	16
98	341	154	343	255	200	288	290	143	6	304	315	17
190	90	141	109	246	333	5	340	146	280	128	208	18
227	316	311	83	177	228	241	74	203	252	240	249	19
187	120	344	69	63	261	192	196	185	98	135	218	20
27	356	291	50	204	68	243	5	156	35	70	181	21
153	282	339	250	160	88	117	36	9	253	53	194	22
172	172	116	10	119	206	201	339	182	193	162	219	23
23	360	36	274	195	237	196	149	230	81	95	2	24
67	3	286	364	149	107	176	17	132	23	84	361	25
303	47	245	91	18	93	7	184	309	52	173	80	26
289	85	352	232	233	338	264	318	47	168	78	239	27
88	190	167	248	257	309	94	28	281	324	123	128	28
270	4	61	32	151	303	229	259	99	100	16	145	29
287	15	333	167	315	18	38	332	174	67	3	192	30
193	221	11	275	...	...	79	311	...	...	100	126	31

name, are assigned numbers according to the following number should be drafted first.

| 7-Z | 8-T | 9-W | 10-P | 11-Q | 12-Y | 13-U |
| 20-L | 21-M | 22-A | 23-R | 24-E | 25-B | 26-V |

273

INDEX

Abbreviations: 2
Active duty. *See* Military service
Address, informing board of: 23, 48, 93
Addresses of Selective Service directors: 269
Administrative disqualification. *See* Disqualifying conditions
Administrative remedies, exhaustion of: 243
Advisors to registrants: 28
Agricultural deferment: 49, 133
Aliens: registration, 32, 33; exemption (IV-C), 50, 154; prior military service (IV-A), 48, 160; travel outside U.S., 155
Allotments for dependents of men in armed forces: 150
Alternative service. *See* Conscientious objection
Amnesty: 222
Appeal: 7, 20, 22, 29, 30, 61, 68, 71; while outside U.S., 62, 68, 96
Appeal agent. *See* Government appeal agent
Appeal board, State: 29, 70
Appeal board, Presidential: 30, 71
Apprentices: 49, 130, 136
AR. *See* Army Regulations
Armed forces: *See* Military service
Armed Forces Examining and Entrance Stations: 78, 166
Armed forces physical examination. *See* Pre-induction physical examination
Armed Forces Security Questionnaire: 172, 174
Army Regulations: 3, 161
Arrest: 92, 242

Attorneys: 65, 73, 92, 109, 241, 255, 256

Basis in fact: 184, 245
Black Muslims: 239, 248
Breen v. Selective Service Local Board No. 16: 97, 243
Broyles, U.S. v.: 246
Bureau of Prisons: 109, 248

Canada. *See* Emigration
Carey v. Local Board No. 2: 128
Changes in circumstances: 23, 54
Children: 23, 48, 139
Citizenship, effect of renouncing: 222
"Civil Disobedience": 233
Civilian alternative service. *See* Conscientious objection
Classification, draft board procedure: 51
Classification, reopening of. *See* Reopening of classification
Classification Questionnaire: 35
Classifications, list in order: 3
Classifications: I-A, 4, 51, 79; I-A-O, 49, 179, 198; I-C, 101, 110, 199; I-D, 48, 107; I-O, 49, 74, 75, 82, 129, 179, 200, 239; I-S(C), 113, 125; I-S(H), 49, 114; I-W, 213; I-Y, 50, 161; II-A, 49, 103, 113, 130; II-C, 49, 103, 130; II-S, 49, 115, 124, 139; III-A, 48, 103, 139; IV-A, 48, 51, 101, 110, 159; IV-B, 103, 131; IV-C, 50, 154; IV-D, 49, 152, 239; IV-F, 50, 161; V-A, 6
Clerks, local board: 26, 64, 66, 69
Coast Guard: 102, 109

College students: 115, 125, 137, 139, 154
Commissioned officers: 101, 103, 107, 109, 110
Congressmen: 32, 73, 131
Conscientious objection: 179, 198; after ordered for induction, 185; effect on career, 251; effect on deferments, 49, 129, 185; in armed forces, 108, 198; Public Health Service and Environmental Sciences Services Administration, 110; "selective" objection, 182; unsuccessful claims, 197, 239, 248; when to apply, 49, 184
Constitutional defenses: 244
Conviction for draft violation. *See* Courts, Prison
Convictions, criminal. *See* Disqualifying conditions
Copies. *See* File
Counseling. *See* Draft counseling
Courtesy hearing: 55, 63, 196
Court-martial: 109, 242
Courts: 241
Criminal record. *See* Disqualifying conditions

Deadlines: 20, 23, 62, 68, 71
Defense, legal: 241
Delaying: 61, 66. *See also* Postponement of induction
Delinquents: 81, 96, 244
Dentists. *See* Doctors
Dependents: 23, 48, 139; procedural rights, 55, 69; men in armed forces, 107, 150
Dickinson v. U.S.: 184, 245
Director of Selective Service: 31; powers, 69, 71, 89; address, 31, 269. *See also* State directors
Discharge from military service: 107, 159
Disqualifying conditions—medical, mental, criminal, political: 161; evidence, 50, 78, 163, 167; medical discharge from armed forces, 108
Doctors: 89, 133, 139, 140, 158
Draft boards. *See* Local boards, Appeal boards, Presidential appeal board
Draft cards: 34, 54
Draft counseling: 11, 20, 255, 256
Due process: 245

Educational disqualification. *See* Disqualifying conditions
Ehlert v. U.S.: 185
Emigration: 219, 225, 256
Employers: as witnesses, 64; letters and forms from, 48, 49, 131, 137, 151; procedural rights, 55, 69
Enlistment. *See* Military service
Environmental Sciences Services Administration: 109, 110, 159
Estep v. U.S.: 245
Evidence for classifications: 7, 22, 48, 51, 54; at personal appearance, 64; for appeal, 69
Examination. *See* Pre-induction physical examination, Induction order
Executive secretary. *See* Clerks, local board
Exhaustion of administrative remedies, 243
Extended liability: 6, 82, 84
Extreme hardship deferment. *See* Hardship deferment

Farm work: 49, 133
Fatherhood deferment: 139
Federal courts: 241
File at draft board: 50, 51, 64; right to examine and copy, 21, 51, 173
File, personal: 21
Foley v. Hershey: 128

Foreign registration. *See* Registration Forms, Selective Service: deadlines for return, 20; numbers, ix, 51

Government appeal agent: 22, 27, 55, 69, 71, 72, 89
Government Printing Office: 3, 31, 161
Graduate students: 124, 125, 139
Gregory v. Hershey: 139
Gutknecht, U.S. v.: 97

Habeas corpus, writ of: 108, 241, 242
Hardship deferment: 23, 48, 140; men in armed forces, 107
Haughton, U.S. v.: 245
Hearing. *See* Personal appearance, Courtesy hearing
Hershey, General Lewis B.: 31
High School students: 49, 114

Induction order: 79; cancellation or postponement, 60, 72, 89; claims made after issued, 55, 125, 185; physical examination at induction, 92, 174
Information, sources of: 11, 24
Involuntary servitude: 237, 244
Islam, Religion of: 239, 248

Jehovah's Witnesses: 239, 248
Judicial review: 241
Junior college students: 122, 137, 138

"Kennedy husbands": 81, 82

Law school graduates: 89
Lawyers. *See* Attorneys
Legal defense: 241
Local Board Memorandums (LBM): 2, 31
Local Board No. 100 (Foreign): 35
Local boards: 25

Lottery: 81; numbers, 272

Mail: certified, importance of using, 22. *See also* Address
Marriage: 23, 48, 81
McKart v. U.S.: 160, 244, 245
Medical advisor: 28, 162
Medical discharge: 108
Medical disqualification. *See* Disqualifying conditions
Medical specialists. *See* Doctors
Membership on draft boards. *See* Local boards, Appeal boards, Presidential appeal board
Mental disqualification. *See* Disqualifying conditions
Military Selective Service Act of 1967 (MSSA): 2
Military service: 48, 101. *See also* Veterans
Ministers: 49, 152, 239
Mulloy v. U.S.: 55

National director. *See* Director of Selective Service
National Guard: 48, 106
National Institutes of Health: 109
National Security Council: 125
National Selective Service Appeal Board: 30, 72
Noncitizens. *See* Aliens
Noncombatant military service. *See* Conscientious objection
Noncooperators: 236
Nonregistration: 2, 33
Nuremberg trials: 237

Objection to war. *See* Conscientious objection
Occupational deferment: 49, 130
Oestereich v. Selective Service Board: 243
Officers, commissioned: 101, 103, 107, 109, 110

INDEX 277

Operations bulletins: 31
Optometrists. *See* Doctors
Order to Report for Induction.
 See Induction order
Osteopaths. *See* Doctors

Pardon for draft violation: 251
Parole: 250
Peace Corps: 133, 212
Penalties for violating draft law:
 235, 246
Permit for Registrant to depart
 from the U.S.: 93, 155
Personal appearance: 7, 20, 22, 26,
 61
Pharmacy graduates: 82
Physical examination. *See*
 Pre-induction physical
 examination
Physicians. *See* Doctors
Postmark: 20
Postponement of induction: 78, 89,
 123, 128, 130
Precautions: 20
Pre-classification interview: 63, 196
Pre-enrollment in seminary: 49, 152
Pregnancy: 23, 48, 139
Pre-induction physical examination:
 74, 166; failure to take, 74
Pre-seminary students: 49, 152
President: 72
Presidential appeal board: 30, 71
Presidential pardons for draft
 violation: 251
Prison: 248
Prisons, Bureau of: 109, 248
Probation: 246, 248
Procedural errors by draft board:
 32, 245
Procedures. *See* Registration,
 Classification, Reopening,
 Personal appearance, Appeal,
 Pre-induction physical
 examination, Induction order
Professional examinations: 89

Psychological disqualification.
 See Disqualifying conditions
Public Health Service: 109, 159

Qualifications of draft board
 members. *See* Local boards,
 Appeal boards, Presidential
 appeal board

Race: 26, 244
Random selection: 81; numbers,
 272
Ready Reserve: 102, 106, 108
Reconsideration by appeal board:
 70
Records. *See* File
Recruiters: 2, 102, 107
Refusal of induction. *See*
 Induction order
Registration: 2, 32; aliens, 32, 154;
 nonregistration, 2, 33; outside
 U.S., 2, 34; transfer of, 34, 35
Regulations, Selective Service
 (REG): 2, 31
Religious training and belief. *See*
 Conscientious objection
Renouncing citizenship: 222
Reopening of classification: 54; after
 induction order, 55, 89, 125, 185;
 rights after, 61
Reserve Officers' Training Corps
 (R.O.T.C.): 48, 103, 107
Reserves. *See* Military service,
 Ready Reserve, Standby Reserve
Resistance, draft: 237

Security questionnaire: 172, 174
Seeger, U.S. v.: 180, 245
Selective objection. *See*
 Conscientious objection
Selective Service (News): 31
*Selective Service Law Reporter
 (SSLR)*: 3
Selective Service Regulations: 2, 31
Selective Service System: 25

Seminary students: 49, 152
Senators. *See* Congressmen
Sentences for draft violations: 246
Service. *See* Military service, Conscientious objection, Public Health Service, Environmental Science Services administration
Sicurella v. U.S.: 182
Sisson, U.S. v.: 183
Sole surviving son: 51, 160
Standby Reserve: 102, 108
State appeal boards: 29, 70
State directors: 29; powers, 69, 71, 89; addresses, 269. *See also* Director of Selective Service
Statement of Acceptability: 79
Statute of limitations: 2, 34, 222
Stout, U.S. v.: 196
Student deferments: 49, 113; college, 115, 125, 137; disadvantages of, 123, 139; graduate and professional, 124, 125; high school, 49, 114; military training, R.O.T.C., 48, 107; seminary, pre-seminary, 49, 152; study abroad, 93; vocational training, 49, 50, 136
Surviving son: 51, 160
Suspended sentence, 246

Tarr, Dr. Curtis W.: 31
Thirteenth Amendment: 237, 244
Thoreau, Henry David: 233

Toussie v. U.S.: 34
Transfer: of appeal, 69; of induction order, 89; of personal appearance, 34, 62; of physical examination, 75, 78; of registration, 34, 35
Travel: 23; outside U.S., 62, 68, 93; aliens, 155
Trudeau, Prime Minister Pierre: 217

Underground to avoid draft: 2
Unsuccessful cooperators: 236, 238

Veterans: 48, 101, 159, 251
Veterinarians. *See* Doctors
Vocation training: 49, 50, 136
Volunteering for induction: 81, 103

Wallen, U.S. v.: 29
War, objection to. *See* Conscientious objection
Watchtower Bible and Tract Society: 239, 248
Weller, U.S. v.: 65
Welsh v. U.S.: 180, 245
Witmer v. U.S.: 184
Witnesses at personal appearance: 64
Work, deferment for. *See* Occupational deferment

Youth Corrections Act: 246, 250, 251